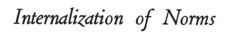

Internalization of Norms

JOHN FINLEY SCOTT

University of California, Davis

Internalization of Norms

A SOCIOLOGICAL THEORY

OF MORAL COMMITMENT

PRENTICE-HALL, INC., *Englewood Cliffs, N.J.*

Prentice-Hall International, Inc., London
Prentice-Hall of Australia Pty. Ltd., Sydney
Prentice-Hall of Canada Ltd., Toronto
Prentice-Hall of India Private Limited, New Delhi
Prentice-Hall of Japan, Inc., Tokyo

Printed in the United States of America

To my parents
Gladys and Frank Scott

Ich hätte gerne ein gutes Buch hervorgebracht.
Es ist nicht so ausgefallen, aber die Zeit ist vorbei,
in der es von mir verbessert werden könnte.
—Wittgenstein

Contents

CHAPTER II

Analysis of Concepts, 42

CHAPTER III

Moral Commitment as Moral Learning: Theory and Hypotheses, 87

CHAPTER IV

Application of the Theory to Socialization, 127

CHAPTER V

*Application of the Theory to
the Maintenance of Moral Commitment in Adults, 177*

Preface

A person "internalizes" or learns a norm to the extent that (other things being equal) he conforms to it at a spatial or temporal remove from sanctions. He learns it through sanctions applied by his social environment. Once the norm is learned, the emergence of deviant behavior following termination of sanctions is slow. But the learning of norms is never complete, and always involves expectations that sanctions will be applied. Thus even when norms are thoroughly learned, when moral commitment is strong and a sense of obligation is reported as keenly felt, the maintenance of both conscience and conformity depends on the exercise of sanctions.

That, in brief, is the theory of normative internalization, or moral learning, of which the following text is an exposition and defense. The theory is an attempt to integrate "operant behaviorism"—better identified as the psychology of B. F. Skinner—with some contemporary forms of sociological theory. Although parts of the argument are new to sociology the theme is one of the oldest in the discipline: that the explanation of human conduct rests more on factors in its social environment than on "psychological" factors conceived to operate apart from that environment. No other process is presumed to depend more strongly on psychological factors in this sense than is moral commitment. Thus the present program for explanation can be stated in a phrase by adapting a Freudian epigram: where psyche was, there shall sanction be.

Much of what sociologists say about socialization and internalization is in agreement with the claims of the operant behaviorists and many of the "learning theorists," the part of psychology to which the operant program is generally thought to belong. I argue below that this program for the analysis of behavior and much contemporary macrosociological theory are *logically* complementary. That claim may well prove to be more novel than the theory of moral commitment itself, for today experimental psychology and theoretical sociology are *intellectually* quite distant. Thus the theory needs a more detailed and discursive presentation than it would were sociologists conversant with learning theory or persuaded of its claims.

The theory is relatively abstract, but it is presented here in a narrative of ordinary language rather than in any formal notation. Those sociologists who advocate the formalization of sociological theory will see this as a defect. There are of course great potential rewards in the use of a formal and artificial language for theoretical exposition. But there are also great (and usually unremarked) risks. The formal sociological theories produced so far have not, on the whole, been well received. Often they are hard to relate to previous theoretical and substantive writing, and often also they are simply less sophisticated than the discursive theories they are intended to replace. Because of this uneven reputation, a highly formal statement of the conceptual links between operant psychology and macrosociology, or of any theory that is derivative from these links (as the theory proposed here is) will fail, in my opinion, to reach the sociologists who will do most to lift the scientific and scholarly reputation of the field in the next generation. In the long run, formalization of sociological theory is both inevitable and desirable. But in the short run I think some of the formalists are moving backwards.

The present theory and arguments on its behalf are sympathetic to the Skinnerian perspective, but they do not agree with every part of Skinner's highly controversial programs for psychology and "cultural design." One disagreement involves the relative merit of experimental evidence. Skinner himself uses the terms "experimental," "functional," and "scientific" almost as synonyms, and most of those who rally round his banner present their case in the context of evidence from closely controlled laboratory experiments. That is not how this theory is presented. Experimental evidence is highly relevant, but for our purposes, also incomplete. The process of moral learning is in one sense very narrow in scope (because "internal" to one person) and in another sense it is very broad, extending in space and time far beyond the range of present and probable future experimental research. Scientists lack the authority to experiment with many aspects of moral commitment and they almost always lack both authority and resources to experiment on anyone over long periods of time. This is not to say that no inferences drawn from a few experimental subjects can be applied to a large population or extrapolated from a short learning process to a lifelong moral career, but only that not all scientifically useful evidence comes from experiments and that (at least for some time to come) the experimental study of human affairs is likely to be most fruitful when complemented by (often highly imperfect) nonexperimental data. The preoccupation with experimentation (by psychologists generally, and not just the new "operant conditioners") criticized in Chapter IV as "experimental positivism" has, in my view, been less fruitful because not so complemented. The defects of casual and uncontrolled observation are of course notorious. But only less notorious and not less real are the defects of experimentation, especially with human subjects, when it is used to assess the variety and magnitude of factors that operate in an extra-experimental universe. Because I have not always found evidence in the experimental literature either for or against many of my claims, I rest my case often on an appeal to commonly observable events and sometimes simply on speculation. Like the great Skinner himself, I am often an armchair Skinnerian.

What this theory shares most with operant behaviorism is its emphasis on the relative importance of social reinforcement in human behavior. Skinner's studied inattention to "mental states" (to which he believes theory construction in psychology always regresses; hence his aversion to it) and his extreme emphasis (at least on first reading) on environmental factors and an "empty organism" may not prove in the long run to be scientifically profitable. Research in genetics, physiology, and biochemistry may someday fill the organism and establish well-determined limiting conditions for environmental effects. But Skinner's approach will benefit the behavioral sciences in the short run, especially sociology and social psychology, because it discourages speculation about matters far removed from the current knowledge in these fields and recommends instead the analysis of variables whose constituent data are readily at hand. The variables that operant behaviorism stresses are the ones we know most about now.

The following theory may appear to some readers to be defective because largely tautological. Its principal empirical claim is simply that moral behavior is an operant; given that claim as a premise together with most interpretations of its key terms, much of the theory turns out to be true by definition. To the charge that this is a defect I offer no defense except to note that tautological propositions abound in a wide variety of otherwise successful theories. Tautology has been cursed since Hume at least, but it remains a type of reasoning that theorists cannot or will not avoid. Perhaps it is better then not to curse tautology but simply to identify it, and so to set it off from a theory's contingent claims which empirical methods may confirm or confute. The literature of the social sciences today is full of pointless empirical "refutations" of analytically true parts of a theory, where the defect is not in the theory but in the uncritical choice of parts of it to test and in the poor design of the operations through which its empirical references are to be made known (usually the refutations are soon forgotten, while the theory lives on to irritate future critics). In what follows, I try to identify whatever tautology in the theory is visible to me, and to marshal evidence of the variety of ways in which human moral commitment is an operant activity.

A theory of internalization as moral learning would appear to be a task more suitable for a psychologist than for a sociologist. Most of the writing and almost all the research specifically on this topic are by psychologists. But the more general and theoretical issues in moral commitment are primarily debated by sociologists. Whatever it is called, the notion of internalization of norms is fundamental to almost all varieties of sociological theory. The present conception of moral learning will not surprise many psychologists, for most of them will be conversant with the approach from which it derives. It is offered rather as an attempt to make sociological theory more complete.

Acknowledgments

My first of many debts to other persons is to my father, Frank Clarke Scott, because he sent me to Reed College when I would not have chosen the school myself, and I have profited ever since from the education I thereby received and which he paid for. I am still using concepts and strategems I learned at Reed from Marvin Levich and Howard Jolly, my first teachers in philosophy and sociology. In my graduate studies at Berkeley I received timely help and encouragement especially from Philip Selznick. I learned much from him, including certainly the importance of cadence and sonority as elements in a sociological prose style. With his characteristic tirelessness, Neil Smelser helped me greatly by reading and criticizing in detail all the written work I ever showed him. My greatest intellectual obligation is to Kingsley Davis. His writing served me, as it serves the profession generally, as a model of clarity and economy in exposition. Those who know his work will see that my citations to it discharge only a part of my debt to him.

Justin Aronfreed corresponded with me throughout the course of this work, and sent me drafts and reprints of his own extensive writings on internalization. Their impact on my thinking goes beyond the several citations to them. Emmy Werner helped guide me through the voluminous literature in child development, while Robert Burgess kept me supplied with current reports in operant psychology and gave me some measure of education on experimental methods. Robert Leik caught some fatal errors in Chapter IV that I otherwise would probably never have noticed. All these persons have done much to improve the manuscript and I bear the sole responsibility for the defects that remain.

Much of this work was written during three years I lectured in sociology at the University of California, Davis. Bennett Berger, then chairman of that department, encouraged my work and provided exceptionally favorable conditions for writing and study.

An early statement of the theory was read at the 1963 meeting of the American Sociological Association. In the discussion afterward, Dennis Wrong expanded my appreciation of theoretical issues. Parts of Chapter II were included in a paper called "Interspecific Comparisons" at the 1966 meeting of the A.S.A., and other parts were summarized as "A Behavioristic Analysis of Normative Concepts" at the 1967 meeting of the Pacific Sociological Association. The criticism of Richard Emerson, discussant at the 1967 session, was incorporated into the present text and made it less obscure than it would be otherwise.

The manuscript was prepared by Robin Pardini, Jeanette Freeman, Ardelle Knudsen, Beulah Reddaway, Margaret Albertson, and Edna Jones. Judy Kotar and Barbara Garner edited the text. Marjorie Donovan, Linda Fritschner, and Mrs. Garner rescued the bibliography from several hundred cryptic footnotes.

To my wife, Lois, there is a special obligation. She has not typed any of this manuscript and has proofread little of it. Rather her own studies in wholly different fields have served me as a welcome recess from the labored abstractions of this essay. She also endured my company during courtship when I was preoccupied with getting something down on paper to start with, and later encouraged me in ways and on occasions past all counting.

JOHN FINLEY SCOTT

Blue Canyon, California
August, 1970

CHAPTER I

Issues in the Study of Moral Commitment

Sociological Theory and the Concept of Internalization

The notion of normative internalization is part of what Philip Selznick has aptly labeled "the enormous corpus of vague sociological concepts." Thus its meanings are diffuse and interwoven. Among other things, "internalization" conveys a distinction between internal or subjective commitment to a norm and external control of behavior through sanctions. The degree of "internal commitment" then becomes, as a remainder, the propensity of persons to comply with or deviate from a norm irrespective of such sanctions. This in turn has suggested that internal commitments may be independent of sanctions, as the voluntarism of Western religion and intellectual life implies, or at least that they intervene, within the individual, between sanctions and his subsequent behavior. Sometimes internalized norms are said to be "part of the personality." Thus, when moral action follows internal commitments, it is generally thought to be more than an immediate response to whatever properties norms may have as external stimuli. Variable properties of the actor intervene between his morally relevant environment and his subsequent action upon it.

This turns out to be about all that is said. In practice, sociologists generally take the process of internalization for granted and treat the concepts involved in it as logical primitives. The word "internalization" thus becomes simply an omnibus reference to the moral vocabulary of natural language and its implicit "folk psychology"—to whatever is signified by such words as "conscience," "guilt," "obligation," and "responsibility." The discussion of moral commitment has of course a long intellectual history, and sociologists have drawn from it. But little of this discussion has been scientific, and, when it has been, it has usually relied upon the psychological method of "introspection upon consciousness," as called by its principal and last systematic advocate, E. B. Titchener. Yet introspection failed to be a profitable method in psychology, and we shall see that it has some special shortcomings when used in the study of moral commitment.

The issues involved in scientific attention to subjective or mental states have a long and stormy history in academic psychology. Behaviorists have repeatedly stressed the methodological problems involved in introspection and the chronic unreliability of its results, while defenders of the subjective methods, though often acknowledging the problems, have argued that these are more than offset by the relevance of the data thereby made available. Both sides of the matter have been argued with great intellectual skill.[1]

These debates have reached only a small audience among sociologists, who generally are much less concerned than psychologists with theories of method. Attempts to draw out the implications for sociology of the problems of subjective reference have been made from time to time, but they have stirred little interest. As a result, most sociologists remain unaware that the analysis of subjective states is controversial. When one of them presents, as important phenomena to be explained, events revealed only by introspection, little if any objection will be raised among his colleagues.

To the extent that they have been aroused to take sides on the issue of subjective data, sociologists are strongly inclined to permit them, a result of the historical involvement of their field with philosophical idealism, especially in Germany and in the tradition of *Geisteswissenschaft*. Sociology never went through the sharp break with idealism that psychology experienced. In the course of setting their discipline off from traditional philosophy in Germany in the nineteenth century, psychologists came to distinguish themselves by their method: if philosophy was speculative and deductive, psychology would be empirical and inductive. It thus quickly aligned itself with the recent successes of *Naturwissenschaft*. One result of this is that no "main-line" academic psychologists with reputations as theorists have ever

---

[1] For a good statement of the behaviorist position, see the various programmatic papers of Edward C. Tolman, mostly written between 1920 and 1936, in his *Collected Papers in Psychology* (1951). For a good statement of the subjectivist position, see various works of Gordon Allport, especially *Becoming: Basic Considerations for a Psychology of Personality* (1955).

gotten very far from the laboratory. They work in basements that smell of rats and are proud of it. But in sociology there are still theorists who do little or no research themselves. Sociology's first two or three generations of theorists sometimes did empirical research—note Durkheim's *Suicide* and Weber's *Die Verhältnisse der Landarbeiter im ostelbischen Deutschland*—but on the whole few of them had any strong ties to "empirical science." They usually relied on ratiocination or interpreted data collected by historians.

Today of course sociology is highly empirical. But it is empirical within a peculiar division of labor that isolates theory to a remarkable degree from research. Sociologists with reputations as theorists are more likely to study the writing of earlier theorists than contemporary research literature, the salient example being Talcott Parsons' profoundly influential volume *The Structure of Social Action*. And the intellectual history of a science, as the psychologist Edwin Boring reminds us, does not depend solely on research anyway (Boring, 1961, p. 344). Research is transitory; the enduring effects are wrought by the theoretical writing that interprets the research. This, together with the isolation of the theorists, is why idealism continues to be so influential in sociology today, and why its effect on the present theoretical treatment of norms, sanctions, and moral commitment is substantial. In this area perhaps more than any other, our theory and method for its verification have changed little since Kant: here work men who still think they see the ghost of *Geisteswissenschaft* in the shadows of variance unexplained.

Not that sociological idealism has had no enemies. The social psychology of George Herbert Mead grew out of a polemic against idealism. But the Meadian tradition, for a number of reasons, has not figured largely in the macrosociological theory that uses the concept of internalization. Mead's own notions of large-scale social organization were merely adumbrated in his own writings and lectures and hardly compare with those of Durkheim or Weber. His contribution lay elsewhere, in his sophisticated conceptions of mentality as process rather than structure, and of the interacting social environment as analytically prior to "mind" and "self." The notion of "internalization" may be interpreted in this way too—as Mead himself did when he referred to thought as an "internalized conversation of gestures."

The term "internalization" is a metaphor: it implies that something moves from outside the mind or personality to a place inside it. The internalized state, even though it may be subjectively expressed, is not conceived as exclusively subjective: thus the concept is contrary to the idealistic conception of subjective states as not describable in the objective terms of the external human environment and therefore not explainable by them. To speak of morality as involving *internalized* norms suggests that, regardless of its properties after it is made internal, it had a prior external status, at least a history of objective events. The present theory builds on this line of reasoning and thus continues Mead's approach.[2] I try to show that many aspects of moral commitment which we usually regard as primarily subjective are also objective in important ways—as Mead showed for the constructs of "mind" and "self"—but I do not mean to explain whatever *irreducibly* subjective properties the process of moral learning may be claimed to produce. The failure of introspection in scientific psychology seems to me to be important, for I believe it to show that the scientific study of methodologically private events is futile. But since many sociologists do not share this view, and respect explanations that are "phenomenologically adequate," a more detailed criticism of phenomenology in sociology therefore follows in the text.

Psychology and Sociology:
Some Lines of Mutual Alienation

The study of human activity is carried on in many separate fields. If we are to undertake a study of some particular topic, to which of the various behavioral or social sciences do we turn for relevant knowledge?

The answer is that we can usually turn to all of them. The *formal* definition of the subject matter of any one discipline—psychology, sociology, anthropology, economics, demography, political science—or of various amalgams of these will reveal that to a surprising extent, they all take their subject to be the same concrete events. Most of the difference lies in the point of view—in the various aspects selected by the method of abstraction from the concrete events for a specialized analysis.

More important than any formal separation of analytical perspectives are the informal separations of actual research operations and of the intel-

---

2 The theory is not, however, "Meadian" in the sense of sharing the viewpoint of those contemporary sociologists who frequently invoke Mead's social psychology. Mead said one thing, but the interpreters of the Meadian tradition, concentrating on certain ambiguous phrases in a stenographic record of Mead's lectures on his notions of the "I" and the "me," have come round to say nearly the opposite. Mead's life work was the development of a theory of outspokenly reductive analytical pragmatism within which the social psychology that has been so influential in sociology was the more specific reduction of selfhood and consciousness to processes based on objective behavior, and he differed from Watson's behaviorism mainly on whether first-person reports of putative internal states should be admissable as descriptions of events, as well as placing more emphasis on social stimuli. The present theory follows Mead in an explanation, in naturalistic terms, of the phenomena of moral commitment—phenomena which the idealism of Mead's day explained on the basis of *a priori* properties. It thus shares Mead's reductionism to an extent that many professed Meadians would find quite unpalatable. For a recent published discussion illustrating the vagaries of Meadian exegesis, see the exchange of letters on Mead between Blumer and Bales (1966).

lectual stances from which the research is interpreted. For the study of moral elements of human behavior I draw mainly on the disciplines of psychology and sociology, relating the findings of each to the other. It proves necessary to attend closely to differences in outlook between the two fields, for a mutual alienation exists that is remarkable in view of their formal proximity. Part of the alienation rests solely on terminology: given the same event, psychologists are likely to stress its individual aspects and sociologists its collective aspects. What the psychologist calls an expression of "personality" the sociologist calls an expression of a "role." What one calls the expression of a "value" the other calls "conformity," or "commitment to a norm." This separation is easily bridged.

Less easily bridged are differences in research method. Scientific psychology is mainly experimental. The controlled experiment is the institutionalized form of research, and psychologists tend to use experimental terminology even when their research is not experimental at all. Sociology, however, is mainly observational. We will see later on how certain sociological processes that are difficult to study experimentally have been overlooked by experimental psychologists even when they bear on the conclusions that the psychologists draw from their experiments (which, in fairness, is not to say that sociologists never overlook relevant psychological processes).

The difference in method between psychology and sociology is really part of a more general difference in present intellectual stance, strongly shaped by different routes of intellectual development. Except for therapeutic specialists, contemporary psychologists are rather self-consciously scientific. But many sociologists still respect a strong literary and historical tradition that resists much of what is regarded as scientific practice in psychology. The differences are well illustrated by habits of scholarly publication. Each field uses a distinctive style and idiom which hinders translation from one to the other even when the concrete events are identical and the analytical frameworks highly complementary. Psychological prose tends toward literal and invariant use of technical neologisms (some authors state with pride that their concepts have been cleansed of "surplus meaning"); sociological prose tends toward metaphor, literary constructions, and natural language. Psychologists follow the citation practices of the natural sciences; some sociological journals still use the footnotes of traditional scholarship, and some sociologists show a historiographer's concern for the exact location of references. But these are only examples of a more general difference in manner that hampers communication. Each group reads little of the literature of the other, and reads selectively when it reads at all.

One important result of this mutual alienation is that specialists in one field tend to hold a layman's view of relevant aspects of the other. Psychologists for example sometimes tend, in their discussion of social effects, to assume the universality of the middle-class environment with which they are personally familiar and to ignore variation among societies and, within them, among strata and inheritance groups. This sociological innocence is exemplified in the review, in Chapter IV of this work, of literature on "father-identification" and learning of the male role, which is based on the assumption that a sociological father is usually there to identify with. Sociologists tend to use psychological constructs based on a mixture of commonsense introspection, popular psychiatry, and (in some cases) the results of their own psychoanalysis, and to ignore most of the concepts developed by non-clinical psychologists. Their psychological innocence is revealed in occasional speculations about feelings of guilt on the part of deviants—after all, the sociologist knows that *he* would feel guilty in such a situation—without considering, on the basis of any psychological theory about the variables of which guilt may be a function, whether certain kinds of deviants will be disposed to guilt at all. What happens is that psychologists assume a middle-class social environment and that sociologists assume a lay, commonsense actor.

There are exceptions of course: each field encompasses many perspectives. The shortcomings that a preoccupation with experimental methods may produce have been capably discussed by psychologists themselves. The psychologist Urie Bronfenbrenner has argued the cause of sociological factors in child development more effectively than any sociologist. And psychology itself can hardly be considered monolithic in view of the great gulf that separates the clinical from the experimental psychologists. A somewhat separate (and not so sharp) split divides them again, on the matter of respect for psychoanalytic theory and method. Dissatisfaction with behavioristic and deterministic perspectives has recently produced a movement of humanistic or existential psychology, which celebrates the phenomenological level of inquiry and has gained many enthusiastic followers. Sociologists, in turn, are distributed along a broad dimension of varying respect for Marxian theory and ideology, which in the last decade has gotten involved in practically all aspects of the discipline. The profession encompasses demographers and "human ecologists" who attend almost exclusively to the spatial distribution of census variables, theorists who strive to organize sociological perspectives in line with the tradition of *Geisteswissenschaft,* its own adamant neo-Freudians, and still others who, like the humanistic psychologists, believe that sociological inquiry is at bottom phenomenological. These diverse alignments need attention because only by reference to the intellectual perspective from which an assertion is made on the present topic can it be compared with other assertions deriving from other perspectives.

But the overall division which I find to be most prevalent between the commentaries of psychologists and sociologists on the matter of moral commitment is this: psychology tends to be behavioristic, preferring methodologically public data; sociology, though it does not explicitly embrace a phenomenological point of view, generally allows that subjective or method-ologically private data are important. I will call these positions, thus divided, *empirical* and *idealistic,* admitting that the terms do not fit all practitioners of either field: In fact, they refer best to past traditions rather than present positions, but the study of human morality is one for which the past governs the present.

Against Idealism

I want briefly to continue the historical polemic against idealism in social thought with which Mead was involved, because his enemy was the same idealism mentioned above, and because a polemic clarifies a positive thesis in specifying the position to which it is opposed. Sociological idealism is still very much alive. Because Talcott Parsons, early in his career, published several persuasive and closely reasoned statements from an idealistic point of view of the role of normative elements in social processes, these statements are the target of the polemic. Indeed it was in the context of a polemic against "behaviorism" and "metaphysical materialism" that Parsons advanced his positive thesis.

There is a sense in which a polemic pays the point of view it opposes considerable respect: it is considered important enough to refute. This essay disagrees with some of Parsons' answers to the question of the role of normative elements and agrees with others, depending on what part of his omnibus commentaries is at issue. But the entire present work is predi-cated on the importance of the question itself, and it has been Parsons, more than anyone else, who has called sociologists' attention to it. His priority in this respect must be acknowledged, along with any claim of the present theory to make some new contribution.

Idealism in philosophy asserts that ideal rather than material states are fundamental. It stresses an introspective method, for this is how such states are made known. The core of morality as revealed by this method is a subjective sense of moral commitment or obligation. For such a thorough-going idealist as Kant, a sense of obligation provided the sole motive for moral action.[3] But the study of moral commitment by a subjective method poses a problem for any science which inquires into its origins, for the sense of obligation is persistently ahistorical. The experience of commitment seems to tell us nothing about its origins. As a result, some philosophers

---

[3] Kant's position can be construed either as a hypothesis (Durkheim read it this way) or as a definition of moral action (that is, action following from motives other than obligation really isn't moral). Either interpretation indicates the idealistic position.

have concluded that moral commitment has no history, that it is timeless and perhaps transcendental (for a modern statement of an ahistorical or innate moral sense, see Bertocci, 1945). Although such speculations are not strongly entertained today in sociology, there persists an inarticulate conception of the human sense of moral commitment, if not as inborn, still as invariably acquired. The belief persists because sociologists have few reservations about introspection, and because they are on the whole very moral men. The notion of a ubiquitous sense of obligation may be called the "idealistic" conception of moral commitment. In its naive form the conception is that the obligation attaches to particular values. Probably very few sociologists hold this view today, for as a whole they have been very much impressed by the diversity of human values among different groups. In more sophisticated versions of idealism, the values themselves are permitted to vary but the ubiquitous sense of obligation to *some* sort of values remains. This is the position that Parsons advanced in his important paper of 1935, "The Place of Ultimate Values in Sociological Theory," in which he offered the ubiquity of a sense of duty as evidence for other points, and treated a binding sense of moral obligation as a settled matter of fact (Parsons, 1935, pp. 288–90). I have argued elsewhere (Scott, 1963) that Parsons appears to have changed his position on this matter, and we shall see that his most detailed statements on internalization as a process (rather than as a result) largely agree with the present theory. Yet the idealistic legacy still lingers. A number of Parsons' students now hold influential positions in sociology themselves, and many studied under him when he was presenting an idealistic conception of normative elements to sociology.

Because it has supplied most of the concepts and categories by which normative elements are analyzed, idealism has given a persistently subjective emphasis to the study of moral behavior. It gives an edge to some scientific questions and makes others impossible to ask. If one such category, for example, refers to some subjective state which by implication is predicable of all men, then it is not hard to invent explanations that use this implied universality, e.g., that social order generally prevails because all men feel obligated to the norms on which it depends. Now this particular explanation may be partly true; and it is argued below that there is indeed a close connection between social order and moral commitment. But the important prior questions—whether a sense of obligation has in fact any existence beyond the name that has been invented for it; or, if it does exist, where it comes from, how it is maintained, and whether it is constant or variable— are thus removed from the level of empirical contingency to repose in the categorical "frame of reference." The categories get taken for granted, not only by those congenial to the idealism they convey but also by graduate students who accept them on the authority of their professors and by others who simply do not imagine that alternate categories are possible. To be sure, the idealism has been attenuated in its passage from Kant to Weber to Parsons and on to Parsons' students. But it is still strong enough to cause Parsons and most of his students to emphasize the importance of internal commitment in social control and, most important, to depreciate the role of sanctions.[4]

The Parsonian perspective is tenacious. It is very hard to reject it by an appeal to any possible evidence, for it prospers on Parsons' indubitable skill in the multiplication of concepts—the strictures of William of Occam are not for him. In terms of his "action scheme," alternate hypotheses get rejected not on the basis of evidence against them but through a suspicion that they must be incomplete or wrong because they fail to take account of the "facts of obligation" or the "universality of the normative element in action"—that is, because they fail to refer to all of the categories derived from the idealistic tradition. Thus in *The Structure of Social Action* Parsons defines "action" in terms of an actor, an end or goal, means and conditions for the realization of the goal, and an "independent, determinate, selective factor," the normative element, which he insists is not reducible to the means and conditions (Parsons, 1937, pp. 44–46. For more discussion of Parsons' reasoning on this matter, see Scott, 1962, 1963, pp. 719–24). While a wide variety of hypotheses about social behavior may be expressed in terms of this "action scheme," one that cannot be expressed is the hypothesis that normative elements have natural causes which sociology, or any other science, can study. Such causes turn out to be part of the "means and conditions" of action, by which normative elements cannot be explained *a priori*. The result of using categories derived from idealistic concerns is the strong tendency in sociology to view norms solely as independent variables. We have many statements of the effects of norms, but very few on their causes.

The introspective *method* of idealism (as distinct from its concepts) leads to similar results. When academicians practice introspection (reading Parsons first is not necessary), the principal result seems to be a peculiar phenomenological record—what I call the "phenomenology of the moral man." This putative account of inner experience rigidly distinguishes sanctions from commitment, celebrates the latter and obscures the former, and supports a view that moral commitment is autonomous and independent—that it is not just an independent variable but an *eternally* independent variable. Indeed, some commentators on the phenomenology of moral experience explicitly reject *any* account of its origins. Parsons did just this in 1935:

---

4 This was one of Parsons' recurrent themes in his advancement of voluntarism in *The Structure of Social Action*; in his review of Durkheim (pp. 382 ff.) he strives to exorcise the latter's emphasis on external control and replace it by internal commitment.

"[T]he inner sense of freedom of moral choice...is just as ultimate a fact as any other. ... *In fact a psychological explanation of moral obligation really explains away the phenomenon itself*" (pp. 288–90, emphasis supplied). Introspection is therefore a poor guide to the discovery of the conditions on which moral commitment depends, because the discovery of an "inner sense of freedom" inspires men to believe that there really are no such conditions. Introspection among Western intellectuals causes voluntarism to become a vital part of the idea of morality itself. There is more to be said on this association below.

Since the present theory holds that moral commitment does depend on external conditions, it denies the implications of introspection. That moral commitment "feels free" does not mean that objectively it *is* free. The following exposition will therefore be more clearly understood if problems with the subjective method and its ancillary concepts are brought up at the start.

The "Fallacy of Reductionism" and the Logic of Explanation

"The analytical independence" of sociological concepts is a key phrase in theoretical discussions, and it is often used by Parsons and his students in reference to norms. We are told that they must not be "reducible to the conditions of action," nor explained in "biological categories." Rather they must be dealt with at "their own analytical level," lest we commit the "fallacy of reductionism." The problem here is one of definition of terms and analysis of concepts. What is "analytical independence?" Is it the same thing as independent variation, so that X, being "analytically independent" with respect to Y, may assume various values irrespective of any value of Y? Or does it mean that X is some determinate function of Y, but that this relation is not a sociological concern? What are "biological categories?" Are variables associated with the sexual division of labor, for example, biological or sociological categories? Is it possible they might be both? How can we study the implications of physiological factors and ecological arrangements for social organization without reference to biological categories? Are variables on the "sociological level of analysis" considered *a priori* to be independent of other levels? What, indeed, *are* levels of analysis? Are they levels of explanation? Of organization? These are only a few of the questions that may be asked.

Since sociologists are so concerned with reduction, it is pertinent to ask what reduction is. A tentative definition is that "reduction" constitutes the explanation of one set of propositions by showing them to be a special case of another set.[5] The set to which the propositions are reduced is thus always more general. Suppose that the claims of sociology constitute the first set, and those of some other field—psychology, ecology, or biology in some general sense—constitute the second. To such a reduction very many sociologists will object. They will, in effect, argue that the more general set of propositions does not in fact account for all the propositions of sociology. But only in effect, for these opponents of reduction are not likely to regard their field of inquiry as a body of propositions or to be much concerned with scientific methods for their verification. The objection is not concerned with the logic of explanation, but with the quality of the subject matter. We are told that the events of social life, not the least of which is the moral commitment of its members, are on such a different level, and possessed of such idiosyncratic qualities, that a reductive explanation is not so much wrong as somehow just irrelevant. The opposition is not simply to "premature" reduction, for that implies that a "mature" reduction would be unobjectionable. What is opposed is *any* reduction, regardless of any warrant for it by the facts of the case or the logic of the explanation. And most of the opposition strives to preserve the relevance for sociology of subjective phenomena, which it is widely supposed a reductive explanation will depreciate.[6]

There is, however, a problem with the characteristic antireductionistic stance in sociology—a problem which I think will become more clear and more severe if scientific explanation advances in the study of human events. Antireductionism evolves into anti-theoretical particularism. Insofar as science explains complex and particular events by simple and general *theories* —that is, hypothetical explanations for which not all the confirming or

---

5 Cf. Marion J. Levy, Jr. (not the strongest philosophical idealist among Parsons' students): "Reductionism may be defined as the attempt to theorize about matters considered to be on one level of generalization in terms of the conceptual scheme of a more general level" (1963, p. 17). This is not an invidious notion of reduction in that it does not imply (as is usually implied) that reduction is illegitimate. Levy deals with the "legitimacy" of reduction by specifying further two "illegitimate forms," which he calls "premature" and retarded."

6 Not all reductions would do so; it is logically possible that a set of propositions which make no reference to subjective events could be explained by a more general set which do so refer. This sort of "idealistic reduction" is found in sophisticated statements of philosophical idealism, for example, Berkeley's "to be is to be perceived" or Schopenhauer's "The world is my idea." Modern phenomenologists within and without sociology seem to invoke this idealistic reduction with their notions of the "social (intersubjective) construction of reality." It is interesting to note that Parsons (1937) argued for a dualism in which *both* mind and matter were equally and irreducibly real, rather than for an idealistic monism. See Scott, 1963, pp. 722, fn. 28, and 723–24. Probably most antireductionistic sociologists would repair to such a dualistic position if they were to make their metaphysical beliefs explicit.

confuting facts have yet been marshaled—then these theories stand or fall in large part according to the test of evidence eventually brought to bear on them, including those which are more or less reductive. When a theory proposes a reductive explanation which evidence later proves to be false, then we can speak of a "premature" reduction in the sense indicated by Levy: it "assumes that a range of (unexplained) variation within limits does not exist, when at a given state of knowledge it does." The facts are more variable than the account of variation offered by the theory.

Historians of the behavioral sciences have traced the rise and fall of many reductions which later proved to be premature, and of other reductive explanations which, if not demonstrably premature, still proved to be dead ends in terms of further scientific development. The apparent differences between the animate and the inanimate, between man and lower animals, between symbolic and infrasymbolic behavior, have long proved to be difficult to reconcile by reductive explanation, and they probably will remain difficult for some time to come. But many social scientists have been so impressed with this difficulty that they have failed to recognize it as one of the essential tasks of scientific explanation: in arguing against premature reduction they have advocated what Levy calls an "untenable nonreductionism," assuming "that a range of (unexplained) variation... exists, when at a given state of knowledge it does not" (1963, pp. 17–18). Levy's remarks on the intellectual history of this tendency are pertinent:

> [I]n the case of biological determinism, some of the victors (and their intellectual descendents) of the fight against premature reductionism were and are in some danger of asserting biological factors to be irrelevant on as cavalier a basis as the biological determinists once asserted their complete relevance. Furthermore, many scholars were so scarred by the struggle that they are far less likely than they might be otherwise to recognize quite tenable grounds for reductionism [1963, pp. 17–18].

An antireductionistic argument probably did serve sociology well in the early effort to establish the field. If social phenomena are not reducible to some nonsocial explanation, so the argument ran, all the more reason to establish a separate discipline of sociology. But sociology today is a going concern, increasingly composed of present results rather than programs for the future. Besides, a discipline can define and claim a specific subject matter without having to claim that the subject matter is idiosyncratic and admits of no reductive explanations. In view of the complexity of the arguments that have hinged on this last assertion and the fervor of the debaters, a proof of it is really very simple.

Assume an explanatory hierarchy, in which the sociological phenomena comprise factor *B*. Factor *B* is shown empirically to explain some factor *C*. Then assume that *B* is subsequently explained by factor *A*. If *B* explains *C*, and A explains B, then A explains C.[7] But this does not mean that B no longer explains C; only that B itself is no longer unexplained. Nor, for that matter, does B necessarily change its properties simply because it is explained. Does a rose smell less sweet because some biochemist knows the formula for its aromatic oils and can even synthesize it out of coal tar? Explaining an object no more changes its properties than giving it a name does. We do, to be sure, have names without objects (such as "unicorn") whose analysis has exercised many philosophers. Many scientific concepts (such as "phlogiston") have proved to be names without objects, or "explanatory fictions." Explanation has removed many such names from the scientific vocabulary. But it cannot make objects disappear, and so long as a specialized field of science studies real objects and not just a set of names, a general reductive explanation will not cause them to disappear either. The modern trend to reduce biology to chemistry, for example, has caused not the disappearance of biological disciplines but rather their tremendous growth. The increasing unity of science brought about by reduction in the natural sciences has enriched many more fields than it has impoverished.

A *particular* reduction may, of course, prove to be wrong. But there is no *general* fallacy of reductionism. If all explanations are reductions, then sociology can reject particular explanations not simply because they are reductive but only because they are wrong. It must either admit the possibility of reduction or abandon the quest for explanation.

The issue of reduction in general is separate from the reducibility of one particular field to another. In sociology, the usual issue is whether sociology should or should not be reduced to psychology.[8] Much of this particular

---

[7] For a quantification of syllogistic inference and an ingenious solution to the ancient problem of the undistributed middle using conventional statistical measures of association, see Costner and Leik (1964). The old problem with syllogisms of the form "All A is B, but only some B is C" is that no inference can be drawn as to whether any (let alone how much) A is C. Costner and Leik show how much of C we can infer is explained by A (the "proportion of variance explained") if, for example, A explains 80 per cent of B, and B explains 75 per cent of C.

[8] That it *should* be reduced is the particular claim of sociology's currently most outspoken reductionist, George C. Homans. In his 1964 presidential address to the American Sociological Association, "Bringing Men Back In," Homans said with respect to the internationalization of values that "the explanation is given not by any distinctively sociological propositions but by the propositions of learning theory in psychology" (Homans, 1964, p. 814). Also, "When a serious effort is made, even by functionalists, to construct an explanatory theory, its general propositions turn out to be psychological—propositions about the behavior of men, not the equilibrium of societies" (Homans, 1964, p. 809). Presumably Homans would mean by "psychological propositions" those about the behavior of men. While this essay closely agrees with most of Homans' substantive sociology and his criticism of nonreductionism in sociology, the relation between psychology and sociology is handled differently. When you look at them closely, propositions about the equilibrium of societies are also statements about the behavior of men. I also think it likely that much of contemporary psychology will be reduced to sociology, rather than vice versa. These matters are discussed later.

debate is pointless. Reduction is an operation of explaining particular events in terms of general theories, and as between psychology and sociology it is not at all clear which theories of the two fields are more general. If social behavior is more general than whatever is judged to be the subject matter of psychology, then psychology could in principle be reduced to sociology instead of (as sociologists fear) the other way round. Our argument, which stresses the primacy of social reinforcement in what is usually regarded as a psychological process, is in some respects such a reduction of psychology to sociology.

Sociology and Reinforcement Psychology

Sociology and psychology are not so much set off from each other by different ranks in a heirarchy of explanation—the question of reducibility of a less general set of propositions to a more general set—as by a study of the same concrete events from different points of view. They are differentiated almost exclusively by their methods of abstraction. It is approximately correct to say that psychology studies individuals and sociology studies groups; the problem is that all humans and most other mammals live in groups and that all groups are composed of individuals.[9] Necessarily, then, the two fields produce parallel discussions of individual and collective aspects of the same concrete events. If the two fields had closely related intellectual histories, these parallel discussions might be closely coordinated, but we have seen that they have not.

The branch of psychology called "learning theory" or (in part) "reinforcement psychology" is, to most sociologists, quite remote. To the extent that they appreciate psychology at all, sociologists are likely to be aware of studies in personality, of social psychology, and of clinical practice; they tend to ignore discussions of more general psychological theory and experiments on nonhuman subjects. Our claim—that sociology and learning theory are complementary—therefore seems novel. Since the book as a whole attempts to show this complementarity, only an outline of it follows here.

---

[9] This concretely inseparable association between individual organisms and group life has not prevented assertions that only individuals or groups (especially the former) are real or are proper objects for scientific predication of properties. Actually, the individual-group distinction is both abstract and relative. Distinctions between simple objects or units of analysis and aggregations of such objects or units can be made at many levels—for example, particle–atom, atom–molecule, molecule–cell, cell–organism. Thus a personality, though a single unit when considered as an individual relative to a human group, can also be considered as an aggregation of individual acts. The individual–group debates have their counterpart, on this level in psychology, in preferences for molecular or molar levels of analysis. If whether a given object is a simple object or an aggregation is a relative matter, then most debates on whether any particular aggregation is the proper level of study are pointless. Unfortunately, this is not likely to put an end to them.

The claim itself is not new. In 1941, Neal Miller and John Dollard published *Social Learning and Imitation,* in which they tried to show how the acquisition of social behavior could be explained in terms of the learning principles advanced by Clark L. Hull. In his Preface to that work, Mark A. May ventured a programmatic statement which still expresses well a practical relation between sociology and learning theory:

[This work] proposes that those who work with the principles of learning (psychologists, social psychologists) cannot evolve a theory of social behavior without understanding the social order which sets the conditions for human learning. Conversely, technicians in the social sciences must consent to take some account of the principles governing that long learning experience which fits any individual for participation in the social order. From psychology, then, are derived the fundamental principles of learning, and from social science its prime conditions [May, 1941, p. viii].

This drives–conditioners division of labor has not been widely embraced. The perspective of *Social Learning and Imitation* seems to have been affected by the separate decline of the Hullian variety of learning theory on which it was based. But the basic distinction is not tied to any one theory of learning and remains generally sound. There *is* a useful psychological literature on the general principles of learning or the shaping of behavior, and the literature of sociology records what gets learned outside the experimental laboratory. Insofar as they are concerned with cataloging the natural reinforcements of human behavior, psychologists will turn increasingly to the social environment and thus to sociology. *It is within the subject matter of sociology that the important conditioners are to be found.*

This claim is perhaps obvious in one respect and surprising in another. The tendency is strong among psychologists to consider as reinforcing stimuli only those that the experimentor is able to present in a laboratory. The assertion that important conditioners operate outside a laboratory goes beyond their habitual use of the concept and thus seems somehow inappropriate. This is one result of "experimental positivism," discussed in detail in Chapter IV. But no branch of learning theory has formally defined its concepts so narrowly: they apply in principle to natural settings (both social and nonsocial), even though the application is not often made.

In the natural setting much of the reinforcement of a social animal comes from the behavior of other animals of the same species. Generally the more complex the animal the more important the social reinforcement.[10] When

---

[10] On the experimental level these statements are supported by the work of Harlow (1959) and Harlow and Harlow (1961); also Mason (1963); all in Southwick (1963). For field studies see any of the other papers in the Southwick volume, and Tinbergen (1953, Chaps. VII and VIII).

we consider the extent to which group life among these animals is instrumental to their survival, it is not surprising that the physiological mechanisms underlying this capacity for social stimulation have evolved. The primate ethologist Sherwood Washburn has written that "most of a baboon's life is spent within a few feet of other baboons" (Southwick, 1963, p. 99), and what is true for baboons is that much more true for humans, whose societies are not less social because they are more complex.

Students of animal and human societies often differ in their conception of what constitutes a society or social system, but it would be difficult to find one in either field who would deny that *interaction* among different organisms (or actors) is a basic part of it. "Interaction," in turn, is variously defined, but the central idea is that the activity of one organism produces certain actions in another, which in turn produce reactions in the first. Some sociologists would stress the importance of subjective factors, such as "perception" or "interpretation," through which they claim the effects of interaction are mediated, but none omit the interdependence of the activity, regardless of how they claim it gets produced. In this step sociologists have already moved close to learning theory, because interaction can be viewed as a special case of reinforcement, that is, as reciprocal social reinforcement.

Both learning theorists and sociologists are concerned with the variables of which behavior is a function. Their styles and perspectives are of course widely divergent, and the sociologists are concerned only with the social variables, but since this appears to be by far the most important subset of all the variables that affect the complex behavior of social animals, the limitation is not great.

Among all the varieties of learning theory, the one that connects most directly to the data of sociology is Skinner's operant behaviorism. This is why the Skinnerian lexicon is used for the exposition of the present theory. Skinner's candid disrespect for methodologically private data, his delight in battle with his more humanistic critics, and his unbounded Harvardian self-confidence probably make sociologists even less receptive to his approach than they are to learning theory in general. Yet many features of the operant approach render sociological materials a good source of data for it. Skinner has, for example, derided the "ghost physiology" of some learning theorists who repair to a convenient "conceptual nervous system" in order to connect stimuli and responses. His advice is to leave physiology to the physiologists, the better for the behavioral sciences to study the other, more readily observable variables of which behavior is also a function. Equally fictitious as explanations in his view are "personality constructs," especially the "three little men" (id, ego, and superego) of the Freudian model. Many sociologists profess to disagree with Skinner's programs, but they have long followed many of his recommendations in practice. Not that they often eschew personality variables; many sociologists (especially those of a psychoanalytic persuasion) would argue that "personality variables" constitute a "separate level of analysis" reducible in principle neither "down" to physiology nor "up" to the social environment.[11] Yet the practical result of sociological research has not been to demonstrate the independence of personality from the social environment but rather its close dependence upon it. Socializing institutions—"persistent patterns of social reinforcement applied mainly to naive organisms," to use a different phrase—are argued to be the *source* of personality. Ellsworth Faris marshaled comparative evidence on social causes of variation in presumably invariant psychological structures over forty years ago in his cogent essay, "Of Psychological Elements" (1937). Willard Waller's chapter, "What Teaching Does to the Teacher" (1928), is an early and still excellent discussion of what is now called "adult socialization," while Kingsley Davis' discussion of isolated children (1948, pp. 204–8) offers a concise and logical statement of what may be extrapolated from negative cases. In this way, sociology meets the canons of the Skinnerian program surprisingly well—better, in fact, than much psychology. Its practitioners are not on the whole fascinated by inborn drives, and many are skilled in the critical dissection of presumably invariant and reinforcement-free personality structures. Since sociology yields information on social reinforcements and their organization, it is not surprising that Skinner, in order to illustrate his argument in *Science and Human Behavior,* becomes a shrewd amateur sociologist, describing the reinforcing properties of commonplace social life. The "empty organism," purged of mentalistic fictions, gets refilled through social reinforcement: <u>where psyche was, there shall sanction be</u>.

One reason why the Skinnerian program has a brighter future in sociology than psychology involves the institutionalization of scientific disciplines. Skinner's conceptual armamentarium is parsimonious in the extreme. Were it to be established as legislative for academic psychology, large numbers of psychologists who now make the analysis of mentalistic constructs and other unparsimonious conceptions their life work would find their efforts to be redundant. Whole specialties in psychology, each with its own traditions, would come to an end. And academic psychology, like other fields, is a veritable institution, infused with value for those who work in it. Since Skinner's program would radically change psychology, most psychologists who value their traditions oppose it; for this reason, among others,

---

[11] See, for example, the attempt to make room for personality variables as not simply a consequence of "organizational roles" in Levinson (1959).

it is not likely to prevail among the next generation of psychologists.[12]

Skinner's program threatens institutionalized aspects of sociology much less than those of psychology. The emphasis on reinforcement, especially on its social forms, integrates easily with the traditional sociological thesis of the importance of group life. Except for some parts of social psychology— a disputed territory claimed by both psychology and sociology, many of whose practitioners have been trained in psychology—Skinnerian concepts render few sociological concepts redundant. Unlike psychological concepts, sociological concepts are not so much logically contrary to those of operant behaviorism as they are logically complementary, expressing modes of organization among reinforcers. Contemporary theories of social organization are already notably complex and cumbersome, and a statement of their elementary constituent units in economical terms is therefore very much to be desired.

One important aspect of this complementarity lies in the method of explanation used alike by operant behaviorism and the more substantive (as set off from conceptual or classificatory) theory of functionalist sociology, differing only in the scale of events to which each is applied. The operant behaviorist typically works on a small scale and observes the relation between an operant and its reinforcers. His population is usually one organism, or at most a small group. The logic of his explanation is essentially that of causation according to Hume: A causes B if the two are regularly associated, spatially proximate, and A precedes B temporally. Any more intimate notion of a causal link is dismissed as "metaphysics" (Hume) or "explanatory fictions" (Skinner). But for resting his case on these "empty correlations" the operant behaviorist is criticized for neglecting an account "more adequate in terms of psychological causation." We are told that his task should be to explain *why* a given stimulus is a reinforcer, or that he should also consider various processes intermediate between operant and reinforcer ("motivation," "drive reduction," "learning," as distinct from "performance," and so on).

The functional sociologist typically works on a large scale and studies relations among broad aspects of social structure. His population is usually

---

12 See, e.g., the polemic of the influential psychologist Sigmund Koch against behaviorism in general and also against much that Skinner advocates (1964, pp. 6 ff.). See also Skinner's comments at that symposium (1964, pp. 42 ff.). What is said here about why psychologists oppose Skinner also applies to the current decline in empiricist programs among philosophers. Several of empiricism's strongest advocates have publicly recanted their earlier views. One severe practical problem with the positivistic program was that, if taken seriously, philosophers would either have to abandon the field or undertake, at a mature age, a laborious education in logic or the technical details of some empirical science. Most of them rejected the positivistic program instead.

large; the behavior studied is usually a massive complex involving many actors (for example, "economic development"). He too uses Hume's notion of causation. But for resting his case on empty correlations (e.g., between fertility on the one hand and economic development, urbanization, or rules of residence on the other) the functionalist is criticized for "talking about explanations without actually explaining anything." An "adequate explanation," he is admonished, "must be on another level—that of the behavior of men." In order to be adequate, the functionalist theory must be more specific about the psychological contingencies involved—e.g., what individual processes intervene between high fertility and low rates of economic development? It is interesting to note that the principal critic of functionalism in this respect, George Caspar Homans (from whose previously cited address of 1964, "Bringing Men Back In," the preceding statements are paraphrased), recommends as a cure for the explanatory defects of functionalism that it repair to "behavior psychology"—that is, the same operant analysis criticized for the same defect on a different scale. But perhaps this merely gives more reason for operant and functional analysis to join ranks: one to study behavior experimentally on a small scale; the other to study societal behavior through observation on a large scale. As between the two the first is molecular and the second molar. Both rely on a skeptical empiricism, and both study relations among observed variables without speculating on whatever unobserved (and sometimes unobservable) variables might be intermediate among them. They both offend critics who insist that some particular level of abstraction or of observational scale be included in all explanation at any level and on any scale.

Many conventional sociological propositions can be readily translated into the terminology of operant behaviorism. The concept of "the significance of the group for the individual," so well promulgated in textbooks in order to convince college freshmen (who imagine that their highly age-specific, sex-specific, and class-specific behavior is unique and voluntary) of the relevance of sociology, becomes "the relative strength of social reinforcers as compared to all others." The organization of such reinforcing effects is what sociologists call "social structure." Most of them would add, of course, that there are limits to the variation in such organization, that it is worth studying in itself, or that not all the properties of such organization can be derived from presently confirmed propositions about single reinforcing stimuli or small aggregations of them.[13] But none of these qualifications

---

[13] Perhaps this is a more tenable statement of some older criticisms of reductionism. Certainly it is preferable to the wearisome contradiction that "the whole is greater than the sum of its parts." Synergistic interaction among some parts of a whole is analytically yet another part.

is inconsistent with the definition of social structure as a massive aggregation of social reinforcements. The psychologists' notion of "discrimination"—the response of an organism to one stimulus out of a larger set of stimuli within which it frequently occurs—can be applied to the sociologists' "role" or "role expectation." Since the strongest reinforcers come from fellow organisms of the same species, the individual will be most rewarded and least punished when he discriminates, among all the stimuli produced by his fellows, those which persistently occur in association with particular activities of his own. This is to say that the most important things an actor can learn are "role-expectations." When the organism learns a response of his own by reinforcements from others which in turn are responses to his own behavior, he has learned his self-concept (Mead was a learning theorist too, at least programmatically).

The concepts of reinforcement theory provide perhaps the simplest and clearest way to distinguish between ascribed and achieved status—a distinction sociologists regularly make, but one that is surprisingly hard to define formally. A status can be said to be *achieved* to the extent that (1) placement in it is a function of operant activity, and (2) its occupants are reinforced on a "ratio schedule," that is, as a function of the rate of emission of activities. A status can be said to be *ascribed* to the extent that (1) placement in it is not a function of operant activity, and (2) its occupants are not reinforced as a function of the rate of activity, that is, on *interval* (so much reinforcement per unit of time) or other non-ratio schedule. Skinner and his co-workers find that ratio reinforcements are remarkable for the high rates of activity they produce in experiments; sociologists observe the same thing on a larger observational scale in the importance of achieved statuses in economic development, as well as in such homely examples as the output of salesmen, baseball players, business executives, and nontenured professors who must "publish or perish," all of whom are paid and promoted largely in proportion to how much they produce. Skinner notes that most natural schedules are a mixture of various analytically distinguishable schedules; sociologists have observed that there are no concrete examples of purely ascribed or purely achieved status, but only statuses that embody elements of each, tending from case to case more toward one element than the other.

These remarks merely adumbrate what might be said on the complementarity of sociology and learning theory. The general point is this: the important reinforcements of social animals are themselves social, and the analysis of social organization into statuses based on patterns of interaction is at the same time a classification of the schedules of the reinforcements of which the interaction is composed. While many sociologists deny in principle that social life is composed of reinforcement, the growing implication of their research is, to the contrary, that it is so composed.

The Impossibility of Scientific Phenomenology

One tradition of sociological thought contrary in spirit to learning theory or behaviorism involves the importance of subjective elements in sociological analysis. Parsons' emphasis on "the point of view of the actor" has encouraged this emphasis on the subjective; he acknowledged the relation of this perspective, as developed in *The Structure of Social Action,* to Husserl's phenomenology (1937, p. 750). Parsons' position since that time has been equivocal, but he still seems unwilling to depreciate the subjective point of view (Scott, 1963, pp. 724–31). A new approach in sociology rejects Parsons' current ambivalence between behaviorism and phenomenology and returns to the uncompromising subjectivism found in *The Structure of Social Action.* This doctrine is based on the work of Edmund Husserl, most of the exegesis and development having been performed by Alfred Schutz (Edward Tiryakian has recently presented this position, together with much evidence of subjectivism among influential sociological writers [1965, pp. 674–88]. See also the comments by various sociologists in the same journal—*American Sociological Review,* 31, 1966, pp. 258 ff.).

As we have already said, the theory to be presented in this volume does not attempt to explain subjective aspects of moral commitment. This is an important and radical omission because, as embodied in such concepts as "guilt" and "obligation," these aspects are ubiquitous in other discussions. The reasons for their omission therefore require some account.

Most propositions about subjective events are impossible to verify, given the general verificatory practices of most scientists, including behavioral scientists. This is not to deny that such propositions may have heuristic value in the formulation, within a theory, of propositions about objective events which present no special problems of verification. If this be the case for a subjective analysis of moral commitment, then it would be an error to ignore it even when one's objective is to formulate a theory solely of the objective aspects of moral commitment. And no doubt some subjective analyses have been scientifically fruitful in this manner. Yet attention to subjective events has not, in my opinion, been heuristically valuable: more often it has led behavioral scientists *away* from the development of good objective theories. But the first problem lies in the scientific analysis of subjective events.

Philosophers, like behavioral scientists, often have trouble sorting out what they believe ought to be from what there is. A recurrent problem in modern philosophy of science is that adherents of particular philosophical positions—especially, perhaps, the logical empiricists or logical positivists—have tended to state their own prescriptions or programs for scientific verification as if they were in fact descriptions of how the persons who engage in what is commonly called scientific activity actually come to assent to particular scientific statements or theories. The clearest example of this has been the "verifiability theory of meaning," which has undergone a number of revisions in the past twenty-five years as its advocates have come to realize that scientists habitually respect a number of theories that are only dubiously meaningful under the criterion of verifiability (see, e.g., Hempel, 1959). Now by adopting an appropriate criterion of verification it becomes an easy matter to rule phenomenological inquiry out of science. It is much harder to dismiss such inquiry by a criterion which most scientists will actually respect, because scientists disagree in their definitions of "sufficient verification" or "relevant evidence."

There does remain, however, one datum that has always been regarded with suspicion. This is the *private event*, the event that only one person can observe. The more public an event, the less debate about its status as a datum. Philosophically this is a very thorny field, for it is easy to argue that all science depends on sense perception and that all sense perception is private, so that scientists cannot really exclude private events (a representative discussion of this issue is found in Malcolm, 1965, pp. 149 ff.). But the scientific preference for proximate—if not philosophically ultimate—publicity still obtains in practice.

Consider the debates over the existence of canals on Mars. The assertion that there *are* canals on Mars was based solely on the observations of a few astronomers who claimed to see more detail, due to their diligent efforts to observe that planet under rarely perfect conditions, than could be resolved in photographs taken under ordinary terrestrial conditions. The acrimonious debate over these claims was precisely a consequence of the inability of their defendents to verify them more publicly. The controversy is now settled by the photographs (by the *Mariner* space vehicles) from outer space—it appears that there are no canals—which provide *public* data not previously available.

Within the behavioral sciences there is a debate over extrasensory perception. Most of the claims about "ESP" are publicly verifiable in principle, and many of its advocates have been careful to use experimental procedures. But in general only those persons who also have a strong commitment to certain religious and supernatural doctrines have produced positive evidence on ESP. When disinterested or critical psychologists have performed the experiments, no positive evidence has been found.[14] Some advocates of ESP

---

14 For a comprehensive discussion, critical of ESP, see Gardner (1957, Chap. 25). The flavor of debates on the matter is well represented in discussions attending an article by Price (1965). See also the rejoinders of Soal and Rhine, comments by Meehl, Scriven, and Bridgman, and a reply by Price, in *Science*, 123, January 6, 1965.

A recent book by Hansel (1966) provides a comprehensive and severe evaluation of research on and advocacy of ESP.

have claimed that it is attenuated or inoperative in the presence of persons who strongly disbelieve in it. This renders public verification—*disinterested* public verification, at least—impossible in principle. Psychologists have also been dissatisfied (though not so much as with research into ESP) with conclusions drawn from psychiatric interviews, especially when the claim is advanced by orthodox Freudians that only a person who has himself been analyzed is competent to interpret the "protocols" (transcripts or tape recordings) of psychoanalytic sessions. Given the ambiguous criteria for successful psychoanalysis, this constraint on verification is logically similar to the parapsychologists' requirement of prior belief in ESP (on psychoanalysis see Boring [1940] and Sachs [1940, pp. 127–42]).

In none of these examples is an exclusively selected verifying audience a *necessary* limitation of the research itself. Presumably any number of astronomers could look, and evidently have looked, at Mars through telescopes, and any number of psychologists could witness an ESP experiment or watch a video tape of a psychoanalysis. The difficulties and arguments have occurred simply because the limitation of the audience was enforced as a matter of *doctrine* extrinsic to the research. When an exclusive verifying audience is a matter of logical necessity, we can expect the conclusions thereby verified to be viewed with at least equal suspicion. When the verifying audience is so limited that it can have only member, suspicion reigns supreme.

This is just the situation that prevails in the analysis of first-person reports, the data of introspection, or the verification of propositions which refer to the "phenomenological level." Edward C. Tolman put the matter very well in the opening apothegm to his *Purposive Behavior in Animals and Men* (1932):

> The motives which lead to the assertion of a behaviorism are simple. All that can ever be actually observed in fellow human beings and in lower organisms is behavior. Another organism's private mind, if he have any, can never be got at. And even the supposed ease and obviousness of "looking within" and observing one's own mental processes, directly and at first hand, have proved, when subjected to laboratory control, in large part chimerical: the dictates of "introspection" have proved over and over again to be artifacts of the particular laboratory in which they were obtained.

The bearing of this judgment on phenomenology and subjective reference in sociology or any other science can be reduced to a simple syllogism. Scientific verification is public; the method of introspection is private: therefore introspection is not a method for scientific verification.

This is too simple of course. The report of introspection is not private but public. It can be written down, recorded, delivered in a packed auditorium. The problem is that the relation between the report and what is presumably reported can never be publicly checked. The relation must be inferred solely from the report: it is logically primitive or "given." This in turn has led some psychologists to regard reports of introspection as indubitable accounts of events which it is the object of their discipline to study. William James put the matter gracefully in his *Principles of Psychology* of 1890:

> *Introspective Observation is what we have to rely on first and always.* The word introspection needs hardly to be defined—it means, of course, looking into our own minds and reporting what we there discover. *Every one agrees that we there discover states of consciousness.* So far as I know, the existence of such states has never been doubted by any critic, however skeptical in other respects he may have been. That we have *cogitations* of some sort is the *inconcussum* in a world most of whose other facts have at some time tottered on the brink of philosophical doubt. All people unhesitatingly believe that they feel themselves thinking, and that they distinguish the mental state as an inward activity or passion, from all the objects with which it may cognitively deal. *I regard this belief as the most fundamental of all the postulates of Psychology.* . .[15]

The good common sense of James's statement masks the fact that it is a very difficult one for a public science to deal with. It is one thing to define introspection, but quite another to assert that "consciousness. . .has never been denied," and still another to venture that there is any equivalence between the conscious states of any two reporters (or even between two reports of such states by the same reporter). The reports themselves may be equivalent, of course, but we listen to them because they are supposed to tell us something about private events. This line of reasoning suggests that there is a problem involved in James's statement and that there is a way to solve it.

---

[15] Quoted in Boring, "A History of Introspection," 1953 (requoted in Boring, 1961, p. 212). Most sociologists, innocent as they are of involvement with the hoary debates about first-person reports, would probably find James's declaration unobjectionable. If so they should read Boring's whole article for an account of how psychologists have dealt with this problem over the years.

Boring was well qualified to comment on this issue, for he studied under E. B. Titchener, the final exponent of introspection as *the* method of psychology, and began his career as a practicing introspectionist. But by the time he wrote *The Physical Dimensions of Consciousness* (1933), Boring shared Tolman's dissatisfaction with introspection. Boring was the first experimental psychologist to chair the Department of Psychology at Harvard (it had previously been chaired by philosophers), and during his long tenure the department gathered such epistemological leftists as S. S. Stevens and B. F. Skinner. It is interesting to note that Harvard's epistemological rightists in psychology, such as Gordon Allport and Henry Murray, have generally been members of the Department of Social Relations, founded by Talcott Parsons, rather than Boring's Department of Psychology.

The problem is this: if we are really serious and consistent about accepting reports of states of consciousness, we end up accepting as scientific data a bewildering, contradictory, and often highly implausible set of statements. Introspection, which seems so easy and obvious at the beginning, in the end reveals private experience to be a chaos. One way to order the chaos and solve the problem is to move to a *public* interpretation of the meaning of first-person statements. We study the statements themselves—as behavior, rather than as reports of private states of consciousness (the public verification of private events is discussed at great length in Skinner, 1945).

Consider the following hypothetical report of a *golem*, stated, as introspection requires, in the first person. "My introspection reveals James to be wrong. I look for my own conscious states and find nothing at all. I have no states of consciousness." However outrageous this statemest may seem to phenomenologists and others who build on James's postulate, it is a consequence of their own emphasis on the "apodicticity" of phenomenological propositions that they cannot prove it to be false. They may suspect that the *golem* possesses states of consciousness, because he is a clever little fellow who can readily be observed making verbal responses and various complex and subtle discriminations among the stimuli with which he is presented, after the manner of humans who do admit to states of consciousness. But what is observed about the *golem* is only his *public* behavior—and, as Tolman pointed out so nicely thirty years ago, this is all that can be observed. The *golem*'s private mind, if he have one, can never be got at, can never be anybody's business but his own. Forced by their own logic to agree with the *golem,* phenomenologists may well suspect that he is lying, that he really is conscious but denies this truth just to confound them. Quite apart from debates on the usefulness of introspection, there are good grounds for their suspicion: as we argue in Chapter III, the verbal report of an activity is itself an activity, separate from the (public or private) activity reported; and the reporter is not always rewarded for providing the most literal and accurate report of which he is capable (the *golem* was designed for operant conditioning). And it is of course also true that a verbal report of introspection which confounds phenomenologists, even if it involves telling a lie, may be strongly reinforced (especially if the *golem*'s designer is a behaviorist).

Yet many behavioral scientists will still judge a theory which makes no statements about subjective events to be somehow the worse for their absence, even though they may agree, upon reflection, that such parts of the theory could never be verified. Now the adequacy of a theory as a whole which includes such statements is a separate matter from the verifiability of these statements alone. It depends on prior conceptions of what theories generally should or should not contain. In practice, scientists have long respected theories which contain unverifiable propositions, and the replacement of one scientific theory by another is not simply a movement away from a theory with many references to unobservable events toward one with few. A theory with many such references may still afford a more parsimonious explanation of observable variation than another with few such references. Then, too, scientists show well-established preferences for elegance in exposition and logic; and unobservable concepts may, because they are not constrained by definition in terms of observable events, be more elegant. Further, a hypothesis referring to subjective elements may (as we mentioned before) be heuristic in that it inspires its adherents to construct a better theory than they would otherwise, even if the subjective elements do not appear in the final version. Subjective concepts (especially those of psychoanalysis) often play this useful role in the behavioral sciences. Finally and most important, many statements which appear to refer solely to subjective events may refer to objective events as well. The language of the contemporary behavioral sciences is only slightly abstracted from the natural language of its practitioners—which, like all natural languages, is generally imprecise. The discourse of the most doctrinaire behaviorist seems often to involve subjective events at its outer edges, and most statements about "constitutive phenomenology" imply a great deal about ordinary public activities.

This last problem is complicated by the tendency of natural language to rely heavily on what appear to be subjective references. Insofar as the behavioral sciences stay close to natural language, this gives an advantage to the phenomenologists. But do the subjective terms in natural language refer *solely* to private events? Language is no less social and public than science: a language may be esoteric—much more esoteric than science, for that matter—but never methodologically private.[16] *What appears to be a private reference therefore has to be also an elliptical reference to something public.* Skinner has outlined the role of this reference in psychological explanations and gives a cogent example in the following discussion (wherein what he calls an "experimental analysis" can be understood also to be an analysis of relations among publicly observable events).

> In an experimental analysis, the relation between a property of behavior and an operation upon the organism is studied directly. Traditional mentalistic formulations, however, emphasize certain way stations. Where an experimental analysis might examine the effect of punishment on behavior, a mentalistic psychology will be concerned first with the effect of anxiety on behavior. The mental state seems to bridge the gap between dependent and

---

16 This is ventured as a statement of fact based on the failure of isolated children to use language except as a consequence of subsequent social interaction. And even if there were a truly private language, a public science would know nothing about it.

independent variables and is particularly attractive when these are separated by long periods of time—when, for example, the punishment occurs in childhood and the effect in the behavior of the adult.

The practice is widespread. In a demonstration experiment, a hungry pigeon was conditioned to turn around in a clockwise direction. A final, smoothly executed pattern of behavior was shaped by reinforcing successive approximations with food. Students who had watched the demonstration were asked to write an account of what they had seen. Their responses included the following: (1) the organism was conditioned to *expect* reinforcement for the right kind of behavior. (2) The pigeon walked around, *hoping* that something would bring the food back again. (3) The pigeon *observed* that a certain behavior seemed to produce a particular result. (4) The pigeon *felt* that food would be given it because of its action; and (5) The bird came to *associate* his action with the click of the food-dispenser. The observed facts could be stated respectively as follows: (1) The organism was reinforced *when* it emitted a given kind of behavior. (2) The pigeon walked around *until* the food container again appeared. (3) A certain behavior *produced* a particular result. (4) Food was given to the pigeon *when* it acted in a given way; and (5) the click of the food-dispenser *was temporally related* to the bird's action. These statements describe the contingencies of reinforcement. The expressions "expect," "hope," "observe," "feel," and "associate" go beyond them to identify effects on the pigeon. The effect actually observed was clear enough: the pigeon turned more skillfully and more frequently; but that was not the effect reported by the students. (If pressed, they would doubtless have said that the pigeon turned more skillfully and more frequently *because* it expected, hoped, and felt that if it did so food would appear.)

The events reported by the students were observed, if at all, in their own behavior. They were describing what they would have expected, felt, and hoped for under similar circumstances. But they were able to do so only because a verbal community had brought relevant terms under the control of certain stimuli, and this was done *when the community had access only to the kinds of public information available to the students in the demonstration.* Whatever the students knew about themselves which permitted them to infer comparable events in the pigeon must have been learned from a verbal community which saw no more of their behavior than they had seen of the pigeon's. Private stimuli may have entered into the control of their self-descriptive repertoires, but the readiness with which they applied them to the pigeon indicates that external stimuli had remained important. The extraordinary strength of a mentalistic interpretation is really a sort of proof that in describing a private way station one is, to a considerable extent, making use of public information.[17]

---

[17] B. F. Skinner, "Behaviorism at Fifty," (1964), pp. 90–91. Quoted with the permission of Professor Skinner and The University of Chicago Press (for Rice University). Copyright © 1964 by The University of Chicago Press.

In the same symposium, the philosopher Norman Malcolm (who does not wholly agree with Skinner) comments:

> I believe that Skinner has stated here an absolutely decisive objection to introspectionism. The intelligibility of psychological words must be based on something more than the occurrence of these words. That we have a common understanding of them proves that their use has to be logically connected with other public behavior [Malcolm, 1964, p. 149].

The objection to introspection presented by Skinner and Malcolm applies to its use in the study of moral commitment. It is in respect of these and the preceding objections that the present essay concentrates on the public aspects of morality and moral commitment. Commitment itself is not regarded here as a subjective sense of obligation, but as conformity in the relative absence of sanctions. Norms are not viewed as derived from conceptions of desirable courses of action, but as names for patterns of sanctions. Normative elements are not said to be perceived but to be discriminated. Conscience is not a subjective sense of duty or obligation but a report of a generalized disposition to conform. The existence of subjective aspects of moral commitment is not denied. Individuals often report that they feel guilty or righteous, or that they possess a sense of obligation, and we cannot prove that they are mistaken. The point is that insofar as these events are truly subjective, neither we nor they can prove that they are *not* mistaken, because the scientific determination of a mistake—that is, a discrepancy between the report and what is reported—would, if possible at all, have to compare two public events, and one of the events in question here is necessarily private. Conventional scientific verification of a first-person report of a subjective state is therefore impossible. The study of the reported *events,* in and of themselves (not of the *reports* in themselves, nor as part of some other study or as an heuristic aid to drawing other conclusions), will be fruitless, and will come in due course to no more adequate conclusions than those reached about the existence of ESP. The terms which have traditionally referred to subjective aspects need not be wholly abandoned, for Skinner and Malcolm show that any common meaning they have is "public property." Our emphasis will not be on the "mental way stations" they imply, but on the observable social behavior from which their public meaning derives. Skinner states the general point well in his influential *Science and Human Behavior:*

> The practice of looking inside the organism for an explanation of behavior has tended to obscure the variables which are immediately available for a scientific analysis. These variables lie outside the organism, in its immediate environment and in the environmental history [Skinner, 1953, p. 31].

The Phenomenology of the Moral Man

There is another problem with subjective perspectives—a problem which remains even if they *can* tell us something about the outside external environment, even if they *are* heuristically valuable, and which is particularly troublesome in the study of morality. If introspection is private, it is *a fortiori* parochial. Even if it does provide information about the social world, its range must be very narrow, for it tells us only about the social world of one man. If every man's social world were the same as every other's, this would pose no difficulty. But societies are in fact differentiated, often to an extreme degree. The range of possible experience of social life is therefore vastly greater than the range of the experience of any one man. This would still pose no problem if the social scientists who seek to extrapolate the general social environment from their own subjective experience were representative of all parts of that environment. Their collective extrapolations would then also be representative. But of course social scientists are not representative at all. The mechanisms whereby they are recruited and selected for professional work result in a highly concentrated selection mostly from one sex, from certain strata, and disproportionately from particular educational, occupational, and ethnic backgrounds. Their own subjective experience of moral commitment represents not all degrees and kinds of commitment but rather generally strong commitments to major institutional norms, together with some commitment to others that they chronically judge to be more fully institutionalized than they actually are. They are *moral* men, and their reports of the subjective experience of morality are therefore a phenomenology of moral men.

Indeed, not only sociological discussions of morality but most abstract discussions of it generally have derived from the phenomenology of moral men. Especially is this so for philosophers, who have usually been even more moral than sociologists and psychologists, and who have relied on ratiocination almost exclusively. Who but a moral man could have written *Principia Ethica,* with its lucid abstractions on the one hand and its artless provincialism on the other?[18] Whatever the other divisions in ethical theory, the

---

[18] It was written of course by George Edward Moore, fresh from the sanctuaries of English public schools and Cambridge and published in 1903, when Moore was twenty-six. The parochialism revealed even in Moore's quite abstract argument was sensed by George Santayana, who argued the relevance of conditioning to ethics in his classic rejoinder to Bertrand Russell's exposition of Moore's doctrine. Russell's background at this time was similar to Moore's. See Russell (1910) and Santayana (1913).

Moore himself subsequently was strongly affected by Charles Stevenson's "emotive theory of ethics," as presented in his *Ethics and Language* (1944). See his equivocations on the validity of the argument of *Principia Ethica,* in Schilpp (1942, pp. 536–47.)

observations of the cynic have usually been considered only that they might thereby be better deplored, as in Socrates' sophistical rejection of Thrasymachus' quite tenable assertion that "justice is the interest of the stronger." Thomas Hobbes is one of the few traditional thinkers to attend to the calculations of amoral and immoral men. He used this to unique advantage in his classic exposition in *Leviathan* of the conditions of the "war of every man as against every man." Hobbes also saw one deficiency inherent in *verstehen*—the attempt to know another man's private mind through introspection upon one's own. Although men are plainly unequal in their objective capacities, they are all equal in their conceits:

> For such is the nature of men that they may acknowledge many others to be more witty or more eloquent or more learned, yet they will hardly believe that there be many so *wise* as themselves, *for they see their own wit at hand and other men's at a distance* [Hobbes, 1651, p. 105].

Hobbes' reasoning shows, first, that subjective estimates of attributes which are subject to objective reward (wisdom is rewarded) are prone to parochial exaggeration; and second, that such estimates cannot actually be compared as between two or more men. If this is true of wisdom, so also for goodness—goodness of *intent,* at least, if not goodness in consequences of action. All men mean well; just ask them and they will tell you so.

To reflect on the environment and history of the typical scholarly commentator on morality is to note how unrepresentative his own introspective discoveries are likely to be of the private moral consciousness of mankind in general. Academicians generally are not well exposed to the mainstreams of society; many of them have spent their lives in systematic isolation from major social processes. Anyone who travels far enough along the academic road to write on morality has almost certainly already been "quite well socialized." He is unlikely to have deviated far from major institutionalized roles, for the contingencies attached to such deviations almost certainly would have interfered with his protracted education. His family will have reinforced the high levels of performance in symbolic skills without which he could not have survived academic competition. In the process he is almost certain to have acquired deep and general obligations, including commitments to abstract and generalized ethical doctrines. His adult situation is also exceptional. The status of the scholar is relatively high (if not always as high as scholars desire), either because of its traditional class origins or, more recently, because of its occupational prestige. The scholar has little need for deviant means of gaining economic advantage: because the symbols that convey his status are so cheap for him, he often fails even to imagine the monetary temptations that afflict men in less favored statuses, whose only effective claim to good opinion rests in what Thorstein Veblen identified so well as "unceasing evidence of the ability to pay." The academic commentator on morality will also be held in high esteem by his colleagues, for few write on so lofty a topic who have not already reached high rank in their field. Because a well-integrated society connects stratification and major institutional norms generally (some details of the connection are considered in Chapter V), discussions of morality have long been a specialty of Brahmins and others of high rank, and it is not surprising that the situation of the lowly (and chronically immoral) is not well represented in their work. But the most exceptional characteristic of the professor's status is its security. He is insulated to an extreme degree from the temptation to seize some opportunity now because it may well be gone tomorrow; and here, too, professors fail to see how moral commitment erodes in less secure men when they are faced with a strong, fortuitous temptation. A "rich" schedule of reinforcements effectively socializes the professor in his youth; it isolates him from temptation and molds him as a moral man, while the prestige and security of his adult status sustain his commitment later on.

It is a credit to the academic profession that it excludes felons, egregious and clumsy psychopaths, and many other varieties of moral derelicts. But this is precisely what makes the introspective findings of professors so poor a guide to a general conception of moral behavior. *A general theory of moral commitment must explain not only the presence of commitment in some persons but its absence in others.* Those men who gain the specialized skills needed to invent such theories have acquired moral commitments and entered a social environment profoundly different from those of many to whom the theories presume to apply. The introspection of moral men tells us little about the habitually immoral.

Accounts of any kind which presume to report the phenomenal life of moral derelicts are really very rare. A few works may be considered here —narratives of alcoholics, prostitutes, professional thieves, and the literary efforts of Jean Genet, Donatian de Sade, and the pornographers of North Hollywood or the Olympia Press—but these hardly represent most deviants. For one thing, the authors are literate and well educated, whereas we know that deviation occurs most frequently in the lower classes, where few are well educated and many or most are illiterate. The protocols of psychotherapeutic interviews might tell us something more about the phenomenology of the habitually immoral, but the gain is only one of small degree. Persons who undergo psychotherapy hardly constitute a better sample of the varieties of human morality than professors. Prison psychiatrists frequently lament that their "depth interviews" with convicts seem on reflection to be less a virtual account of the convicts' subjective states than an effort, often highly skilled and sometimes successful, to emit a dissembling narrative of contrition and "emotional maturation" which leads to favorable prognosis and quick parole.

The *general* reason why the phenomenology of the deviant actor is so little reported is simple. We shall see, in Chapter III, that the deviant is liable to punishment not only for his acts but also for his verbal reports, either of the acts themselves or of the subjective states which are supposed by laymen and mentalists to motivate the acts. Since talk is cheap and action dear, the verbal report of a person's immorality in action or fantasy is more readily suppressed by punishment than is the action or fantasy itself. Small wonder then that the bias inherent in the phenomenology of the moral man cannot be made explicit by comparing it with the phenomenology of the immoral man: the latter finds it to his interest to withhold from the sanctioning community both the record of his secret transgressions and the range of his private designs.

If the preceding analysis of the phenomenology of the moral man is plausible, it follows that attention to private events experienced by moral men is not warranted by their pertinence to a general theory. When this consideration is added to the more basic problems involved in using *any* private event as scientific evidence, it seems clear that the study of moral commitment can most profitably concentrate on its public rather than its private aspects. That, at any rate, is the methodological stance of this essay. Others write of the phenomenology of conscience and commitment: let us see what can be said about them in terms of ordinary social behavior.

The Role of Norms in Social Organization

Although most theoretical writers in sociology deal with normative elements—in terms of rules, "natural law," custom, mores, and so on—they have been incorporated most systematically in the work of the functionalist school, and most specifically in the writings of Emile Durkheim, Talcott Parsons, Marion J. Levy, Jr., and Kingsley Davis.[19] The following discussion of the role of norms in social organization generally follows the approach of Levy and Davis.

---

19 It would be difficult to name any one work of Durkheim's which did not involve an analysis of normative elements. The analysis is especially concentrated, however, in his essay "The Determination of Moral Facts" (1903), which contains his definition of sanctions (see also Chapter II of this volume). For a bibliography on Parsons' "social psychology" of normative elements, see the references in Scott (1962, 1963). Parsons' integration of these elements into larger-scale theory is found in his book *The Social System* (1951), Chaps. 6, 7, and *passim*. Levy presents his analysis in *The Structure of Society* (1952), especially Chaps. 3 and 4. Davis' exposition is found in *Human Society* (1949), Part I, especially Chap. 3. Davis has contributed, with Judith Blake, a more extended discussion in "Norms, Values, and Sanctions" (1964).

If a species of animal lives in societies this means by at least one definition of "society" that the social interaction among its members is instrumental to the survival of the species. But among the more complex social animals (whose range of behavior is not narrowly fixed by instincts and physiology), not all the activities of which the members of the species are capable contribute equally to its survival, and many possible activities are inimical to it. In the reproduction of primates we find a good example. Primate fertility is comparatively low, which means that a high proportion of all the infants born must live and grow if the species is to maintain its numbers. Yet the primate young are relatively helpless, and depend in the early part of their life not just on the mother but also on a larger group which can protect both the infant and the mother (herself disadvantaged during pregnancy by the large primate fetus). Thus among all the activities which it is physically possible for primates to perform, only those which do not interfere with the protection of infants are consistent with the survival of the species. This results in a complex social organization (see, for example, Washburn and DeVore, 1961). Yet laboratory work with primates shows that the behavior of which this organization is composed is not instinctive, but requires extensive learning, mainly as a result of reinforcements resulting from the organism's presence in an ongoing group (Harlow, 1959; Harlow and Harlow, 1961).

If this is true of primates generally, it is that much more true of human primates. In human society, many socially fatal activities are not only possible but, in a complex social organization, can even reward individual actors. Every persistent society—one that survives over many generations— therefore sets conditions for learning which tend to delimit the individual's range of activities to those that are consistent with the society's survival. These conditions are provided by what sociologists call *institutions,* that is, complex patterns of interaction that produce the division of labor necessary to viable organization. Sociologists stress the *normative* character of institutions, asserting that they represent complexes of norms. Some will add that the normative character of institutions is more fundamental than the interaction said to result from the norms. But whatever the basic nature of institutions, they serve to *limit human activities, narrowing them from all that is physically possible to some smaller range*—often a range consistent with persistent social organization. This limiting function is the core of the definition of norms presented in the next chapter.

The question of whether norms or interaction is more fundamental to institutions is resolved by defining sanctions as social reinforcements (that is, those reinforcements provided by interaction), and norms as patterns of sanctions. This is a more general conception of norms than is commonly advanced: in respect of an idealistic heritage, norms are usually defined as possessing an essentially symbolic form. The conception of this theory not only extends to symbolic forms (although we will see that not all normative statements are actually norms), but also includes as normative the processes that have sometimes been considered under the somewhat separate rubric of "social control," or, in Hobbes' terms, "a power to hold all men in awe." Yet these processes too have been used to explain social order and the maintenance of conditions under which society can continue and the species survive; indeed, Hobbes' analysis of the conditions that render "the life of man solitary, poor, nasty, brutish, and short" is also an analysis of some of "the functional requisites of any society," as Levy has called them, and of the need for such delimitations of possible activities as norms (as conceived above) can establish.

Variations in the formal content of a concept affect its use in explanation. The formal conceptions of norms vary considerably. In practice, however, norms are regarded mainly as *controls on learning*. We see in Chapter IV that Parsons, who generally advances an idealistic concept of norms in abstract contexts, regards them as patterns of sanctions when discussing concrete cases of socialization. The controls that norms produce result in the performance of the functions necessary for the continuity of society. There is therefore a close connection between ubiquitous norms—those that occur with little variation in their major features in all persistent societies (such as incest taboos, principles of legitimacy, rules of economic exchange, and structural concentration of the most forcible sanctions)—and the functions that must necessarily be performed in any society.

Much more indeed remains to be written on the relationship between norms and social organization. It is evidently not yet possible, and in all likelihood never will be possible, to generate, by deduction from the functional requirements for societal persistence, an explanation either of social structure or of the normative elements in that structure which will satisfy all sociologists. The "functionalist" theory of norms is essentially an evolutionary one: only those norms will become ubiquitous that contribute to the survival of a necessarily social species. It is not a complete account either of species or societal survival (which, as Levy has pointed out, may be undone by a number of factors that have nothing to do with "functional requisites" [Levy, 1952, p. 14]), or of the totality of norms—if indeed any limits to such a totality can be specified. The theory accounts best for institutionalization and thus for long-range norms; other types of explanation may be more useful in accounting for shorter-range normative variations (an example based on economic analogy is Smelser, 1963, especially Chapters 7, 9, and 10).

These and other limits of "functional" explanation have been widely remarked. But the critics of functionalism have not followed through with any alternative theory of normative elements. The functional explanation does account for the ubiquity of normative elements and for their similarity insofar as they relate to events that in the nature of the case must occur in all societies. The salience of normative elements, however variously conceived, has been consistently recognized wherever men have reflected on societies as wholes and not simply on aspects of societies selected for study by some special method. They deserve an attempt at explanation.

The Ubiquity of Moral Commitment and the Social Utility of a Premise of Moral Autonomy

The internalization or learning of norms, as well as the norms themselves, also contributes to species viability. Since conformity to norms entails an avoidance of socially fatal activities, and since a given level of conformity can be obtained with fewer or weaker sanctions when the norms are learned, a society which maintains a high rate of moral commitment arranges for the performance of necessary functions at a lower cost in sanctions, and thus has more resources deployable for other activities. This gives it a competitive advantage in contending with other species (predators, insects, bacteria) or with other human societies. The morally committed society can marshal bigger armies for defense and conquest or advance further in agriculture, industry, or control of morbidity and mortality. The society with a low level of moral commitment, in contrast, spends so many of its resources on immediate social control, maintaining necessary activities in the face of disinterest and calculation, that it has fewer to deploy elsewhere. Morally committed actors, conforming to sanctions which are at a spatial or temporal remove, can follow organized and long-range courses of action such as a complex division of labor requires, whereas the behavior of the uncommitted actor is more of an immediate response to the transient vagaries of reinforcement.

Probably the most incisive illustration of the personal as well as social disadvantage in a condition of freedom from all moral commitment is Durkheim's hypothetical example of an absolute despot, given in his lectures on moral education:

> Imagine a being liberated from all external restraint, a despot still more absolute than those of which history tells us, a despot that no external power can restrain or influence. By definition, the desires of such a being are irresistible. Shall we say, then, that he is all-powerful? Certainly not, since he himself cannot resist his desires. They are masters of him, as of everything else. He submits to them; he does not dominate them. In a word, when the inclinations are totally liberated, when nothing sets bounds to them, they

themselves become tyrannical, and their first slave is precisely the person who experiences them. What a sad picture this presents. Following one upon the other, the most contradictory inclinations, the most antithetical whims, involve the so-called absolute sovereign in the most incompatible feelings, until finally this apparent omnipotence dissolves into genuine impotence. A despot is like a child; he has a child's weaknesses because he is not master of himself [Durkheim, 1903–1906, pp. 44–45].

Utterly unconditioned by normative patterns, the despot responds to every positive reinforcement and can sustain no abiding course of action. Therefore, because it contributes so much to efficient social organization, normative learning—though variable in content and degree—is as universal in human societies as the norms themselves.

Western societies feature a widespread doctrine that builds on the ubiquity of moral commitment. This is the doctrine of "free will" and its associated concepts of moral autonomy and responsibility. The doctrine holds that part of human activity has no efficient cause. This part is then linked to areas of moral concern, so that moral actions are usually said to be those which the individual did of his own free will. It is only for moral acts that individuals are held to be responsible, that is, liable to subsequent sanctions. Thus, if it can be plausibly argued that a given act followed from an efficient cause, the act is not regarded as a moral issue and the actor incurs no liability to sanctions. Debates on the scope and limits of free will are common in English and American law; and, in different terms, it has been incorporated into theories in psychology and sociology through the work of such writers as Talcott Parsons (1934–1935) and Gordon Allport (1937, 1955). But in fact the doctrine is ubiquitous: the speculations of jurists about the line between criminal responsibility and insanity and the abstracted voluntarism of scholars both simply reflect a common theme in their cultural environment.

Free will is impossible to explain directly. Insofar as "explanation" requires the specification of an efficient cause of an event, then explanation of a freely willed act, defined as an event that has no efficient cause, is a contradiction in terms. The attempt to explain it, as Parsons pointed out so neatly many years ago, really only "explains it away" (Parsons, 1934, p. 290). The doctrine of free will also exchanges support with the phenomenology of the moral man. Free will supports phenomenology by claiming that external conditions do not determine part of human activity, whereas the phenomenology of the moral man reveals no causes of moral commitment and thus concludes that the doctrine of free will is correct.

But it is not impossible to explain more indirectly why men *believe* in free will and in phenomenological revelations of it. If we can assume that beliefs, like norms and other abstracted aspects of social structure, affect the competitive position of the societies in which they are held, then, *ceteris paribus,* those beliefs are more likely to persist which give a competitive advantage in the society that holds them. This is indeed what is claimed for religious beliefs (that they contribute, for example, to the socially useful integration of conflicting personal interests) in "functional" theories of religion, as first stated by Durkheim and developed further by Davis (1949) and Johnson (1960). We argued earlier in this chapter that the process of moral commitment gives such an advantage, by reducing the cost of sanctions needed to produce a given level of social control. It can be similarly argued that the belief in free will—the belief that moral commitment has no causes—reduces the cost of sanctions still further.

A man who believes in free will, and thus that he alone is responsible for his moral actions, is not going to spend his time examining the conditions which may be prerequisites for such actions. He believes that there are no such conditions. He sees his task rather as determining the practical consequences of various courses of action, among which he believes he is free to choose and for which his acts are the prerequisites. This determination alone is an enormous task. When the further requirement of determining which among these choices is the right thing to do is added, the resulting labor of analysis and speculation can quite fully occupy the most intelligent and industrious of men. *This is precisely the advantage of the doctrine of free will to economy in social control.* The intellectualization of moral choice that follows from faith in free will absorbs energies that might otherwise be invested in a subtle analysis of the relation between conduct and sanctions. Then the maintenance of social control would require very costly sanctions, more subtle than the intelligence marshaled against them. The socially dangerous answers that might be provided to the question, "What is most rewarding?" are deflected into the less dangerous answers to the question, "What is right?"

If moral choice were a limited undertaking, the intellectualization of choice through the supposed exercise of free will would produce only temporary economies. But intellectual questions about voluntary responsibility have the further advantage of being (by all inductive evidence from law, ethics, and theology) inherently insoluble; they will therefore reduce the cost of sanctions so long as men believe that the attempt to answer them is worthwhile. The intelligence of the human species—its ability to make, retain, and communicate fine discriminations among stimuli—is of course its greatest resource in ecological adaptation and interspecific competition, but it is at the same time the greatest potential challenge to normative control in human society. The social utility of a premise of moral autonomy is found in what it adds to the effects of moral commitment: it further disinclines men to the intelligent study of sanctions.[20]

---

[20] Perhaps some limited and indirect ethnographic evidence for our abstract argument is provided in Edward Banfield's study of southern Italy (1958). In that society, the Protestant voluntarism of educated men in northern Europe does not exist;

The Morality of Theories of Morality

Respect for the phenomenology of the moral man requires that theories of moral commitment be parochial, and a belief in free will requires that they be inconclusive. These two requirements in tandem impose the further requirement that theories of morality be themselves morally persuasive. Intuitionists and many others in philosophy have only recently distinguished theories of morality in general from advocacy of particular moral doctrines or rules.[21] Most of them have served both as analysts and advocates without ever giving much thought to the possibility that analysis and advocacy might be distinguished, and we should therefore not be surprised that their analysis generally supported their advocacy. The pervasiveness of faith in the phenomenology of the moral man is revealed in the repugnance with which intellectual communities have historically viewed theories of morality that are *not* morally persuasive—that is, theories which purport to explain moral behavior but which do not assent to particular moral rules or at least respect the sense of commitment in general.

The best historical example of a writer cast into disrepute for a morally unpersuasive theory of morality is Thomas Hobbes. The general line of refutation of Hobbes has not been that his premises were unsound or that

---

instead there is fatalistic determinism, lack of interest in abstract morality, shrewd (if often uninformed) calculation of sanctions, and consistent distrust of all persons outside the nuclear family. The competitive disadvantage of southern Italian and Sicilian society and its long history of domination by other societies no doubt involve many factors, but Banfield states that since no one trusts anybody outside his family, all extrafamilial relations require that a large proportion of time be spent in surveillance of the other party, thus making the relative cost of social control in such relations very high. Secondary organization (for example, municipal government) beyond the family is described as limited and ineffective, partly because administrators regularly convert the prerogatives of office to their family's short-run advantage. In northern European and American society, administrators are more likely to conform to the abstract norms that apply to their office and to ignore, at least to some degree, the rich opportunities for graft inherent in delegated authority.

Justin Aronfreed, who reviews "culture-personality" studies in many societies, concludes that Western societies show a relatively high level of internalization (1968).

[21] Thus in a fascinating critique of the sociological school of Durkheim and his followers, Sir David Ross was able to write, in 1930:

> [A]ccording to this school...no one moral code is...any nearer the apprehension of objective moral truth than any other; each is simply the code that is necessitated by the conditions of its time and place, and is that which most completely conduces to the preservation of the society that accepts it. But the human mind will not rest content with such a view.... It is [at least] competent to see that the moral code of one race or age is in certain respects inferior to that of another. It has in fact an *a priori* insight into certain broad principles of morality.... There are not merely so many moral codes which can be described and whose vagaries can be traced to historical causes; there is a system of moral truth, as objective as all truth must be, which, and whose implications, we are genuinely interested in discovering...[Sir David Ross, 1930, pp. 10–11].

his reasoning was faulty (although both these questions can be raised about his work), but that his view of human nature must be wrong because it affronts moral sensibilities. He was a cynic, and while a cynical theory might be scientifically correct, in moral rhetoric (the function of which is to persuade others to conform) the cynic is of course always wrong. We still judge theories of morality by a canon of moral persuasiveness: the label of "cynic" has been used to depreciate such diverse and instructive commentators on norms and morality as La Rochefoucauld, Voltaire, Santayana, Freud, Willard Waller, Charles Stevenson, Kingsley Davis, B. F. Skinner, and Erving Goffman. We paradoxically expect a theory of morality to reward our moral commitment by supporting the belief that commitment needs no reward.

Some readers will therefore find the theory to be advanced in this book unsatisfactory because, if taken seriously, it seems to undo the very process that is its subject. It is not so much that the theory is obviously false as that it challenges what is revealed in the experience of good men. This is an application of the criterion of phenomenological adequacy to theoretical construction. The theory explains what introspection reveals as voluntary action (traditionally commendable in the West) as dependent on social reinforcement (traditionally not so commendable). But there is no good *scientific* reason (to admit only a concern with the morals of science) why a theory about morality need itself be moral or morally persuasive, "any more than theories of gases need be gaseous, or botany vegetable or geology mineral." (Russell, 1910. Russell made the same point—that ethical theories need not be ethically commendable—but the requirement he challenged proved subtler and more pervasive than he realized at the time.)

It is possible that a morally neutral theory of morality may, if widely promulgated, corrode moral commitment. This is another reason why cynical discussions of morality have been depreciated and why good men find it so easy to believe that the source of conscience must be more than (as Hobbes averred) the fear of death, that justice must necessarily be more than the interests of the stronger, or that "good" must be objective just as "round" and "square" are. I have already suggested that such beliefs may be socially important, apart from their truth. But historical fears that an amoral analysis of morality would advance immorality have been groundless. Both moral and immoral action depend not so much on abstract debates (whose direct effects scholars and intellectuals chronically overestimate) as on more concrete reinforcements organized into strong social institutions. Except as they might be embraced by otherwise powerful groups and incorporated into less abstract ideologies, theories of morality are feeble reinforcers, effective only in a few specialized situations, and with little power to produce social change, either institutional or subinstitutional. Thus, no general attempt to explain human morality (such as Adam Smith's

Theory of the Moral Sentiments) has by itself had any significant effect on moral action. Young women may have abandoned their chastity after reading *Madame Bovary* but, if so, it was not because their minds had been poisoned by the narrative—it is still the case that no woman was ever seduced by a book—but because the men near them offered the prospect of adventure or marriage, escape from parental domination, or flattery, and thus rewarded carnality more than chastity. Our theory holds that good men stay good not simply because of what they believe, but also because their beliefs are reinforced. A theory of belief may corrode belief, but a theory of sanctions hardly makes sanctions disappear.

Conclusion

In this chapter we have dealt with only a small part of the contemporary controversies revolving around normative elements. Unlike the contemporary accounts of psychologists, which stay close to the research literature, our chapter has surveyed broader intellectual and philosophical themes. I think this is warranted as a starting point, because it is to broad intellectual traditions rather than narrow empirical contingencies that most of the controversy eventually repairs. As we will see in Chapters IV and V, current evidence is highly inadequate to resolve current theoretical issues; moreover, differences of opinion as to what constitutes adequate evidence suggest that the massing of evidence alone will never be adequate. All the introspection in the world, however carefully reviewed and cross-indexed, will not impress a behaviorist; scores of charts of learning curves and printouts without end of attitudinal factor analyses will not satisfy a man who wants a theory "adequate on the level of meaning." If a scientific issue is conceptual, then it should be handled on a conceptual level. And while research is increasingly dear, conceptual analysis remains relatively cheap. The attempt to solve purely conceptual issues by amassing research results wastes scarce scientific resources.

Some account should be given for the relative neglect in this work of Freudian concepts and psychoanalytic research. Freud's original emphasis on both socialization and morality led him to develop a number of elaborate concepts and theories about the internalization of norms. His impact on psychology, sociology, and intellectual life generally has been enormous. Freud's thought influences even these opposed to it: Skinner, for example, pays Freud the considerable tribute of interpreting him as a somewhat misled reinforcement psychologist. But today the ideas of Freud are so diffused, modified, and interwoven with other traditions that the variety of concepts and hypotheses in which they are incorporated runs past all enumeration. As a result the writings of sociologists and nonclinical psychologists will receive more attention than do those of psychoanalytic writers in what follows. The exclusion may be regrettable, because much discussion of morality in the psychoanalytic tradition (by Freud and others) is valuable and relevant to the present theory, whatever may be said of the substantive and heuristic impact of psychoanalytic thought as a whole. (For a sociological review of Freudian concepts, especially as applied to psychopathology, see Scheff [1966, especially Chap. I].) But there simply is not space to consider everything.

The present theory can be summarized as follows. Moral commitment is treated as a case of learning generally, using the perspective of operant behaviorism largely developed by B. F. Skinner. Normative concepts are defined in terms consistent with that perspective and in polemical opposition to an idealistic one. The basic element of the norm becomes not its symbolic form but what the symbol represents: a pattern of sanctions. Sanctions are in turn defined as social reinforcement: thus, most of the operant behavior of complex social animals is seen as normative. Phenomenological adequacy is ignored, because propositions on this level are impossible to verify publicly and because introspection about morality leads to parochial, moralistic, and incomplete hypotheses. The theory contains several subordinate assertions of a sociopsychological character, but these do not closely relate to most contemporary theory and research in "social psychology" as practiced either by psychologists or sociologists and as collected in treatises and textbooks on that subject. Our concern is, first, to relate reinforcement psychology to macrosociological theory; and second, to show that the variables of sociology, if irrelevant to the strictly experimental analysis of behavior, still are profoundly relevant for the application of that analysis to the natural activities of complex social organisms. Whatever the merits or demerits of this exposition, the issue of moral commitment is an important one; and its resolution will make sociological theory more complete.

CHAPTER II

Analysis of Concepts

Concepts Make a Difference

One reason most discussion of normative elements is vague and discursive is that the concepts on which the discussion must rely are vague and discursive. In quest of greater precision, we present in this chapter an analysis of concepts and definition of terms.[1]

It is easy to make too much of purely conceptual analysis; it is hard to resist the judgment that too much is made of it already in sociology. The work of Talcott Parsons is often cited in this connection, yet his great influence shows that conceptual analysis cannot be ignored. To start with the right concepts is half the battle won. In *The Structure of Social Action* (1937), Parsons never stated unequivocally the great thesis of voluntarism that the book was supposed to be all about, but he did offer a subtle and

---

[1] A difference in concepts provides the major distinction between this essay and the important paper by Blake and Davis (1964). Both advance similar points, especially on the importance of sanctions in normative processes and the ubiquity of some calculating attitude toward norms. Blake and Davis criticize Parsons and his recent followers in this respect. But their article tends to use many of Parsons' constructs (cf. Davis's earlier statements [1949, pp. 122 ff.]), including many concepts with a conventional subjective reference. In this way their argument tends to sustain the phenomenological moralism to whose conclusions they are otherwise opposed. Further comparisons of their paper with the theory advanced here follow in the text.

extended analysis and classification of normative elements which ha.
profoundly shaped subsequent discussions.

Concepts restrict hypotheses. In *The Structure of Social Action* Parsons defined normative elements as essentially independent variables, thereby excluding at the start hypotheses which might treat them as dependent variables. Two generations of sociologists since then have failed to get beyond this construction. Nevertheless, the hegemony of norms in society that is so pervasively implied in the writing of Parsons and his closest followers has had many critics (e.g., Dahrendorf, 1958; Wrong, 1961). Insofar as these critics have tried to depreciate the role of norms in general, however, they have—in my view at least—been unsuccessful. They would have been more successful had they reached the level of concepts, because this is where the difficulty they sense really resides. In the remainder of this chapter and in the following exposition, normative elements are considered to be as pervasive as they are in Parsons. The difference lies in our avoidance of the traditional connotations of the idealistic perspective.

Parsons' critics have done little to modify the idealistic conceptions of normative elements. They generally allow that norms possess the characteristics that voluntaristic introspection and the phenomenology of the moral man reveal them to possess. They then find that such conceptions do not serve well in the explanations of social organization where norms are used as independent variables. If the integration of society is achieved fundamentally through the internalization of common values, as Parsons emphasizes, then how do we account for integration in the face of "value pluralism" by the forcible sanctions of despots and dictators? How many values do lower classes really share with upper classes, or slaves with masters? But these may be admitted as reasonable problems requiring explanation without rejecting Parsons' emphasis on normative integration.

Most of what gets represented as a conflict between "norms" and "power," or between "norms" and a "refractory unsocialized organism" can be better represented as simply a conflict among norms. It is practically impossible to advance any persuasive *general* definition of "norms" such that any exercise of power is not, in the final analysis, in support of some norm. In this debate, Parsons' critics often implicitly assume that the totality of norms is limited to those implicated in the phenomenology of Western intellectual moral men—a *mélange* of Judeo-Christian liberal-enlightenment optimism. This assumption is fatal: among other defects it leads to a conception of social virtue that makes it almost impossible to explain evil. Perhaps Parsons himself is sympathetic to this optimistic ideology, but here the fault is with his critics: his theoretical constructions, whatever their other shortcomings, are not this parochial. The abstract terms of his notions of "value-integration" fit the concrete case of American society, even though some of the integrated values may include economic imperialism, slavery, or a racist policy of genocide with regard to the nation's aboriginal population. That such values are repugnant to Western intellectuals does not mean that they cannot be integrated into the society or even be the basis of consensus. History suggests that the decimation of a defeated enemy can be a popular and highly valued course of action. Now the norms and values of other groups may be in our own judgment contemptible. But unless we adopt the explicit idealism and parochialism of Sir David Ross's moral conception of the "plain man," with its singular "system of moral truth, as objective as all truth must be" (1930), we cannot conclude that other groups, including murderers and racists, simply lack norms and values altogether.

Much the same point can be made about the claim that certain kinds of acts are not normative but fundamentally contra-normative. Usually it turns out that they are not generally contra-normative at all, but simply counter to certain institutionalized norms. Thus the "primordial id" that Wrong has rescued from monolithic social control in his eloquent essay, "The Over-Socialized Conception of Man in Modern Sociology" (1961), is probably no more than a romantic idea of a presociological neo-Freudianism. "Id" appears to be almost as much a social product as "superego." The complete absence of sexual norms, for example, does not lead to sexual hyperactivity but to sexual apathy.[2] It is true that high rates of casual sexual liaison will occur where norms of sexual property are weak, as in the lower classes of many Caribbean societies. Norms of sexual property are not easy to sustain in any society. But descriptions of Caribbean life reveal no parallel weakness in the equally normative institutionalization of nubility, or in norms defining manly prowess in terms of successful liaisons with nubile women. It is behavior socially learned in response to these norms, not the unchanneled energies which Wrong alleges are "forces...resistant to socialization," that produces high rates of masculine sexual predation. Only where *all* norms sustaining sexual behavior break down, and not just those from which a high degree of chronic deviation from the primary pattern is itself widely institutionalized, will we find "primordial id" in empirically direct view.

Any conception of normative elements consistent with the preceding remarks will have to be very general, and such a general conception is what we are about to present. The basic concepts of the scheme are the *conditioner,* the *sanction,* the *norm,* and *value.* Except for the concept of "value"—whose level in the definitional hierarchy is roughly parallel to that of the norm—particular concepts are defined in terms of more general ones. The most general concept in the hierarchy is the conditioner.

---

2 See Blake and Davis in rejoinder to Wrong (1964, p. 471). The socialization of human sexuality can be inferred *a fortiori* from monkeys in Harry Harlow's work, especially "Social Deprivation in Monkeys" (1962).

Our definitional hierarchy is "reductive," in the sense spoken of in the previous chapter. But its purpose is not to eliminate the more particular terms from sociological use. A scientific language composed solely of a few very simple and general terms, with no special or particular references, would be too iterative and tedious for describing or explaining anything but the simplest and most abstracted phenomena. A strict reductionist still needs to use the very concepts he has reduced to simpler and more general terms, for unless those concepts referred to relevant events there would have been no point in bothering to define them in the first place. This applies directly to the concept of the norm. The following analysis of norms emphasizes the most general aspects of their operation in a social structure, but it is not offered in order to terminate analysis of other aspects of norms. I merely hope that this analysis can help clarify and extend the range of other analyses.

Our discussion of concepts is long and labored, at times generating distinctions that may seem to make no difference later on. In part this is the result of trying to anticipate possible criticisms of the theory that really are objections to its constituent concepts. The concepts have therefore been defined so that, if they are taken as given, many grounds for rejecting the theory will have been cut off in advance. In this sense, the statement of the theory may seem tautological. But it is not tautological as a whole, for there still remain empirical grounds on which the theory could be tested and, in principle, shown to be false.

The Conditioner

Conditioners are stimuli that, preceding or following a particular act, change the rate at which it gets performed. In learning theory, conditioning is usually distinguished according to the sequence of the stimulus and the act. When the stimulus precedes the act it is called Pavlovian, classical, or "respondent" conditioning; when it follows the act it is called instrumental or "operant" conditioning. The second type of conditioning is Skinner's specialty: in his terms, the act becomes (with some further qualifications) the "operant" and the subsequent stimulus the "reinforcer" (see Homans, 1961, pp. 18 ff.; Skinner, 1953, p. 65).

For present purposes the following aspects of conditioners will be used: *rewards* and *punishments, orders* of conditioners, *symbolic* and *nonsymbolic* conditioners, *vicarious reinforcement,* and the *relativity* of symbolic reward and punishment. Although some reference is made to respondent conditioning, most of the discussion derives from Skinner's concepts, and thus uses *reinforcement* (of which reward and punishment are special cases) as its fundamental process.

A *reinforcement* is any event or process possessing stimulus properties for a particular organism which, when it follows the occurrence of a particular repeatable act, increases the rate at which that act subsequently occurs. This corresponds to the more popular term "reward." A *positive* reinforcer produces this increase by the addition of stimuli; a *negative* one by their removal. "Negative" reinforcement, where the rate of the reinforced act is decreased rather than increased, consists of withdrawing positive reinforcers or presenting negative ones. "An example of the former would be taking candy from a baby; and an example of the latter spanking a baby" (Skinner, 1953, pp. 59–65, 184 ff.). This corresponds to the common term "punishment." These are the basic elements of operant conditioning.

In practice "reinforcers" are usually stimuli applied in a psychological experiment. But the extreme generality of the *concepts* of reinforcement and conditioning is clear. They are nothing less than the process occurring when an organism changes its rate of activity in response to stimuli from its environment. Such a conception of relationship can express nearly all relations between the behavior of organisms and events in their environment. The only events excluded are those with no stimulus properties. Particular events which we may wish to study may not have such properties, but almost invariably they will be correlated with other events that do. The birth of a child in India does not in itself stimulate a wheat farmer in Kansas and thus cannot reinforce his behavior. But the single birth is part of a larger-scale demographic event, the growth of a population; this growth in turn reinforces the decision of Indian and American government officials to use American wheat to feed India's population, thereby reducing American grain stocks, strengthening the aggregate demand for wheat, and driving up the price. The farmer reads of this in the *Wall Street Journal* and decides to buy a self-propelled combine. The causally efficient reinforcer was, of course, the "conditioned reinforcer," the small print on the *Journal*'s commodity page. The Indian birth rate, however, was an essential part of the larger *reinforcement process*. Such a general process seems a safe place to begin a hierarchy of definitions. The only thing excluded from respondent and operant conditioning, combined, is behavior that shows no association with environmental events, that is, innate or instinctive activities. These are weak in higher animals; hence the great importance of conditioning in shaping their behavior.

All this may seem obvious, and obviousness to the point of vacuity is a charge often hurled at reinforcement psychology. Yet other men still write that the "concepts of learning theory are too narrow and restrictive" to cover all of human behavior. The truth is that if they are defective in the dimension of generality it is because they are too broad.

So far, these concepts are quite distant from our ultimate concern, moral behavior. The first step in reducing the distance leads us to orders of conditioners; the second, to their derivative, the symbolic conditioner. We begin with a paradigm of respondent conditioning because it describes well (if not completely) how a child learns a language presented to it by its environment. Then we will see how operant conditioning describes the way in which the child learns to present his verbal repertory to his environment.

The essential point in Pavlovian, or respondent, conditioning is that a previously established connection between a stimulus and a response can be generalized to a later and separate stimulus. When a dog's nose is rubbed with meat powder (the stimulus), the animal begins to salivate (the response). Next, nose rubbing is paired with another stimulus, the ringing of a bell. Eventually nose rubbing is terminated and only bell ringing maintained, but the response of salivation continues. It now follows from a new stimulus, which is to say that it has become conditioned.

Experiments have shown that, just as the stimulus can shift from nose rubbing to the bell, so (once the association with the bell is established) it can shift again to a new and previously nonreinforcing stimulus (Staats and Staats, 1963, pp. 39 ff.). A black square (a visual stimulus) is presented together with the bell; eventually, the black square elicits salivation without the bell. What is going on here is an *order,* or *sequence,* of conditioning, and two aspects of it are worth noting. First, the process implies that the transfer of response from one stimulus to another can go on to great lengths: in the higher animals it has been extended until the connection between the original unconditioned stimulus and the ultimate conditioned stimulus has become so remote that the basic principle of conditioned-reflex sequences and the wide range of its application has been obscured by the distance between the original stimulus and the final conditioned response. Second, the effect of the conditioned stimulus does not here depend on its properties as an unconditioned stimulus, but on its association with a prior stimulus-response set, or reflex, and the possible range of such associations is so great that the relation between the new stimulus and the old reflex can justifiably be described as arbitrary. Until research proves otherwise, it is economical to assume that practically anything that can serve as a stimulus at all can come to serve as a conditioned stimulus.

Language and Symbolism

The process of conditioning, and the wide range of conditioning it permits, provide the basis for the use of symbols, especially in verbal behavior, as stimuli in the behavior of higher animals. Here we need some more definitions. The terms "sign," "symbol," "verbal behavior," and so on, have been variously defined from a behavioristic or learning-theoretical point of view (for example, in Morris, 1946; Osgood, 1956; Skinner, 1957. For a discussion of some criticisms of Skinner's views on language, see pp. 52–53 of this text). The range of definitions is suggested in Morris's criteria for a language. In his terms, a language (1) has a plurality of arbitrary signs; (2) the signs have a common or shared significance to a group; (3) the significance is relatively invariant; (4) the signs can be emitted as well as "received" as stimuli; and (5) the signs together constitute a system following certain rules of combination (cited in Osgood, 1956, p. 25). For the present task, points (1) and (4) are most important. The arbitrary character of a conditioned stimulus permits arbitrary signs to be such stimuli, and the capacity of the higher animals to vocalize not only in respondent but in operant fashion means that their vocalizations play a central role in social behavior, especially among humans.

When a stimulus is associated not with another stimulus from the environment, but instead with a repeatable response from the organism, then the increase in the rate or the subsequent probability of that response is the result of operant conditioning. Homans (1961, pp. 18 ff.) gives a very human example of operant behavior: "You can put the baby on the pot but you can't make him perform—at least not then and there. You can only wait until the blessed event occurs and then reward him—with coos of approval, or, better still, by taking him off the pot." In reinforcing the response, defecation, the mother has increased the probability that the infant will defecate when he is again placed on the pot (and, of course, eventually *only* on the pot).

The immediate task, however, is to demonstrate the involvement of operant behavior in learning language. Part of a human infant's repertory of operant behavior—behavior for which there is no apparent prior associated stimulus—is vocalization. Though many other animals vocalize, some in socially functional ways, the vocal repertory of the human is utterly unmatched, because of the elaborately evolved physical structure that makes it possible, the variety of sounds of which it is composed, and the extent to which it can be conditioned. Further, the human environment is social and verbal to an extreme degree, and the response of other humans to an infant's vocalizations is not random but profoundly patterned into language, even though the patterns vary. The first vocalizations of children are undifferentiated and more or less random. But the infant's social environment (mainly his mother) does not respond randomly. On hearing the child's first vocalizations she is likely to respond with such positive reinforcers as fondling, feeding, and so on. She does this because in every society vocal behavior is encouraged: the rule is that children should learn to talk, although later on they will also be expected to learn when they should talk and what they should say. At first, however, reinforcement follows upon any vocalization. The first thing the child learns is that it pays to vocalize.

Eventually, the reinforcements become contingent on the child's uttering different sounds in the presence of different stimuli. Particular sounds are rewarded sometimes and not others. In English-speaking societies, when the father of the infant is present, "da-da" is more likely to be rewarded than when the infant's brother is present, because of its similarity to the colloquialism "daddy." "Da-da" is especially likely to be rewarded when the father serves as a massive stimulus, lifting the child, bouncing it on his knee, and doing other things fathers are expected to do in societies that lack any extreme sexual division of labor.

Eventually, the presence of father elicits "Daddy!" consistently, and the child is off and away on applying the general theory of ostensive names. "Daddy" names a particular stimulus; and the name is learned through the selective reinforcement of particular vocalizations "emitted the first time as if by chance." It is the capacity for such elaborate discriminations of stimuli, and for the conditioning of responses so extremely abstracted from the original act, that so very profoundly differentiates the human infant from chimpanzee playmates with whom, in certain exotic households, he might have been brought up as an equal.

Operant conditioning puts language into the growing child's behavioral repertory, but it is not the only process involved in learning language. Respondent conditioning is involved as well, quite importantly in some distinctively normative functions of language. Suppose a household pet has defecated on a rug, or a toddling infant broken some household treasure. The master of the pet and parent of the child, on discovering either misdeed, is likely to take corrective measures, including saying "bad!" or "naughty!" These expressions may be just that—expressions—with no intent to reinforce the organism whose behavior elicited them, but if accompanied by other stimuli they will serve as reinforcements anyway. The household dog has a very limited repertory of vocalization, but he hears well and learns to discriminate among the more extensive vocalizations of his human masters. If the dog's nose is rubbed in its feces at the same time it hears "bad doggy!" the phrase becomes a conditioned stimulus by the mechanism of respondent conditioning. In due course, some control over the dog's behavior is gained simply by calling him "bad." Thus begins the moralization of the dog.

What the dog can learn, the trinket-dropping infant can learn much better. The infant can be conditioned more rapidly and at a greater remove from the original unconditioned stimulus; he can discriminate more finely among stimuli, especially among the arbitrary sounds of linguistic conditioners; and he can generalize widely from one reflex to another—from the association of treasure-dropping with a verbal response to the association between a general class of prohibited actions and the application to him of reinforcement, particularly of punishment and negative reinforcement.

Most important of all, he can learn by operant conditioning to talk back to his environment and to talk about it. He learns what follows when his own behavior elicits a flow of moral language from his parents. Although these are but the first small steps along the extended course of the present analysis, the way ahead becomes increasingly clear.

Here is a good place to define two popular concepts: "symbol" and "meaning." These in particular need attention, because many sociologists believe that they cannot be interpreted in reductive or learning-theoretical terms. A "symbol" may be defined as a stimulus whose reinforcing value is based on conditioning rather than on unconditioned effects. Symbols generally are considered to possess meaning. Symbols may be defined as "meaningful" to the extent that they elicit a consistent response independent of other reinforcers or stimuli with which they may be variably associated. Thus the sound of the bell was a symbol to the dog who had been conditioned by it, and it meant that food was on its way. The dog showed the meaning of the bell by responding, as it were, to food. Some epistemological conservatives speak as if signs operate by a *natural* association between the sign and the thing signified, and symbols by an *artificial* and somehow non-natural relation; but this distinction makes sense only if we assume that human society is non-natural. A better distinction is between unconditioned and conditioned stimuli. Similarly, "meaning" is often considered to be some kind of intrinsically subjective or phenomenological representation. Although there may be fields in which this conception is helpful, it is no help to sociology. Such representations are private events, and thus cannot operate in interaction between organisms. The significance of the symbol used by individual A in the presence of individual B does not derive from the subjective state which B infers to be present inside A.[3] It derives rather from the information it provides to B about what A is going to do. The ancient habits of the language of which the symbols are a part may of course incline B to speculate about A's "internal states," but until A *does something,* these speculations will never be confirmed: "Another organism's private mind, if it have any, can never be got at." *Behavior rather than intent gives the symbol its meaning*: "intent" is just a way of denoting meaning—that is, of indicating that a particular activity associated with a symbol or gesture is likely subsequently to be performed.

Returning now to our earlier example, we can see how the first, rather concrete meanings are attached to the symbols of "bad" and "naughty." "Bad" means to the dog that it is about to be forcibly presented with a

---

[3] However, for sociological interpretations of symbolic meaning as the representation of a subjective state, see Davis (1949, pp. 149–50) and Parsons (1952a, p. 544).

noxious stimulus; "naughty" means to the child that milder but more general deprivation is on its way. The difference lies in the variety of stimuli which the child, as compared to the dog, can discriminate and from which he can generalize. Symbolism is profoundly more important for the child than for the dog, but so far this does not mean that the general mechanisms by which he learns symbols are any different. They *may* ultimately prove to be different, and they certainly appear different in particular details. The human near-monopoly of language depends not only on species-specific physical capacities for vocalization, but in all likelihood on species-specific neurological processes of which we doubtless have much to learn (despite the confidence of some champions of "cognitive processes" and some theorists of the nature of language who claim to comprehend them whole either through revelation or introspection). Until these factors stand revealed through conventional scientific evidence—and not just hypothesized in one or another of the schemes that Skinner has referred to as "conceptual nervous systems"—it remains safe to say that the difference lies not so much in the qualitative difference, *how* the child and the dog learn, as in the vast quantitative difference—*how much* they learn.

Language can certainly be analyzed on its own level—that is, without always starting out from the conditions under which the developing, symbol-manipulating organism moves from nonverbal behavior to the use of symbols. The direct analysis of language, without this constant reference to language learning, is a major concern of the discipline of linguistics, and represents a major contribution to the social and behavioral sciences. But there is also a persistent notion in sociology and social psychology that symbols are somehow potent conditioners in and of themselves, without any need to be tied into a sequence of conditioning that began with concrete reinforcement. This is to overlook the notorious impotence of symbols when they are presented to something that cannot learn their meaning, including unsocialized children. And often children who have not yet discriminated the conditions under which symbols possess potency will bring to bear on their unconditionable, inanimate environment the same symbols that they have learned are rewarding when used in their conditionable, human environment—as in "Rain, rain; go away."

This error is commonly made in a more profound way when the symbols have the form of a norm. It follows from the preceding discussion that a symbol that is meaningful in one situation or to one audience may not be so to another, because the conditioners for each may be different. Thus the symbolic form of a norm is not effective in and of itself, but must be learned first—that is, it has to be tied into a sequence of conditioning that starts with an unconditioned stimulus. The same norm can mean different things (or nothing) to different audiences and under different conditions.

Linguistic Platonism and the Critique of Behavioristic Conceptions of Language: A Note on the Views of Noam Chomsky

Even in its heyday, the behavioristic persuasion in psychology and the social sciences never swept away all opposition. There was always a "mentalistic underground." Today behaviorism is nearly three academic generations old and it no longer has the force of new and fashionable doctrine. Many new perspectives are polemically opposed to behaviorism, from humanistic psychology to sociological phenomenology and "ethnomethodology." The old theses of subjectivism have found new supporters.

It seems prudent in this connection to take some account of the meteoric rise in the influence of the views of the linguistic theorist Noam Chomsky. Chomsky's view of language represents a radical shift from the widespread acceptance of the idea that language is a changing and adaptive aspect of human behavior. Emphasizing the formal aspects of language, Chomsky appears to conceive of it as some sort of "eternal object." Such a view is highly congenial to an idealistic ontology.

Chomsky's opinion of a behavioristic approach is made plain in his widely cited review (1959) of Skinner's *Verbal Behavior*. Even though Skinner's book was long in preparation, it is highly programmatic and has few connections with prior research and theory in the field. It is not surprising that specialists in linguistics and psycholinguistics have been critical of it, and Chomsky—well-grounded in the philosophical style of careful, analytical criticism—has had a field day.

Many of Chomsky's criticisms of particular points in Skinner's analysis are persuasive. In my view, however, what his criticism really hits hardest are certain foibles in scholarly style that are endemic, not just in Skinner's work but in entire ranks of Harvard faculty (not to mention many senior professors elsewhere). Chomsky extrapolates from his success in exposing these foibles to the conclusion that *any* behavioristic analysis of language is inadequate. For this he receives exceptional acclaim, partly because he had the temerity to take on a Harvardian *guru* and partly because the mentalistic underground is eager to hear that behaviorism is wrong.

Chomsky graphically mocks Skinner's seeming inattention to understatement and irony (1959, pp. 34–35). But in doing so, he fails to consider how easily alternate yet still quite behavioristic analyses of these and other subtleties of language might be constructed. The analyses of Erving Goffman (throughout *The Presentation of Self in Everyday Life* [1959]) and even Stephen Potter (throughout Gamesmanship [1948]) are highly instructive in suggesting the perfectly public variables of which a broad class of ironic and otherwise subtle uses of language may prove to be functions.

Part of Chomsky's dissatisfaction with reinforcement psychology derives from a much more "molecular"—and hence narrower—view of the possible range of reinforcers than is held either by Skinner or the present author. Following a discussion of Old's research on direct stimulation of the brain and of animal ethologists on imprinting, Chomsky declares (p. 41) : "Everyone engaged in research must have had the experience of working with feverish and prolonged intensity to write a paper which no one else will read or to solve a problem which no one else thinks important." Evidently he believes that a reinforcer of which a person is not aware does not exist. This is a generalization of the phenomenology of the moral man. In fact the experience of "working with feverish and prolonged intensity" to which Chomsky refers commonly occurs among men who are well rewarded for it. Few may read the paper, but academic review committees will count it as one more publication, on which important rewards are often contingent. It is indeed peculiar that Chomsky—no innocent in the ways of academic gamesmanship—should have overlooked so obvious a reinforcement.

In comparison with most recent writers, Chomsky's conception of language and its relationship to human affairs is so uncommonly archaic that most contemporary readers mistake it for a new theory (although Chomsky acknowledges his archaic affinities). He aggressively presents a doctrine of innate mental faculties, assessible through introspection, which elsewhere has been in general retreat since Kant. The syntax of language derives, in his view, from such a faculty (1965, Chap. 1. See also the partisan exposition of his position and some application to sociology by Omvedt [1967]). Consider, for example, the striking Platonism of Chomsky's conception of the object of linguistic theory:

> [It] is concerned primarily with an ideal speaker-listener in a completely homogeneous speech-community, who knows its language perfectly, and is unaffected by such grammatically irrelevant conditions as memory limitations, distractions, shifts of attention and interest, and errors (random or characteristic) in applying his knowledge of the language in actual performance [1965, p. 3].

Evidently the real world with which sociologists, sociolinguists, and other grubby empiricists have the bad fortune to deal consists merely of shadows on the wall of the cave.

Within the field of linguistics, a substantial critic of Chomsky's conception of language is Charles F. Hockett, who plays the Holmes to Chomsky's Moriarty. Hockett first adumbrated his criticism of Chomsky's views in a somewhat after-the-fact introduction to his monograph, *Language, Mathematics, and Linguistics* (1967, pp. 1–10, also pp. 51 ff. of the text). He develops the criticism fully in a later volume, *The State of the Art* (1968). Hockett offers "a critical review of current American linguistic theory, directed principally—indeed, almost but not quite exclusively—toward the views of Noam Chomsky" (1968, p. 3). This small book is veritably an exemplar of scholarly refutation, with its historical setting carefully reviewed, its sources meticulously checked (a propositional outline was submitted to Chomsky for his criticism and comments), its arguments carefully marshaled, its conclusions reached with confidence and stated with clarity and force. This is not to say of course that everybody will be persuaded by it, but it is a delight to read.

Hockett is no ranting behaviorist, but he prefers a more empirical conception of language than Chomsky's. According to Hockett, Chomsky considers language as an ideal structure or "well-defined system," of which no physical systems are examples. But natural languages, rather than formal and artificial languages, are presumably the major concern of linguistics (and, incidentally, sociolinguistics); and natural languages change and are probably also incomplete and inconsistent at any point in time. Hence the more closely a formal analysis of natural language approaches a well-defined system, the farther it gets from empirical application—because an important part of what sets off natural from artificial languages has been omitted. Whatever the utility of a "well-defined" model in some aspects of linguistic analysis, there are other aspects of language—such as exogenous changes, or its capacity to serve as a variable conditioned stimulus—with which it is unable to deal.

It would appear from the highly systematic limitations of his scheme that Chomsky is not concerned with those aspects of language with which we are concerned here, that is, its role in socialization and moral learning. It is worth noting that Chomsky's recent writing in defense of student radicalism and his criticism of recent American foreign policy in southeast Asia strongly suggest that he assents to some kind of moral objectivism such as Sir David Ross's (1930) conception (cited in the previous chapter). In another essay (1967), Chomsky strongly respects the phenomenology of the moral man.

Why this concern with a Platonic theory of language in a book which presents a non-Platonic theory of moral commitment? There are two reasons. First, Chomsky's timely appeal to the mentalistic underground has extended the influence of his ideas far beyond the technical field of linguistics. In this larger area he has been nothing short of charismatic, and his words are invoked by persons with little interest in or knowledge of the theoretical controversies in which his concepts are implicated. Today Chomsky is widely, if loosely, cited as having presented an "unanswerable rejection" of behaviorism. Since ours is a behavioristic theory, it is well for us at least to contend with (if not to reject) the views of Chomsky (for a view by a linguist more sympathetic to empirical sociolinguistics see Hymes, 1967). Second, an ideal, formal, and timeless theory of language is an obvious analogy to an ideal, formal, and timeless theory of norms. The idea that the mind apprehends the ideal, formal, and timeless aspects of language (its "competence," in Chomsky's terms, as distinguished from a speaker's "performance") by the exercise of an innate faculty suggests that, by the exercise of a similar innate moral faculty, the person may know the ideal, formal, and timeless aspects of the Right and the Good (the mind's values, as distinguished from the individual's behavior). Chomsky has done for language what the ethical intuitionists did earlier for "conscience"—that is, he has rendered it perfect and turned it to stone. Their view of a morality unsullied by the exigencies of life is now moribund, but the appealing analogy of Chomsky's notion of language might give it the breath of new life. In this respect, Chomsky continues an old line of seductive idealists that runs from Plato to Whitehead.

Meanwhile, debates on behavioristic theories of language also rage elsewhere. (See, for example, Fodor [1963], responses to Fodor's critique of behaviorism by Charles E. Osgood and D. E. Berlyne [1966], and Fodor's rejoinder, [1966]. Fodor depreciates inferences from animal studies by reminding us that *"animals can't talk"* [1964, p. 415; emphasis in original].)

Vicarious Learning

The generalization and discrimination of stimuli make possible an important process in human conditioning: "vicarious learning," or *learning produced by evidence of the reinforcement of others.* Often this is called "empathy" or "identification." These are usually defined as subjective processes, but this interpretation is not necessary. The process consists in an individual's learning that he is similar to others in his social environment. (Research into vicarious learning as "imitation" is presented in Bandura and Walters, [1963], especially Chap. 2.) The process of reinforcement of others is a potential stimulus to a given actor and thus can serve as a reinforcement of his own behavior. He learns that what happens to others can happen to him too. Because a given status is composed of stable patterns of reinforcement, the person learns that the same conditioners are likely to be applied to him as to the others who share his status. If a child steals cookies from a jar, gets caught in the act by his mother, and is punished in the presence of his brother, the brother who neither stole nor got punished can still learn something by generalizing. Whether he learns not to steal cookies or simply not to get caught is a question dealt with in following chapters. Whatever he learns, however, depends on his already having learned, more generally, that what happens to his brother can happen to him too; both are of a similar age status when it comes to cookies. The child can learn that status is a criterion for punishment even though he may not be able to name this criterion. Similarly, as sex roles become differentiated, he will learn that there are some acts for which his sister will be rewarded but for which he will be punished, and *vice versa*.

The boundaries of vicarious learning are primarily set by the organization of conditioners, through norms, into statuses. As a corollary, vicarious learning and generalization from it are the bases for learning about status. It is not learned solely in this manner, for symbolism and language permit of symbolic representation—the process whereby a symbol, a name for something, can elicit a response similar to the thing itself, *without* that thing having been a part of the original conditioning sequence. That sequence must of course begin with *some* unconditioned stimulus, but the distinctive aspect of symbolic representation is that the range of objects and events to which a response can be learned is vastly greater than the range of unconditioned stimuli by which a conditioning sequence need be begun.

Symbolic representation makes possible what is called "cultural" learning, the principal method of learning in human societies. Monkeys, for example, are highly intelligent animals, and under both natural and experimental conditions have shown themselves impressively intelligent about such matters as the acquisition of food. An individual monkey can often work out a very ingenious routine for getting food—sometimes more ingenious than the experimental design of his human masters. And probably another monkey that observed the first one going through his routine could learn it too. But what handicaps monkey society as compared to human society is its failure to evolve a "culture," a *system of efficient symbolic transmission* that would enable a monkey at a physical or temporal remove to respond to the symbolic representation of food, rather than responding first to food itself or even to the sight of another monkey working for food. Symbols, as compared to less elaborately conditioned stimuli, are much more portable, repeatable, adaptable, and economical in presentation, and their inclusion in the vocal repertory of humans makes it possible for humans to use as well as to be stimulated by them. As the essential vehicle, therefore, for all but the most rudimentary aspects of culture, language thus not only enters into social interaction but comes to dominate it, giving rise both to a vast increase in the scale of learning and to a parallel increase in the complexity and differentiation of human societies. Whereas every monkey has to learn directly or by vicarious experience how to get food—which limits infrahuman primate social organization to face-to-face or primary-group interaction—a human can also learn through symbolic representation, thereby building through abstraction and generalization on the adaptive learning of thousands of generations that preceded his own. Thus are the labyrinths of human social organization made possible.

If the phenomena of morality are to be reduced to the concepts of reinforcement, symbols quite obviously have to be taken into account, not only in the two types of learning—respondent conditioning to the symbol and operant conditioning of its use—but in the generalizing and abstracting mechanism of symbolic representation. It is through symbolic representation that very many norms are learned, especially those that relate mainly to adult life but require thorough learning in childhood. Many prohibitions need to be learned before the prohibited acts can actually be performed. Most of the strongly internalized sexual taboos, for example, get learned before we are physiologically capable of performing the prohibited acts. Then, too, humans in a complex society often must produce a complex and crucial learned response under infrequent and diverting conditions; only by symbolic representation can such a response be learned. But symbolic representation is notoriously inexact; and, as we see abundantly later on, the symbolic representation of events that are learned through the moral world-view—itself a system of symbolic representations—systematically misrepresents the events themselves.

The Relativity of Reward and Punishment

Before getting on to sanctions it is probably advisable to comment on the difference between technical and popular meanings of punishment and on the relativity of symbolic reward and punishment. While reward and punishment are fairly well defined in learning theory, their sociological and popular meanings are broader and less consistent. Moreover, the use of reward and punishment in human society has been the object of a great deal of ideological debate, which has influenced sociological discussion. Judged by a diffuse ideology which its adherents claim to derive from psychoanalysis, reward is "good" and punishment "bad." Punishment has been said to be "traumatic" in its effects, over and above the immediate restraint involved. Then too psychoanalysis within recent times has been a somewhat *avant-garde* movement attracting urban middle-class intellectuals, whereas punishment was given much support in the child-rearing folklore of more traditional and unlettered groups. This gave the concept of punishment the worst possible stigma: a reputation of use by a disreputable stratum. The vulgarization of Freud led to "permissive child rearing" as part of the life style of upward mobility.[4] Skinner paradoxically adds to this position with his own insistent depreciation of punishment because it fails to work efficiently in his usual sort of experimental work (Skinner, 1953, pp. 86 ff.). However, much experimentation by others with punishment suggests that

---

[4] I draw here from Aronfreed (1968, pp. 49 ff.). For a brilliant account of the absorbtion of psychoanalytic doctrines into existing American patterns of motive and belief, see Fred H. Matthews (1966).

under some conditions it may work efficiently; and punishment is often applied in ordinary social life simply because it is the only available controlling resource.[5]

As a technical term in reinforcement theory, "punishment" is defined as the termination of a positive reinforcer or the inauguration of a negative one. For example, if the operant activity of, say, one of Skinner's pigeons consists of pecking a target, and the reinforcer is food, then cutting off the food supply contingent on continued pecking constitutes a punishment in this technical sense. But in the popular and sociological sense punishment more commonly connotes only the inauguration of a stimulus, especially a sanction. Technically this can be punishment, but it is only one form. In operant conditioning by negative reinforcement, the activity may be followed by termination of a positive reinforcer as well as by presentation of a positive one. Here lies another difference, for in natural language a reinforcement is implicitly considered to be a conditioner that produces a *positive* emotion, although emotions, or affective states, do not enter into the technical definition. One lay account of negative reinforcement would be that the organism behaved as it did because it didn't like the negative reinforcer and its behavior was instrumental in terminating it. Suppose, however, that the pigeon is operantly pecking away, and the psychologist dumps cold water on him. The pigeon continues to peck. The psychologist dumps more and more water, until the "Skinner box" is awash and water is all over the laboratory floor, but still the pigeon pecks. Technically, the cold water is not a punishment in this case: since it did not change the response, it is therefore not a reinforcer, positive or negative. In the popular sense, however, a stimulus is much more likely to be construed as a reward or punishment *not according to its effects in behavior but according to the emotional state produced in oneself, revealed by introspection and imagined to have been produced in others*: thus the pigeon was punished by the water but persevered nevertheless (good puritan-ethic pigeon!).

In substantive sociology, punishment, as in the negative sanction, is ambivalently defined—both by its effect on behavior and by its effect on an emotional state that is somehow to be distinguished from behavior. Thus the sociologist will regard many stimuli as punishing which technically do not punish because they do not change behavior. Middle-class legal

---

5 See Aronfreed (1968) and cf. with Homans, who follows Skinner much more closely, and emphasizes the relative inefficiency of punishment (because imprecise) as compared to reward because it increases the probability of any behavior that terminates the punishment (1961, pp. 24 f.). In "natural" situations, however, the reduction of the probability of the act that brought on the punishment (for example, a child's running into a heavily traveled street) may have been the sole criterion for efficiency and precision of behavioral control.

analysts, for example, sometimes conclude that imprisonment is an efficient punishment which reduces the subsequent rate of the activity for which it is imposed, because if *they* were sent to prison the effect would be punishing, both in terms of their subsequent behavior and their private emotion. But when this "punishment" is actually administered to adolescent boys among "the disreputable poor" (to make David Matza's nice distinction [1966] between the decent poor who are ashamed of their lot, thus assenting to the higher stratas' scale of values, and the unrepentant remainder who are not), it may serve instead as a reward. Incarceration can become a symbol of a status of overriding value, postadolescent manhood, and thus increase rather than decrease the subsequent rate of the undesired behavior. When imprisonment increases crime, then the punishment has technically become a reward—a consequence that those who define reward and punishment in terms of the subjective states they produce (usually their own middle-class subjective states) are unlikely to notice.[6]

In the hypothetical case of the pigeon that was drenched with cold water, a supposed punishment did not technically punish, because it did not reduce the subsequent rate of an activity on which it was contingent, that is, the pecking. Such punishments may, however, punish others by a mechanism of vicarious learning: conditioning may occur through vicarious punishment as well as vicarious reward. Persons are also punished for what amounts to "ascribed deviation," in which sanctions are evoked by an action or property of an individual which is not in fact part of his operant repertory. Thus society shuns the dwarf and turns in disgust from the harelip's friendly smile.[7] Punishment can do little to affect appearance when it is based on a genetic defect (although it conditions the defective individuals in other ways), but it still can reinforce the operant behavior of others. The sanctions applied to genetic defects of appearance maintain norms of physical attitude and sumptuary detail among those who are genetically normal, thereby demonstrating the norms to those who are able to comply. From such cases as these we can infer a more general point: *a stimulus that does not condition one particular person may still serve, by example, to condition others.* We often observe that particular institutionalized punishments seem to fail in regard to their intended effect on a particular "victim," or produce it only at great cost or with unwanted side effects (such as death or disablement of the victim). But more generally, as exemplary punishments, they may be successful. The behavioral sciences have tended to consider only the individual and not the social effects of psychological processes. The im-

---

6 For an extended discussion which assumes that middle-class subjective states prevail across the whole society, see Inkeles (1963, pp. 336 ff.) and especially his list of the contents of an "adequate superego."

7 "Ascribed deviation" is discussed at length by Goffman (1963); the degree to which it may be an operant especially on pp. 73 ff.

portance of the social effect was long ago well expressed in Seneca's explanation to a horse thief as to why he was being hanged: "We kill you not because you stole a horse, but that horses will not be stolen."

In *Social Behavior* (1961), in which he applies Skinnerian concepts to interaction, George Homans has developed a "principle of distributive justice" (pp. 74–75), which may be summarized as the maxim that "for equal investment and equal costs, men expect equal rewards." Because social conditioners are organized into levels of status and because equivalence of status is a good measure of equivalence of cost and investment, one derivation from the principle of distributive justice is that equal status deserves equal reward. Although the concept of status is not a major one in Homans' scheme, he uses instances of equal status leading to unequal rewards as examples of situations in which distributive justice is violated.

One consequence of the principle of distributive justice is that violations of it are punishing to those who expect it to prevail. This may seem peculiar, because the punishing effect is wholly dependent on what happens to others in the same situation. Consider a group of status equals—students, clerks, or apprentices—all of whom, save one, are promoted. Popularly, and perhaps technically also, those promoted have been rewarded. It may appear that the person who did not get promoted cannot have been punished, since no new stimuli appear to have been presented to him or old ones removed. In fact, however, an important new stimulus has been added, likely to be overlooked because it is symbolic and relative: evidence of the greater reward now received by others who before got the same as he, that is, evidence that distributive justice is being violated. This element of relativity, this dependence on what happens to others of one's own status, must figure in the analysis of social reward and punishment, for it figures large in many social situations. What constitutes a reward or punishment for an individual is not invariant: it is itself a function of what happens to groups to which the person in question belongs and whose history he shares. Indeed, group membership can be entirely symbolic because anticipatory, and the effect of the reward or punishment may then depend on what it means to groups to which the person *aspires* to belong. This is the phenomenon of orientation to a "reference group."

Sanctions

The preceding discussion of the conditioner suggests that sanctions can be viewed as the sociologically relevant aspect of conditioners, and this is the interpretation to be followed here. The usual sociological practice is to define sanctions in terms of norms; here, we define them instead in terms of conditioners.

Many sociologists have described sanctions as the "external element," the "strong arm," the "cutting edge of social control" behind the norm, intimating that sanctions are vitally involved in normative control.[8] Few indeed have neglected them altogether. But sanctions themselves have seldom been explicitly defined. Here we will review some of the concepts of sanction used by other sociologists, in roughly chronological order.

Durkheim (1903) holds an interesting position between the idealistic and empirical traditions that we distinguished in Chapter I. He took Kant's position on morality—that "obligation" or "duty" is the sole motive for moral action—as his point of departure, but amended that position so that these aspects of internal commitment were not the *sole* motive (pp. 36–37). A moral act also has to be "desirable"—a term which it is probably fair to read in this context as "gratifying" or "rewarding." Durkheim used his concept of the sanction to locate the rewarding and punishing aspect of morality. Here is his statement of the relation of the sanction to "the moral rule" or, as we call it, the "norm":

> The violation of a rule generally brings unpleasant consequences to the agent. But we may distinguish two different types of consequences: (i) The first results mechanically from the act of violation. If I violate a rule of hygiene that orders me to stay away from infection, the result of this act will automatically be disease. The act, once it has been performed, sets in motion the consequences, and by analysis of the act we can know in advance what the result will be. (ii) When, however, I violate the rule that forbids me to kill, an analysis of my act will tell me nothing. I shall not find inherent in it the subsequent blame or punishment. There is complete heterogeneity between the act and its consequence. It is impossible to discover *analytically* in the act of murder the slightest notion of blame. The link between act and consequence is here a synthetic one.
>
> Such consequences attached to acts by synthetic links I shall call sanctions. . . . [It] is the consequence of an act that does not result from the content of that act, but from violation by that act of a pre-established rule [1906, p. 43].

Although his terminology differs, what Durkheim states here is the central part of our own concept of the sanction. The notion of a "mechanical consequence" of an act is not entirely clear because unless social interaction is explicitly excluded from such consequences it would seem possible to show that probably all "synthetic consequences" also meet the criterion for the

---

[8] The clearest statements of the importance of sanctions are made by Blake and Davis (1964, pp. 461, 465–66). Gibbs presents a conceptual analysis in his paper, "Sanctions" (1966), concluding with a taxonomy of sanctions based on dimensions of perceived effect, moral intent, and legitimacy (p. 153). Our own emphasis is of course solely on actual effect, whether perceived or not.

"mechanical consequence." Yet Durkheim clearly suggests a distinction between social and nonsocial consequences of an act: the "mechanical consequence" is what follows *regardless* of social interaction, whereas the "synthetic" consequence follows *only* through interaction—that is, when the act is the stimulus to a social response.

Durkheim accounts for this social response in terms of a "pre-established rule"; thus his concept of the sanction requires a prior conception of the norm. The principal question here is whether the criterion of the "pre-established rule" is sufficient. If Durkheim had carried this point through, he might well have concluded that the best criterion for the presence or absence of the pre-established rule was nothing other than the sanctions it was invoked to explain. It is not a perfect criterion nor an easy one to use, but it appears, with all its imperfections, to be better than any other; and it is the one we have chosen in what follows.

Durkheim's influence in American sociology is due largely (though to be sure not exclusively) to the writing and teaching of Talcott Parsons. In *The Structure of Social Action* (1937), Parsons does not define "sanctions" as such. In discussing Durkheim, he speaks of "internal" and "external" aspects of morality, intimating at several points that the external aspect alone is not adequate for the maintenance of social order. His remarks on the term "constraint" suggest how he might have defined "sanction," had that term been part of the "action scheme" which it was his main concern to develop. Constraint means "that a person's will is constrained by the applications of sanctions—that is, that he is coerced" (1937, p. 379). Parsons had an axe to grind here: not only was "external constraint" inadequate in his view as a mechanism for social order, it was also inadequate as an explanation of internal commitment. The latter was not simply important to social order but also autonomous; it was "voluntary," creative, and in vital respects separate from and independent of the natural world (see here not Parsons, 1937, but Parsons, 1934–1935). The notion of sanctions or "constraint" was introduced only to be depreciated. This procedure exemplifies the idealistic method for analysis of such a concept as the sanction: the subjective factors celebrated, the objective ones obscured.

In his postwar writings Parsons goes into much greater detail about the sanction, and we can see Durkheim's thought reflected in Parsons' discussion in *The Social System*. Sanctions are defined in terms of values:

> A value pattern...is always institutionalized in an interaction context. Therefore there is always a double aspect of the expectation system.... On the one hand there are the expectations which concern and in part set standards for the behavior of the actor, ego, who is taken as the point of reference; these are his "role-expectations." On the other hand there is a set of expectations relative to the contingently probable reactions of others (alters)— these will be called sanctions, which in turn may be subdivided into positive

and negative according to whether they are felt by ego to be gratification-promoting or -depriving. The relation between role-expectations and sanctions then is clearly reciprocal [1952, p. 38].

Several aspects of Parsons' formulation bear on the following analysis. First, sanctions occur in interaction—that is, where the response of one organism is a stimulus to another and *vice versa*. Sanctions are as necessarily social to Parsons as to Durkheim. Second, Parsons defines sanctions and the role, or "role-expectation," in his vocabulary, in terms of each other. Our own definition of status is not inconsistent with this approach. Third, Parsons mentions positive and negative sanctions, although his criterion— "how they are felt by ego"—is a nice example of the subjective test whose ambiguities have been discussed above. Fourth, as compared with Durkheim, Parsons seems more clearly to include *all* social responses within the concept of the sanction; this inclusion is made here also.[9] It has been widely remarked that Parsons' sociology emphasizes norms and values. But his concept of the sanction is remarkably close to that of the present essay, even though Parsons' context often suggests a considerable difference in emphasis. This congruence appears again in connection with Parsons' more formal statements on the process of internalization. Indeed, in his concrete examples of socialization of children, the difference between Parsons' accounts and those of the reinforcement and other "learning theorists" is almost solely a matter of terminology. Perhaps there is some reason to believe that attention to the empirical details of human socialization will go a long way toward making a "learning theorist" out of anybody. When you really look at the social environment closely you begin to see how very many reinforcements it presents that would never be revealed solely by introspection.

The work of George Caspar Homans is especially relevant here, because his *Social Behavior* (1961) remains the only book by a major sociologist that builds on the Skinnerian analysis of operant conditioning except for Blau's *Exchange and Power in Social Life* (1964), which builds partly on Homans' volume. Homans is vitally concerned with analyzing the sort of activities that most sociologists view as influenced by normative elements. But the Skinnerian concepts on which Homans relies are so contrary to the traditional sociological vocabulary that the relation between the two will not be noted unless a concerted effort is made to relate them, and this Homans

---

9 Parsons' formulations of sanctions in his other postwar works approximate the one quoted here from *The Social System*. See Parsons and Shils (1952a, p. 15; 1952b, p. 154). In a later version of the action scheme (1956), Parsons does not define sanctions, but he does distinguish between symbolic and non-symbolic sanctions (p. 687) in terms not inconsistent with our own preceding discussion of symbolic and non-symbolic conditioners. See also the learning-theoretical application he makes of sanctions in socialization (Parsons, 1964, pp. 86 ff.).

does not do. Most of what he says about the sociology of norms is not presented in his formal, expository chapters, but in an informal concluding chapter to which he alludes as "a primitive orgy after harvest." Here Homans forcibly argues against the idealist thesis that norms can motivate action in the ultimate absence of what he calls "primary rewards" (p. 382). This argument suggests an emphasis on sanctions, but although the idea of the sanction is ubiquitous in Homans' work, he never defines it explicitly.[10]

Homans' contribution to the present volume is his analysis not only of the basis of sanctions in interaction (that can be drawn from Durkheim and Parsons) but also of interaction in terms of reinforcement. Here is his definition of "interaction":

> We use it when the behavior emitted...whatever it may be otherwise, is at least social. Men perform many activities, like fishing, that are rewarded by the non-human environment; but when an activity...is rewarded (or punished) by an activity emitted by another *man,* regardless of the kind of activity each emits, we say that the two have interacted [1961, p. 35].

Perhaps this might be considered, strictly speaking, simply a *re*action rather than interaction; for Homans says nothing to indicate that the rewarding activity emitted by the second man, itself an activity, is reinforced by the activity of the first. But the reciprocal character of interaction is plain in Homans' subsequent discussion and the addition of a "vice-versa" clause is all that is needed to render his definition of "interaction" the same as our own: *interaction occurs when the behavior of one organism serves as a stimulus for the behavior of another, and when that behavior of the other, as a response, in turn serves as a stimulus for the first.* Interaction requires at least two organisms, but the maximum number that can get involved in it depends mainly on the extent to which the behavior can take on symbolic form; in technologically advanced situations, symbolic interaction can involve millions (though of course in such a situation not everybody interacts equally with everybody else.)[11]

---

10 See Homans' otherwise unpublished comment, cited by Loomis and Loomis (1961, pp. 244, 208*n*): "Every small action of a man is sanctioned. It is one of the fundamentals of all human behavior."

11 In mentioning social interaction we should also note the "symbolic interactionist" school in sociology, many of whose advocates stress the necessity of subjective factors in human interaction and deny the adequacy of an account of it which does not use irreducibly subjective terms. This is also the group that reconstructs G. H. Mead's social psychology as subjective and voluntaristic. They hold that the concepts of "meaning" (or "interpretation") and the "symbol" necessarily refer, at least partially, to subjective states; thus interaction, when symbolic, has always a subjective aspect. But this depends on prior definitions of "meaning" and "symbol," and if the definitions we advanced above are allowed, symbolic interaction has no necessarily subjective aspect. Symbols and meaning are wholly public processes, sanc-

A NEW DEFINITION OF THE SANCTION

Now that some prior formulations have been reviewed, we can state our own definition of the sanction: *It is the reinforcement of behavior produced by the behavior of other organisms of the same species.* In these terms sanctions are simply social reinforcers, the sociological aspect of the conditioner. Interaction, as reciprocal reinforcement, is not intrinsic in social reinforcement, but social species are characterized by the fact that most social reinforcement is also reciprocal. Since symbols can reinforce, sanctions can be symbolic, and the complexity of human social organization depends distinctively on symbolic sanctions. Sanctions are the means whereby the range of human operant behavior is delimited to those activities consistent with group persistance. They also serve to elicit respondent behavior, to stimulate activities that might not otherwise be forthcoming (in this our definition relates to the old idealistic notion of "effort"). Sanctions are not defined here in terms of norms, as in Durkheim's "pre-existing rule," or relative to values, as Parsons implies, but solely in terms of conditioners. Norms and values will in turn be defined in terms of sanctions.

This concept differs from what natural language implies—that a sanction is whatever forces compliance to a norm in the event that "voluntary compliance" does not occur. This was Parsons' earlier view. It also differs from the approach of most sociologists, who implicitly define sanctions in terms of norms: since they would probably hold that not all social inter- action is normative, they would conclude that not all of it is sanctioned. This is not the interpretation offered here. It is, to be sure, very useful to consider different forms of interaction as morally involved to different degrees, but this can be expressed in other ways. Here we shall express it in terms of the degree of the institutionalization of norms.

In order for sanctions to carry the explanatory weight with which they will be loaded in the next chapter, it is necessary to distinguish not only between symbolic and nonsymbolic sanctions, but also between empirical

---

tions depend on interaction, and interaction consists of reciprocal reinforcement; and in this sequence of analysis no terms have been introduced that have not been defined in objective terms, applicable to the behavior of organisms for which putative evidence of subjective states can scarcely be imagined.

For a recent review of "symbolic interactionism" see Rose, ed. (1962a). Rose's own essay in that volume, "A Systematic Summary of Symbolic Interaction Theory," pp. 3–19, does not stress subjectivism. He claims that symbolic interactionism ought not to be "in opposition to the behaviorist and Gestaltist theories, but supplementary to them'" (p. 4). On the other hand, see Herbert Blumer's depreciation of sociological "determinism" and the attempt to account for behavior in terms of its environmental antecedents in his "Society as Symbolic Interaction," in Rose, ed. (1962a, pp. 179–92, especially pp. 182–86).

and "superempirical" sanctions. Through symbolic representation, persons learn to respond to certain stimuli not through any prior conditioning to those stimuli directly, but indirectly, through symbols associated with them. Such association or representation is of course notoriously inexact. It can represent events that never come to pass and thus facilitate fiction and fraud in anticipatory learning, as in the creation of moral optimism in youth which leads to disenchantment in later life.

The distinction between empirical and "superempirical" symbolic representations can be made in many ways. Most of these rest on some metaphysical distinction between a real world and something else, and prove unsatisfactory in practice. The distinction made here is between representations of events which themselves can possibly serve as stimuli and those which cannot. In any particular case, the probability that a stimulus will actually occur may be very difficult to determine. Most empirical symbols, however, are subject to a variety of corroborating stimuli which, by abstraction and generalization, confirm their meaning even though the specific events to which they refer may not happen to a given individual. A male cannot experience childbirth, for example, but the properties of the events symbolically represented by the word "childbirth" have so many analogs he can experience that "childbirth" is a meaningful symbol to him, and clearly also an empirical one. Then too both the probability that the event symbolically represented will occur, as well as the number of corroborating stimuli, are matters of degree, so that the empirical-superempirical distinction is itself a matter of degree rather than a discontinuous dichotomy (the probability that a male will experience childbirth approaches zero empirically, and is zero by the definition of "male").

At the purely superempirical pole, symbolic representation necessarily refers to something outside of conventional experience. The best-known examples (as well as the most relevant for morality and social control) are the descriptions of the "afterlife" contained in the lore of various religions. Commentators with interests as diverse as those of Edward Ross (1901, p. 313); Goode (1951, p. 50); Skinner (1953, pp. 352–55); and John Whiting (1959, pp. 180 ff.) have all recorded the emphasis given to sanctions in the symbolic representations of an afterlife. (Ross simply cited the Old Testament, with its awful catalog of negative sanctions, and Skinner notes that "there is...no absolute distinction between a superstitious and a non-superstitious response.") Because they are essentially independent of corroboration, superempirical sanctions are economical and adaptable, and thus widely used in societies with efficient systems of social control. Moreover, the concept of superempirical sanctions can also be used to defend the theory of moral learning when the merely empirical sanctions that would be required to defend it cannot be readily found.

A related distinction runs between *manifest* and *latent* sanctions, separating sanctions of which the parties involved are "aware" (that is, which they have discriminated and verbally reported) from those of which they are not aware. The lay concept of the sanction tends to be limited to such manifest sanctions as legal sanctions, which involve legal penalties designed to affect the persons to whom they are applied. Sociologists would further distinguish "formal" from "informal" sanctions, thus indicating that social control is not limited to legal control; but still they generally refer to informal sanctions as if the persons who applied them were more or less aware of their character as sanctions. Yet it is clear, from our definition of sanctions (as well as Parsons'), that awareness is no requirement of the sanction: behavior can be reinforced without either the person supplying the reinforcer or its subject being aware of the process. The distinction is important, first, because many manifest sanctions have additional latent effects, and second, because most of the sanctions which are included in the present very inclusive definition operate as latent sanctions. When sociologists venture a criticism of the adequacy of an explanation in terms of sanctions, they are generally thinking only of sanctions as they know them personally, and thus it will be only manifest sanctions to which they attend. Much of their criticism would be warranted were the explanation so limited, but in fact sanctions that are both latent and informal (and unrevealed in the phenomenology of the moral man) carry most of the burden of social control.[12]

Norms

The concept of the norm has been singularly resistant to definition apart from the traditions of natural language and idealistic philosophy. A review of the literature shows how traditional conceptions have persisted.

Durkheim used Kant as his point of departure, and his discussion of "the moral rule" sometimes reflects Kant so strongly that it is hard to tell whether his phrase (it is singular in the original French) simply reflects the Gallic penchant for definite articles and singular nouns, or whether he was actually referring to the Kantian "categorical imperative." He does not use the term "norms" as such, but of the moral rule we are told that "obliga-

---

[12] The distinction between latent and manifest sanctions follows of course from Merton's distinction between "the consequences of an act...which are intended and recognized...by the participants in the system...and those which are neither intended or recognized" (1949, p. 51). A related distinction is made by Clyde Kluckhohn, between the "specificity" and "diffuseness" of sanctions (Kluckhohn et al., 1951, p. 431).

tion is one of its primary characteristics," that the moral rule never benefits the individual at the expense of society, and that it has a sacred character (1903, pp. 36–38). Although Durkheim's discussion of morality avoids identifying morality solely with the sense of duty and inner obligation, his conception of "norm" remains fairly close to natural language and thus has a persistently subjective aspect that he might have been able to avoid had he used a different vocabulary.[13]

Among contemporary theorists, we find the norm consistently defined as something embodied in a particular kind of statement—one about what ought or ought not to be. In *The Structure of Social Action,* Parsons ventured the following:

> A norm is a verbal description of a concrete course of action, . . . regarded as desirable, combined with an injunction to make certain future actions conform to this course. An instance of a norm is the statement "Soldiers should obey the orders of their commanding officers" [1937, p. 75].

In his postwar writings, Parsons does not define norms at all, but instead discusses normative elements in terms of "value-orientations." Here too he emphasizes symbolic representation and, though the discussion is discursive, it appears to be consistent with the formal definition he gave in 1937. A similar definition of norms as statements is also used by Blake and Davis (1964, p. 456): "[T]he term is presumably employed, as is done in the present chapter, to designate any standard or rule that states what human beings should or should not think, say, or do under given circumstances." Since their essay criticizes the "fallacy of normative determinism" and its commission by Parsons, Kluckhohn, and some of Parsons' students, it is interesting to note that it starts with a conception of norms that gives a big advantage to the position to which Blake and Davis are opposed. Later on, these authors face the difficulty of identifying values through verbal professions "which conceal as well as divulge," and consider the problems in the identification and distinction of concrete norms. Yet, as we shall see, such problems are unavoidable, given the definition of norms with which they work. Even sociology's foremost epistemological leftist, Homans, still formally defines norms as symbolic in a book that is exquisitely aware of the non-symbolic (or at least nonverbal) aspects of normative control:

> A *norm* is a statement made by members of a group, not necessarily by all of them, that its members ought to behave a certain way in certain circumstances. The members who make the statement find it rewarding that their

---

13 This is not to deny the pervasiveness of the idea of normative regulation throughout Durkheim's sociology, seen in his discussions of *anomie,* the relation of types of social organization to types of legal and social control, and so forth. See here Alpert (1939, Part III, especially pp. 205–6).

own actual behavior and that of the others should conform to some degree
to the ideal behavior described by the norm [1961, p. 40].[14]

Certainly there are grounds for interpreting norms as statements—or at
any rate as something represented in symbolic form. An increase in the
proportion of norms that are represented in explicit propositional form—
most concretely as "black letter law"—is closely associated with the growth
and structural differentiation of societies, as the legal institutions of complex
societies illustrate.[15] Because normative factors in human society operate
so largely through symbolic representation, and so often in explicit propositional form, it is understandable that the symbol has been taken to be the
essential characteristic of the norm. But there are costs as well as benefits
in this approach. If symbolic form is taken as a criterion together with a
subjective or phenomenological notion of symbolic meaning, then such
symbolically mediated aspects of human behavior as culture or most moral
learning get involved with a timeless realm of Platonic "eternal objects,"
which turn out to reside (as the neo-platonist A. N. Whitehead, who
thought them up, intended them to) beyond the reach of science. Another
problem is that the interpretation of norms as statements suggests an analysis
of their meaning on the basis of logical form, such as inquiry as to whether
the norm "X ought to do Y" implies the proposition: "Y is good," as well
as whether either or both of these statements are true or false. The path of
such analysis has led time and time again to a lion's den from which no
tracks return, and it therefore will not be followed here. We propose an
alternate procedure: to outline only the general symbolic form of the norm,
and then to illustrate some of the problems symbolic form presents as a
general sociological criterion of the norm. In order to solve these problems,
a conception of the norm is then advanced in which symbolic form, though
included in the concept, is not its criterion. We then show how this conception relieves the problems.

Natural language is a subtle thing, and nothing in it is subtler than its
rhetoric of moral persuasion and interplay of literal admonitions, understatement, irony, and circumlocution. Still there is a formal or schematic sense
in which the symbolic form of a norm can be generally represented, and this
may be called the "normative statement." It is in practice the verbal form

---

[14] An interesting variant on the norm-as-statement theme is Harry Johnson's
definition (1960, p. 8): "A norm is an abstract *pattern,* held in the mind, that sets
certain limits for behavior." By this criterion all norms become internalized and
subjective representation completely replaces symbolic content.

In his paper, "Norms: the Problem of Definition and Classification" (1965),
Jack Gibbs offers a general review of literature on the topic and a taxonomy of
norms in terms of structural conditions under which they operate.

[15] See, for example, the discussion of written and unwritten law in Malinowski
(1926, pp. 12–15).

to which moral persuasion repairs when polite indirection fails and explicit meaning is required, and it is also how Parsons, Blake and Davis, and Homans have defined the norm. The normative statement is defined by its *modal predicate,* the verbs (implicit or explicit) of "ought" or "should" or "must" or "deserve" that distinguish normative statements from existential statements, that is, statements about matters of fact. Not all modal predicates are normative; the distinction is that existential predicates refer to an actual or determinate condition, whereas modal predicates specify one indeterminate empirical possibility among several such possibilities. Thus an existential statement, referring to human behavior, says "X does Y," a modal non-normative statement says "X may (or 'might,' or 'could') do Y (but in fact he may end up doing something else)"; and a normative statement says "X ought to do Y (but he may fail this obligation and do something else)." There are practical variations: an authoritative statement or command uses the determinate descriptive form and is thus ironic: the command "X will do Y," when asserted by a person in authority, actually functions as "X ought to do Y, and if he does not, sufficient sanctions will be brought to bear to cause him, in all likelihood, to do Y in response to future commands."

Some ethical philosophers claim that their subject is the direct analysis of normative statements, apart from the behavior to which such statements may refer or be otherwise associated. But until sociologists, as distinguished from philosophers, assent to some version of the doctrine of natural law and come to believe that normative statements are formally derivable from statements of fact, their science must continue to deal with normative statements not for their own sake but solely as they relate to actual behavior— because the social aspects of behavior are their subject matter. Statements of the form "X ought to do Y" should concern them only as they provide information about what X actually does or about the conditions under which Y is performed.[16] Normative statements provide this information only when they are considered together with a number of other factors. Just as existential statements do not by themselves imply normative ones, so normative statements do not imply existential ones: the relation between "X ought to do Y" and "X does Y" is logically indeterminate.

Consider the problems that follow simply from the possible range of reference of normative statements. A complex society always presents a great variety of such statements, including that X ought to do any number of things Y which may lie outside the range of his possible behavior or which would require extravagant and impossible rewards in order to be reinforced at a level competitive with alternate acts. To be sure, some normative state-

---

16 Not excluding the activity of asserting normative statements. But the study of the conditions under which normative statements are asserted is quite different from the direct analysis of the statements themselves, as this has generally been carried out in ethics.

ments that prescribe seemingly impossible acts, or that proscribe seemingly inevitable ones, or whose conditioning would require reinforcers beyond any society's resources, do appear to have affected the merely possible range of human conduct. These effects are important, but clearly they cannot be predicted from the formal content of the statement alone. The assumption that they can be so predicted is a "rationalistic" or (better to say) "moralistic" fallacy against which the sociological study of human morality has long been directed.[17] Norms prescribing some period of celibacy, abstinence from alcohol, and a familial monopoly of sexual activity are regularly asserted in the face of the veritable institutionalization of just what the normative statements claim to prohibit. Thus, societies which prohibit alcohol have high rates of alcoholism, and prostitution flourishes where the formal norms of a familial monopoly on sexuality are strong. By itself, the ubiquitous and infinitely variable exhortation that "X ought to do Y" provides no information about whether X will in fact do Y or whether he will instead do any number of other things. It is this sort of information that sociology requires, and an adequate conception of the norm should therefore make it an object of inquiry.

It is because the conception of the norm solely as a statement is so inadequate that many sociologists, even those who define the norm just in this way, are reluctant to regard the entire process of morality as equally symbolic as the norm itself. They deny the determinacy of purely symbolic norms, and hasten to add what is needed to make more determinate the relation between the norm, "X ought to do Y," and the matter of fact, "X does Y." What is added is a sanction, a socially mediated stimulus presented to X that affects the probability that he will subsequently do Y. The concept of the norm thus tends to be linked to reinforcers, as in the following: A norm is a statement that X ought to do Y, which is associated with rewards for doing Y and punishments for not doing Y. The norm, conceived as a symbol, is imperiled by the impotence of pure symbols, and is rescued by the capacity of symbols to signal reinforcement. Sociologists think of the norm as something different from sanctions, but never really separate from them.

Perhaps the most economical replacement of this conceptual circumlocution—the problem posed by the problematic relation between "X ought to do Y" and "X does Y"—is to change the criterion of the norm itself from the symbolic representation to the reinforcement. The reinforcing effect is after all what the norm produces whenever behavior is actually controlled by it—the effect whereby one act is first selected from among all the differ-

---

[17] Cf. Blake and Davis (1964, pp. 461 ff.) on "the fallacy of normative determinism" (that is, that the content of the norm determines the behavior to which it refers).

ent acts of which an actor is physically capable of performing, with the probability of performance of that act then increased by differential rewards and punishments. Although in the technical sense such rewards and punishments may come from the actor's total environment, the rewards and punishments from the social environment are always stressed in the sociological discussion of norms. Such social reinforcements are equivalent to "sanctions" as they were defined in the preceding section. The criterion of the norm becomes the application of sanctions.

THE NORM REDEFINED

It is now possible to move directly to an explicit definition of norms by a straightforward generalization of Holmes' definition of the law (1896, p. 63). If law is "the prophecies of what the courts will do in fact, and nothing more pretentious" then norms are the prohibitions (or positively, the encouragements) which the sanctions reinforce, and nothing more pretentious. A short formal definition is this: *a norm is a name for a pattern of sanctions*. More exhaustively, a norm consists of changes in the rates of emission of activities susceptible to reinforcement by social reinforcers (sanctions). These may be either nonsymbolic sanctions, or symbolic sanctions, which may include representations of nonsymbolic sanctions and nonsocial reinforcers.

Some implications of this definition need discussion. A norm requires an effect. This is because we have defined sanctions in terms of reinforcers, and because these in turn are defined by their effects. Putative norms and sanctions that have no effect are thus not norms and sanctions in these terms. A norm is *not* identical with the behavior on which sanctions are contingent and of which its effects are a part: norms affect the rates of activity but so do other factors (metabolism, nonsocial reinforcers, and so forth). In this connection, it is probably useful to point out that "the" norm is an abstraction; concrete behavior is usually influenced by a multiplicity of norms. Norms, as names, get used both by persons involved in the sanctioning process and by those who study the process, and thus are subject to the risks inherent in the use of names generally. A major risk is that of naming objects that do not exist. We can name unicorns that do not exist and norms that nobody obeys, and social scientists (largely because they rely on the phenomenology of the moral man and thus mistake conceptions of the good society for descriptions of actual societies) name such norms chronically. But this is a problem of evidence, and certainly not a problem limited to the present discussion. Our reference to "nonsymbolic sanctions" is fairly straightforward; these are simply social acts considered in terms of their primary effects (presenting food to a hungry person, taking food away from him, throwing a rock at someone). The phrase "symbolic representation of nonsymbolic sanctions and nonsocial reinforcers" can be illustrated by the claim that sanctions follow deviation (debtors are thrown in jail for bankruptcy) or that nature attends to human morality (the bridge collapsed because a wicked man was passing over it). The event represented may not be social, indeed may not even occur, but the reference to it is social and, to the extent that it affects behavior, is thus a sanction.

One advantage of this conception of the norm is that it includes more than normative statements (as sociologists have in practice found it necessary to do) without also including all normative statements, with their bewildering variety and frequent irrelevance. Normative statements are norms only when they have an effect on what somebody does—that is, to the extent that they are part of a process of reinforcement. The fact that not *all* normative statements that claim "*X* ought to do *Y*" actually reinforce *Y* does not mean that *none* of them do; and they may reinforce some other activity, even if not *Y*. A normative statement, then, is a norm when it meets the criteria for a norm; such a statement can be called an "effective statement," to set it off from others that are not effective. As a pure symbol, the statement of a norm is always impotent; any potency it has derives from a sequence of learning that began with a nonsymbolic conditioner. The test, in brief, is not one of grammar but one of consequences in behavior. And this will involve not only the normative statement's learned (and variable) general meaning, but also the particular conditions under which it is made—the status of the speaker and the sanctions he can bring to bear, the value (as defined below) of the sanctions to the person to whom they may be applied, and all the other things that sociologists take into account whenever they try to specify actual normative effects, and not just give a formal definition of the norm.

Qualifications. Several further points should be made by way of clarifying our concept of the norm. A plausible objection to the concept is that it is too broad—that, in seeking to relieve the narrowness and avoid the problems of an essentially symbolic conception, it has reached too far and identified the normative with the whole of social reinforcement, and thus with all interaction. "Normative determinism" is established as a matter of definition. The idea that social interaction is variably normative in some respect other than simply its capacity to reinforce is likely to find many supporters. Thus Blake and Davis, opposing the emphasis Parsons places on "major value-orientations" in "basic personality structure," assert that:

[A]n assumption of normative primacy renders it difficult to explain deviancy and crime, although the real world plainly exhibits a great deal of normative violation. If one is to understand deviancy one must ask why societies frequently reward violation more heavily than conformity to the norms; why legitimate authority is one of the most widespread bases of illegitimate power, . . . why any action, no matter how atrocious, can be justified in terms of the verbal formulas in which norms and values are couched [1964, p. 63].

It seems to me, however, that their objection may not apply to Parsons; and it definitely does not apply to whatever "normative primacy" our own scheme implies. Blake and Davis are not discussing a contest between the normative and the non-normative, but simply the effects of interaction among a plurality of norms—what in a more ideological lexicon is called a "conflict of norms." The real world does indeed exhibit a great deal of deviation and normative evasion, but these are always relative. Adolescents whose delinquencies get so much popular and professional attention some-times turn out on a closer look to be very moral fellows, simply marching to a different drummer, responding to different and stronger norms—such as those defining prepotence and exploit as part of the manly role. Moreover, when a society appears to reward "violation" more than "conformity," is it not likely that we have simply made a mistake in identifying the norm?[18] Blake and Davis seem to assume that "normative primacy" means the primacy of institutionalized norms, and perhaps also that institutionalized norms never conflict. Yet it was Davis who earlier identified prostitution as a "veritable institution" sustained by prescriptions linking sex to reproductive institutions, and who pointed out that illegitimacy was sustained, in the face of strong proscriptions, by interaction between norms of chastity and rules of descent (Davis, 1937, 1939).[19]

The questions that the critics of normative primacy have raised are important. But the conception of norms advanced here does not preclude answering them. The definition of the *general* concept of the norm in such inclusive terms does not mean that other more special distinctions among

---

[18] Here again the problem may be linked to the phenomenology of the moral man. The assumption is common among intellectuals that norms that preoccupy them (that is, the mélange of Judeo-Christian, liberal-Enlightenment optimism mentioned earlier) are the institutionalized norms of the whole society. Of course, insofar as such a group can marshal potent sanctions (for example, through a monopoly on force or, more indirectly, through education or because they hold strategic administrative positions), their norms can become institutionalized. But the question is empirical rather than phenomenological. A thoughtful discussion of the primacy of norms and the problem of their empirical identification is found in Melford E. Spiro (1951, pp. 32 ff., especially pp. 34, 47*n*). Spiro discusses Myrdal's postulation of an American "norm of equality." Without qualification and limitation (especially of age, sex, social class, and ethnicity, the major axes of status ascription) such a postulate is dubious, although it is revealed forcefully in the phenomenology of liberal intellectuals. The postulate can, however, become a norm of considerable importance when such persons occupy influential positions (for example, clerk to a Supreme Court Justice).

[19] Actually, further on in their article, Blake and Davis make a related point, in part contrary to their preceding criticism of normative primacy. They note that such critics as Dahrendorf, Mills, and Wrong seem to assume that norms consist of "demands for the peaceful, the static, and the homogeneous." This, in the view of Blake and Davis, confuses "the normative with the changeless and 'utopian'" (1964, p. 467). But the broader the content of norms, the more tenable becomes the premise of normative primacy: again, the matter is conceptual rather than empirical.

particular norms cannot be made. The major distinction in sociological analysis is probably between institutionalized and other types of norms.

Institutionalized Norms and the Subinstitutional. The normative regulation of some forms of behavior is more important than other forms to viable social organization. This statement brings us back to the role of norms in social organization.

Since everything social is normative, the choice of a necktie is normative. "Good taste" in ties is socially learned, and ties are worn in a social context. Indeed we can name rather specific and well-recognized norms that apply to this situation, such as, for example, that patterned ties should be worn only with plain shirts. Insofar as the viability of familial organization is concerned it matters little whether a particular husband (bemused perhaps by the studiously bad taste of dandies and entertainers) violates this norm and wears a Paisley tie on a Madras shirt. But it matters much if the husband is choosing sexual partners rather than neckties and selects his daughter rather than his wife, because rules of incest are a major support for family organization. Hence one important distinction among types of norms has to do with the contribution of the activity to which the norm relates to the viability and efficiency of social organization. This is especially the case for social organization in the long run, as discussed in Chapter I. Salient activities are encouraged or discouraged by constellations of particular norms called *institutions,* and thus we can corollarily refer to the degree to which norms are institutionalized.

It is not trivial to say that some norms are institutionalized, because many norms are not. The varieties of norm formation and change that get studied under the rubric of collective behavior include many with strong but transitory effects, recorded today only as historical curiosities. In terms of our definition, vagaries of adolescent dress represent the operation of norms, just like some quite different acts that are often presented as exemplars of high morality. The difference between adolescent fads and high morality does not lie in whether they are both normative behavior, but in whether they involve institutionalized norms. (Cf. Levy [1952, pp. 101–9] on "institutions.") Sociological terminology is misleading on this point, for often it assumes (as Blake and Davis seem to in the passage quoted earlier) that anything called a norm must have the properties —especially the property of widespread structural significance—that are better regarded as properties only of institutionalized norms.

Abstractness. In another essay, Davis presents and metaphorically labels another useful dimension of norms:

> Norms exist in "layers," so to speak. At the top are remote and official ideals; then follow secondary norms that conflict with the official ideals that regulate behavior because conformity to them is rewarded and deviation

punished. Beyond these are tertiary norms, and so on down the scale of respectability and rightness.... In practice, normative rightness is relative rather than absolute. Bad behavior has extenuating circumstances; good behavior impure motives and dubious consequences. In comparing societies one should therefore compare similar gradations on the scale of normative rightness...[especially as between, e.g.,] the more puritanical sections of the Bible [and] day-to-day norms in a savage society.... An illiterate society has no sacred books in which to encrust an unused set of norms [1966, pp. 328–29].

What Davis recommends here is attention to the *degree of abstractness of norms*. The "top layer" of abstraction, the "remote and official ideals," may indeed be very abstract and diffuse in reference. It is tempting to conclude that such abstract norms are only putative norms, mere names for patterns of sanctions that do not actually exist, and doubtless many claims of abstract norms have this empirically false character. But not all of them do; many high abstractions are backed by powerful concrete sanctions. What seems distinctive about these sanctions, however, is that they apply to competing abstract norms and to the specific symbolic gestures by which men assent to such norms. Torquemada required the Jews of Spain to assent to Christ as the true Messiah, on pain of torture and death. A dreary fate falls on Soviet artists who neglect the canons of "socialist realism."

Since abstract norms (both putative and virtual) are stated symbolically, they partake of the economy and adaptability of all symbols and are thus easy to study. Sociologists generally know more about such norms than about the day-to-day norms governing ordinary behavior. Such ordinary norms are often latent, and their explication is perhaps sociology's most persistently iconoclastic specialty.

Scale.[20] Closely related to the degree of abstractness of norms is the dimension of "scale," or magnitude of the behavior to which they refer. Just as sociologists tend to concentrate on abstract and institutionalized norms, so they also concentrate on those that affect large rather than small populations or that endure for a long rather than a short period. There is of course a body of literature under the rubric of "small-group" research on processes that are quite directly normative within our present definition. But the processes are likely to be labeled in terms of "communication" or "influence," rather than in terms of "norms" and "sanctions"; and where normative concepts are used directly, the ancillary concepts are likely to derive from psychology rather than sociology. "Small-group" research on norms tends thus to get involved in the mutual alienation of these two fields, and has little influence on those sociologists who work on the "institu-

---

[20] This dimension was suggested by Richard Emerson.

tional" level. Between micro- and macrosociology there is much less communication than there might be, and one result is that a norm is implicitly thought to be more genuinely a norm the larger the scale of the behavior to which it applies.

Intrinsic and Extrinsic Reinforcement. Another important distinction among norms is whether the activity that the norm prescribes or proscribes is likely to be reinforced apart from the norm in question, either through the operation of other norms or through inherently reinforcing effects of the activity. Behavior that serves vital physiological functions such as eating, sexual excitation, excretion, and sleep, has persistent and strong inherently reinforcing properties; in Hullian terms these are the "primary drives." Thus, to use an exceptionally homely example, all societies place little normative emphasis on eating as opposed to fasting (although they do of course encumber the act of eating with all sort of rules linking it to major statuses and institutions, regulating when and what to eat, with which hand, and so forth), because eating is so strongly reinforcing in itself that there is seldom a need to reinforce it extrinsically. Thus the presentation of food is often used to reinforce other activities which in themselves may not be reinforcing (for example, rituals symbolizing familial, economic, or religious solidarity). But all societies put a strong normative emphasis on the division of labor that produces food, because this activity, though just as necessary as eating, is not so intrinsically reinforcing.

Another way of looking at the "alternate reward" distinction is in terms of what Homans, blending learning theory with economics, calls "cost" (1961, pp. 52–61). In his terms, the cost of an activity is the value of other activities that had to be foregone in order to carry it out. Thus any prescribed activity is costly to the extent that other rewarding activities could have been performed in its place. The cost of marital fidelity is the forfeit of the variety, excitement, and sense of sexual conquest that extramarital liaisons might provide. Any institutionalized norm is likely to entail costs; moreover, the value of the activities that might have been performed, were it not for the norm, is characteristically great (otherwise they would not require proscription on the institutional level). Alternate rewards, either as the intrinsic reinforcement involved in what are called the "primary drives" or the extrinsic reinforcement of particular deviant acts, are important factors in determining rates of conformity to norms.

Legitimacy. Questions may also be raised as to how this conception of the norm can contend with such attributes of norms as "authority" and "legitimacy." It may be argued that a definition of norms solely in terms of conditioners cannot take account of these properties. We may hear that people do not respond to a norm solely in terms of its capacity to reinforce, but that they also reflect on its authority or its relation to some principle of justification.

It should be noted that such questions arise most readily in connection with norms which are in the form of statements. The statement "X ought to do Y" differs from "X does Y" only in its modal predicate; it is otherwise formally identical. Just as it is possible to evaluate "X does Y" as true or false, so the same operation of validation may be attempted for the statement "X ought to do Y." The analysis of "moral authority" that follows from this analogy operates by deducing "X ought to do Y" from some more general normative statement that is presumed to be true: thus the reasoning may run, "X ought to do Y" because God has ordained that "A ought to do B," and X and Y are members of the classes A and B respectively.

The main problem with this type of analysis, however interesting it may be in its own right, is that it bears on sociology only if it meets one criterion: that the analysis increases our knowledge, not of the properties of "X ought to do Y" purely as a symbol, but of the relation between assertion "X ought to do Y" and the probability that X actually will do Y.[21] If the appeal to the authority behind the statement "X ought to do Y" actually increases the probability that X will do Y, then the appeal to authority operates as a symbolic reinforcer of Y and thus is one mechanism whereby the statement "X ought to do Y" actually operates as a norm and is not simply a statement of a putative norm with no effect on behavior. Not all appeals to the authority behind a normative statement reinforce it, but probably some of them do. To distinguish those appeals which reinforce from those which do not is a difficult empirical task. Indeed, the assumption that the moral authority of a norm is a reliable guide to its role in actual human affairs is part of a doctrine of moral rationalism or idealism in which sociologists, on the basis of quite convincing comparative evidence, strongly disbelieve— except, it seems, when fabricating their formal definitions of normative elements.

The term "legitimacy" describes for sociologists a relation between norms, or between norms and some other normative element. Thus we hear that the mores legitimate the formal law, or that values legitimate norms. For the present, however, we shall treat legitimation as the process of applying norms not directly to immediate activity, but instead to its conditioning: that is, *legitimation is the application of one norm to another*. Thus, Sumner's theory that a society's mores, the mass of informal, strongly held sentiments, can legitimate the formal law can be interpreted as the claim that the mores, as informal norms, are reinforcements which enhance the probability of conformity to formal norms. Similarly, Parsons' claim that

---

[21] A formalistic effort in this direction, limited to "normative statements," has been made recently in philosophy as "modal logic." A statement of this approach to a sociological audience is made by Anderson and Moore (1957).

"values legitimate norms" means that values held by persons determine the probability that a norm will actually prevail. Whether either or both of these hypotheses are more or less true is an empirical question. The bearing of the concept of legitimacy on the present discussion is purely conceptual: it leads to the notion of a hierarchy of norms.

THE HIERARCHY OF NORMS

Though all operant social behavior is, by the present construction, normatively controlled, the controls never seem to be completely orderly. There is evidently a plurality of norms. But it is a most reasonable assumption that in any universe of activities subject to normative delimitation, not all norms contribute equally to the aggregate probability that any activity or combination of activities will occur. More simply, some norms are more powerful than others; thus, any given activity will be affected by some norms more than by others. Norms can therefore be ranked according to their power. Such a hierarchy is not constructed on an axiomatic or deductive basis, although there may well be some degree of analogy between a deductive heirarchy and a hierarchy of power. Here again, the "rationalistic" habit has been to presume that the hierarchy of moral or ethical beliefs can be deduced like theorems of logic or the theories of an advanced science, but the data of comparative sociology and anthropology have cast much doubt on this presumption. The formal norms of codified law do stand to a large degree in a deducible relation between fundamental principles and specific applications, but no one has been able to get very far in working out an axiomatic theory for even small segments of human morality as it actually operates more generally. The many statements that purport to represent actual social norms are manifestly inconsistent.

At the same time, the inconsistency and conflict of the norms themselves are never complete. Their degree varies among societies; some norms affect more activity than others; and, at the least, those norms which maintain patterns of behavior necessary to the functioning of society must prevail. For a society as a whole, therefore, those norms that most prevail—that are the strongest reinforcers—may be called "ultimate" or "basic," and, except as modified by conditions producing social change (population, technology, or interaction with other societies or with the non-human environment), these will be the norms eventually most institutionalized.[22] Those norms which prevail least—whose prescriptions are most quickly ignored when they inter-

---

22 A norm may "prevail" even though the activity that it appears to prescribe is seldom realized. Here again, the meaning of the norm lies in its effect on behavior. Few societies which prescribe marital sexual fidelity actually succeed in rendering infidelity uncommon—but they may succeed in reducing the *rate* of infidelity and

fere with those of ultimate norms—may be called something else—"ephemeral," perhaps. As with the idea of institutionalization, it is to the activities required for viable social organization that we can profitably look first for the explanation of the place of a particular norm in the hierarchy of influence in human affairs. This touchstone may not immediately provide a complete explanation, but it has already provided a partial one.

NORMS IN PRIMATE SOCIETITES

A final point about norms as names for sanctions or schedules of social reinforcement concerns their operation in infrahuman societies. Primitive norms these are indeed, but primate ethologists have often remarked that what they see in the natural setting of their subjects—so much more a challenge to animal intelligence than the laboratory or the zoo—can only be described as "cultural behavior." The complexity and regularity of patterns they report suggest that it is quite appropriate to speak of norms in primate troops. The problems of social organization are much the same as for human societies. A round of activities has to be performed—care and training of the young, protection of weaker members, defense of territory and food supply against other species and even other troops of the same species, regulation of conflict within the troop. Yet the activities are not instinctive, have to be learned, evidently are far more than a response to short-run environmental changes, and have to compete with alternate rewarding activities. Thus the ethologists have reported that the maintenance of these activities—surveillance of the behavior of the troop and the subsequent application of sanctions—tends, in the primate division of labor, to become the function of the dominant adult males, and that the behavior of these adult males is largely limited to these functions by the reinforcing properties of the behavior of other members of the troop. (See several papers collected in Southwick [1963], especially Carpenter on gibbons [p. 22]; Haddow on African redtail monkeys [p. 53]; and Emlen and Schaller on mountain gorillas [pp. 133–35].)

If normative control is to be defined as essentially symbolic, then these relations between behavioral control and societal survival, with their striking analogies to institutionalized human norms, must be explained away—all simply to preserve the idea that morality is a distinctively human affair. A definition of the norm that applies to all learned social organization, one

---

increasing its cost to the philanderer. It is to such consequences, as well as to the specific reference, that the sociologist should look for the content of the norm. The effect of norms of fidelity is found not only in the rates of liaison or concubinage, but also in the degree familial solidarity and the conditions for divorce.

that can build on interspecific comparisons, will serve sociological theory better than an anthropomorphic concept which imposes purely termi-nological barriers across an otherwise continuous dimension of activity.

Values

The import of the preceding discussion of norms for a complementary discussion of value is not hard to divine in advance. Whereas the usual treat-ment of values in sociology stresses their subjective and symbolic aspects, ours will be neither subjective nor limited to symbolic representation.

There are many conceptions of value in sociology. Talcott Parsons' influ-ence has, again, been great, but his notion of "value-orientation," on which so many of his more specific concepts depend, is so protean that no single formal definition of it can be extracted from his texts. The gist of his post-war conception is that "value standards" are what provide "criteria of selection" for the various types of activity (or "courses of action") of which the "actor" is capable (Parsons and Shils, 1952b, p. 56). Our own con-ception of the norm thus parallels Parsons' conception of value. This is not surprising, for Parsons makes no explicit statement about norms as such in his postwar work, using "value-orientations" to account for what most other commentators explain by norms. Moreover, the concepts of value and norm are among the most persistently interrelated and vaguely distinguished con-cepts in sociology, so that Parsons is not singularly culpable but merely in bad company. A related and more specific conception of value, however, of which Parsons probably approved at the time it was written, is that of Clyde Kluckhohn, one of the more substantial collaborators in the formally concerted statement that *Toward a General Theory of Action* was originally meant to be. In his paper on values in that volume, Kluckhohn, after a lengthy review of the analysis of valuation by philosophers and linguists, defines a value as "a conception, implicit or explicit, distinctive of an indi-vidual or characteristic of a group, of the desirable, which influences the selection from available modes, means, and ends of action" (Kluckhohn et al., 1952, p. 395).[23]

Although Kluckhohn goes on to specify the constituent terms of his defini-tion, he tends to identify values fairly strongly with subjective conceptions, on the one hand, and with verbal representations, on the other: insofar as values are "internalized," *verstehen* is called for; and they must be "for-

---

[23] See also the related and rather discursive definition given in Kluckhohn and Strodtbeck (1961, p. 4). Their discussion of Tinbergen's concept of "directiveness" is related to points made in this text in the analysis of the norm.

mulable...by the observer in such terms that the subject [of whom they are predicated] can understand and agree or disagree" (Kluckhohn et al., 1952, pp. 396, 397–98).

If a value is conceived as a statement of what somebody desires, then all the problems of relating norms as statements to norms as behavior, discussed above in terms of relating "X ought to do Y" with "X does Y," will come up again, *mutatis mutandis*. Thus, "X values Y" (which means, in Kluckhohn's terms, that X *says* he values Y) does not by itself provide any information on X's behavior. An abiding suspicion is that Y is an activity that X can perform, but the assertion by X that he values Y may have little or no relation to his actual performance of Y. A drunkard can profess between straight shots that he values sobriety. The literature of interrogatory sociology is full of divergences between what people say they value or say they plan to do in respect of that value, and what they actually do. (The "principle of hypocrisy," advanced in the next chapter, attempts to explain the discrepancy.) Unless a sociologist is concerned solely with verbal behavior and never aspires to study its relation to other activities, he may be tempted to use a conception of value that includes verbal expression but is not limited to it, for the same reasons advanced above for an equally general concept of the norm.

Fortunately, in this case no originality of conception is required, as it was for the definition of the norm. We can simply use Homans' definition of value in terms of quantity of activity (1961, p. 41): "The value of a reward is the amount of activity put out to get it." This is to construe value as *the relative strength of a reinforcer*. If a person values A more than B, he will produce more activity when reinforced by A than by B.

The more important distinction between Homans' definition of value and the conception of value as a statement of preference is that in the former case the test of value is the *whole* amount of activity put out in response to the reinforcer, not just the response of naming the reinforcer as the predicate of a statement of preference. Returning to our hypothetical drunkard, we see that the value he places on sobriety under Homans' definition is negative: it is punishing for him, since he will put out a lot of activity in order to avoid it. But if we use as our criterion for value his statement of preference, and agree that the criterion of value "must be formulable to the subject in terms to which he can agree or disagree," then so long as he is not too deep in his cups to answer "Yes" to the question "Do you value sobriety?" he has to be judged to value it. To make the statement of preference the criterion for value produces endless variations of this paradox, and has caused many sociologists to avoid using verbal expressions of value as their ultimate data just as they have similarly avoided a final criterion of the norm as a statement. In moments of dark suspicion, faced with evidence of the frequent gulf between verbal preferences and subsequent courses of action, good phenomenologists often become crypto-behaviorists.[24]

There is a sense in which values and norms refer to the same thing from two abstractly different points of view, the norm representing a social perspective and the value an individual perspective. Norms were defined above as necessarily social. Value, on the other hand, is to be measured by the amount of activity produced by a given reinforcement, and reinforcers may be nonsocial. Nevertheless, social animals respond so strongly to interaction that their strongest values will usually be social, which is also to say that norms will be their strongest values. In fact, the norms valued most will be institutionalized; for, if the reinforcements embodied in institutions were not widely effective—if they were not widely valued—they would not be institutions. This is one way to resolve some of the seemingly endless arguments about whether values legitimate norms or whether institutionalized norms prevail. To conclude that values and norms are complementary and that institutions prevail by definition has at least the charm of economy.

The discussion can then move to the question of whether a *particular putative institution*—kinship rules, property rights, representative government, religion, or whatever—really meets the criteria for valuation and institutionalization for the group in question. Such a conception does not make empirical solutions easy, but it permits such solutions in principle and is in this respect an improvement on some earlier notions.

Status

Some comments on the concept of status or role are in order, because much of what follows about norms and moral learning depends on our relating norms to roles.

---

[24] The interrogation, in one form or another—interviews and questionnaires—is the preferred sociological method today not because it is good, but because it is cheap. There are very few if any sociological propositions that would not be better verified by evidence from the whole range of behavior to which they refer instead of just the verbal report of it by the people involved. The question that affects research design is whether the better information about the whole range of behavior—and it usually would be very much better—would be worth the astronomically greater cost. If verbal reports alone must be studied and resources do not permit their systematic comparison with the activities reported, then they should be studied under conditions where candor is well rewarded or where there is little to be gained from a false report. Studies which deal directly with "values" and "morality" are particularly susceptible to reporting merely the artifacts of hypocrisy. For more detail on such a study, see Scott (1965).

Irwin Deutscher has published several papers on the relation of activities and their report. For a comprehensive statement see Deutscher (1966).

Linton's original distinction between "status" and "role" has probably been confused or ignored more than it has been respected. Linton himself artfully depreciated the distinction as "of only academic interest," and even academicians have not used it. A status, in his terms, is a collection of rights and duties that defines a position in a social structure; a role, on the other hand, is the behavior that occurs in the status (1936, pp. 13–14). Today, the term "role" is used where Linton's "status" fits better: a person's role is what he is expected to do (as in Parsons' reference to "role expectations"); what he actually does is described, if at all, by other terms, like Erving Goffman's "role distance."

In fact, there are three aspects of status, or role, and performance that in practice need to be distinguished. First is the ordinary verbal statement of a role, usually in formal terms better fitted to a bureaucratic office than anything else. Then there are the concrete sanctions that define a position in a social structure. These can be named, but the names used by laymen are often misleading and incomplete, reverting to the notion of limited office. Sociologists borrow these names instead of attending to the sanctions themselves, and thus produce pale and inadequate descriptions of concrete statuses. Finally there is the actual behavior in the position, which insofar as it is operant is a function of the sanctions which locate the position (and usually of other reinforcements as well) and insofar as it is not operant is also a function of other variables (for example, fatigue).

All the problems that inhere in the analysis of pure normative statements apply to the delineations of status on the basis of laymen's names for their rights and duties. Just as there is a quandary about the relation between the statement of a norm and its effect on behavior, so there is a similar quandary between "pure" status and the behavior of the person who occupies it. There are, however, two reasons for this quandary. The first is simply the risk in the use of names: a given status may be ineptly named, so that we cannot adequately locate and define it from the name alone. The second is that the sanctions which serve to locate a status in a social structure are not the totality of the sanctions that affect the behavior of people of that status. The remainder of these sanctions account for most of what Goffman has identified as "secondary adaptations" and "sullen and reluctant performances." For example, the status of an elementary school teacher is pretty well located in terms of her involvement with children, to whom she is supposed to be a monolithic exemplar of morality. Her classroom posture may, however, reinforce her use of exceptionally coarse language in the teachers' lounge. The latter reinforcement is largely derived from a position that is already well fixed, but it may also vary according to her previous background.

Status is defined with regard to sanctions, and not to persons. Linton, and several commentators after him, went to some lengths to distinguish the status from the individual who had the status. This distinction cannot be absolute, however: any status is limited by the properties of the persons who will be called upon to occupy it. A status, or role, cannot combine activities which are mutually exclusive, or require activities outside the repertory of persons who occupy it. Husbands cannot be expected to bear children. Less obviously, the norm that admirals should stand and wait in mixed queues with enlisted men cannot be incorporated into the status of "admiral," because equality of treatment would be inconsistent with the requirement of respect and awe of the admiral that helps to locate him in the naval hierarchy of command. Nor can a status or role contain norms that reinforce only behavior beyond the limits of conditionability set by physics and physiology.

It may be objected that many roles seem to call for the impossible. The answer is that such norms actually operate by reinforcing the possible: the apparent symbolic reference to the impossible is not, in fact, what is meant. This is one advantage of the behavioristic criterion of meaning. A position may appear to call for unlimited exertions, but a man cannot be required to work 168 hours a week, 52 weeks a year (although it is *said* that assistant professors at Harvard are). Men cannot be required to walk on water (although some graduate students at Harvard expect their full professors to walk on water). These impossible prescriptions still inform us about the operating norms: assistant professors at Harvard work very hard, and the respect and envy accorded Harvard's full professors cause them to be very sure of themselves. This leads us to a further specification of status, role, or position: *it is a collection of norms delimited by what a single actor can be expected to perform.*

Summary

In this chapter we have applied some learning theory concepts, largely those of Skinner's operant behaviorism, to some of the normative concepts that sociologists apply to human behavior. First, we defined conditioners as reinforcers, with some discussion of symbolic conditioners. Next, sanctions were defined as the reinforcing effect of interaction, and norms as patterns of sanctions. A complementary definition of value was taken from the work of George Homans and, finally, Linton's concept of status was interpreted as one way whereby norms are organized.

The analysis and exposition of concepts is tedious, but the concepts found in the existing literature are vague, and many controversies about the attributes of norms can only be resolved when differences in meaning are made explicit. To start with the right concepts is to build half a theory.

Now these concepts will be used to build the other half, the theory of moral learning (Chapter III), to illustrate the process in socialization (Chapter IV), and to show that the moral commitment of the adult remains an operant activity dependent on social reinforcement (Chapter V).

CHAPTER III

Moral Commitment as Moral Learning:

Theory and Hypotheses

The theory we shall advance in this chapter is implicit in the preceding pages. If learning is a function of reinforcement, then moral learning is also a function of reinforcement. What we call "moral commitment" or the "internalized response" to a norm is the same behavior that follows upon learning a response to any conditioner: "When learning is established, extinction of the response by stopping the reinforcement is slow" (Boring, 1950, p. 651).

The processes to which sociologists refer when they use the phrase "internalization of norms" are those referred to in lay terminology as "conscience" and "moral commitment." But "internalization" is also often used in a more general sense. Parsons mentions the "internalization of objects": in his neo-Freudian scheme, internalization reaches not only the supergo—the psychoanalytic location of "conscience"—but realms of ego and id as well.

We have no dispute with Parsons' claim that internalization is general and that even the id is socialized. But some objection can be raised to the idea of internalization itself. To be sure, the term is used very widely among sociologists, and to some extent elsewhere in the social sciences. Freud used the term "introjection" and in some articles written in the 1940's one finds the clumsy neologism "interiorization." "Internalization" appears in the title of this book in place of a more exact reference to its mission because all the more exact references seemed either to have the wrong connotation or to be hopelessly esoteric.

The problem is that "internalization" is a metaphor, suggesting that what is presently internal was once external. If this is taken literally—and very often it *is* taken literally—it often re-erects the old distinction between "mind" and "body." That distinction then becomes a barrier to explanation and to discovery of the variables of which "mindedness" may prove to be a function. It also leads to more immediate problems. Where, for example, is the boundary between "internal" and "external" located? Is it psychological, fixed between "self" and "other"? This is a problem that G. H. Mead addressed—the natural constitution of elements taken as evidence for a mental life autonomous from nature. But if this boundary be used we then discover, as Mead did in his programmatic solutions, not only that all our originating events are on the external side of our boundary, but that the contents of "self" and "ego" are themselves perfectly external, composed of the responses that an organism elicits through interaction from its social environment. No interaction, no self. Only phenomenologically is "ego" internal, distinguished from something else that is external; and since we are not dealing with phenomenology here, we shall excuse ourselves from any concern with internalization so conceived. Perhaps a better way to draw the line between internal and external is in terms of physiology: inside the "skin" of a concrete individual organism as distinguished from outside it. We can speak of internalization in terms of ingestion; then, bananas can become internalized objects but only in the most unlikely circumstances can kinfolk become internalized objects. Norms as defined earlier cannot be internalized in this physiological sense, because they are composed of social reinforcements, symbolic and nonsymbolic, and both are public and external. What is "internal"—that is, predicable of the individual organism relatively apart from its environment—is the propensity to produce a conditioned response at some remove from stimuli. Thus the *"internalization" of a norm is the propensity to conform to the norm—to behave in the way the norm reinforces—at a spatial or temporal remove from its sanctions.* Normative internalization is, in this sense, a particular kind of learning: it is social or moral learning. Since most sociologists implicitly limit their reference of "norms" to "institutionalized norms," what they refer to as "normative internalization" is translatable as "moral learning in response to institutions."

Parsons and Allport:
Two Theories of Emergence

The premise of moral autonomy or voluntarism is fundamental to the idealistic tradition. The claim that moral learning depends on the same process as a pigeon training to stretch its neck in a "Skinner box" will therefore be resisted in psychology and sociology in part to the extent that the idealistic tradition prevails. But this resistance is not uniform: also widespread is the somewhat disparate idea that internalized norms are not given but acquired. Sociologists, and many psychologists, take the process of moral learning largely for granted. They assume that the actions of men are somehow influenced by norms at some time or place separate from the actions, but they neither analyze the properties of norms nor study the mechanisms whereby their effects are produced.

Parsons is an important exception, for he has discussed the process of internalization on a theoretical level at some length. In several papers written over many years and collected in *Social Structure and Personality* (1964), Parsons uses the concept of internalization very widely (see, for example, 1952a), but he actually illustrates what he means in a more recent paper. First Parsons describes the steps that an infant goes through in learning to nurse. Starting with an assumed "inborn sucking response,"

> The child early learns to suckle better than he is equipped to do by sheer "instinct." He learns how to move his lips, what posture is best, when to exert effort, when to relax, and so on, for the amount of milk he gets and the ease with which he gets it are contingent to an appreciable degree on his own goal oriented action [1958, p. 85].

This is to say that the child learns to discriminate among the properties of his environment (in this case the properties of his mother) and of his own behavior in response to the controlling reinforcements. So far, this is easily interpretable as operant conditioning. Parsons stresses the reciprocal response of the mother to emphasize the social nature of the learning:

> Thus the infant in the first few weeks, if not days, of life comes to be integrated into a social system. Relatively definite expectations of his behavior are built up, not only in the predictive sense, but in the normative sense. He nurses "well" or "badly," he cries only when he "should" and is quiet the rest of the time, or he cries "when there isn't any good reason." Inevitably, the behavior of adults takes on the character of rewarding him for what they feel to be "good" behavior and punishing him—including omitting reward—for what they feel to be "bad" behavior, and otherwise manipulating sanctions in relation to him [1958, p. 86].

We have already asserted that attention to the details of infant learning would make a reinforcement psychologist out of any reasonable man. Evidently Parsons is a reasonable man: the difference between Parsons and Skinner at this point is almost entirely a matter of terminology. Parsons continues, illustrating how "it may be assumed, on learning theory grounds, that [in learning] there will be generalization from the more specific items to the pattern."[1] The result is that his summary, as far as it goes, makes approximately the same claim as the present thesis:

> The essential point here is that this system of internal control over the child's instinctual or impulse system has become established through a generalized pattern of sanctions imposed by the mother. . . . One can clearly say that, at the same time, [the child] is learning to act in conformity with a set of norms [1958, p. 88].

So much the worse, one might say, for the voluntaristic thesis. Unfortunately for such a tidy conclusion, Parsons is a master of equivocation (see Scott, 1963). Although he seems willing to reduce the *acquisition* of normative internalization to a principle of reinforcement, Parsons' position on its *maintenance* is ambiguous, at least in his earlier statement (by eight years) in *The Social System* (1952b). Here he appears to refer not so much to the acquisition of internalization as to its subsequent development or maintenance as part of the actor's behavioral repertory:

> There is a range of possible modes of orientation in the motivational sense to a value-standard. Perhaps the most important distinction is between the attitude of "expediency" at one pole, where conformity or nonconformity is a function of the instrumental interests of the actor, and at the other pole the "introjection" or internalization of the standard so that to act in conformity with it becomes a need-disposition in the actor's own personality structure, relatively independently of any instrumentally significant consequences of that conformity. The latter is to be treated as the basic type of integration of motivation with a normative pattern-structure of values [1952b, p. 37].

Now, in these terms, does internal commitment depend on latter reinforcement, or not? How independent is "relatively independently"? Does it mean "independent of instrumentally significant consequences in the short run, but dependent on them in the longer run"? If so, then Parsons substantially agrees with our own interpretation of moral learning as conformity to a norm at a spatial or temporal remove from sanctions (since sanctions provide most of the "instrumentally significant consequences"). But he does not elaborate this point further, and in the text cited Parsons equivocates on the subsequent influence of reinforcement.

The position of Gordon Allport is less ambiguous. Allport joined the issue of voluntarism v. determinism candidly, definitely rejecting the thesis that

---

[1] Continuing in the same vein, Parsons remarks on the concepts of "meaning" and "intent" in roughly behavioristic terms.

moral commitment always depends on reinforcement. Allport was an outspoken defender of the "epistemological right" and of much of the tradition of *Geisteswissenschaft*; of the idea that the natural and the human sciences are fundamentally distinct, and that so human a phenomenon as morality deserves an explanation in terms that do not violate the subjective experience of it. His general position was clearly set forth in his paper of 1937, "The Functional Autonomy of Motives," and is developed most fully in *Becoming* (1955). But even Allport accepts a learning-theoretical paradigm for the *origin* of conscience. What he rejects is the view that it *remains* a function of reinforcement (1955, pp. 70–71).[2] He writes:

> If early prohibition and parent identifications were the only source of conscience there would certainly be a fading of conscience in time. *It is the generic self-guidance that keeps conscience alive and applicable to new experience.* The generic conscience tells us in effect, "If you do this, it will build your style of being; if that, it will tear down your style of being." In proportion as the generic conscience becomes the monitor of growth, emphasis shifts from tribalism to individuality, from opportunistic to oriented becoming. Fear becomes ought as propriate development begins to outweigh opportunistic [1955, p. 74; emphasis added].

Now, we certainly agree with Allport that conscience would fade if it depended solely on "early prohibition." But his interest in phenomenological adequacy leads him to ignore the effect of *later* prohibitions, of sanctions continually applied to adults. Because moral commitment "feels free," and because it is useful for society to tell men that morally they *are* free, analysis of moral commitment on a phenomenological level obscures its relationship to other factors. Rather than "generic self-guidance," it may be the pattern of social interaction, sometimes stable and sometimes changing, that keeps "conscience alive and applicable to new experience." Allport is mainly concerned with answering the Freudian thesis that behavior is determined by events in childhood. He has not considered social determinants contemporaneous with adult life at all. For all of the erudition and clarity with which he argues his cause, Allport's whole position is based on the "phe-

---

2 Yet Allport, too, finally equivocated on this point. In his text *Pattern and Growth in Personality* (1961), a revision of his *Personality: A Psychological Interpretation* (1937), Allport allows (p. 188) that conscience may not be wholly independent of reinforcement, at least in "extreme" conditions such as studies of Korean War "brainwashing" provided. "Even under...*anomie*...the person manages to retain his personality system more or less intact. And yet beyond a certain point he cannot do so. In the present troubled era we have vivid proof that a person, however intense his efforts, cannot permanently withstand complete collapse of his social supports." The point that he failed to grasp is that this "present troubled era" is no more dominated by social determinants of what is perceived as voluntary than any other.

nomenology of the moral man," with all the risks attending that position, which we have already reviewed.[3]

In the example cited, however, Allport unequivocally denies that the adult conscience depends on reinforcement, and he gives in this respect a better theoretical example than Parsons, who does not commit himself. Our own position is also unequivocal, and contrary: we hold that moral commitment requires subsequent reinforcement. Because it has been learned, extinction of the moral response in the absence of reinforcement is slow. This lends credibility to the idea that it is "relatively independent." The point however is that in the long run, it is *absolutely dependent*. In his moral action as in his behavior generally, the organism interacts with his environment. In view of the vitally social nature of the human environment, the idea of moral independence is a sociological anomaly. Where psyche was, there shall sanction be.

Theory of Moral Learning

If moral learning is a function of reinforcement, what are the reinforcers? Norms are the reinforcers, and these were defined in the previous chapter as patterns of sanctions. Sanctions, in turn, were defined as social interaction. Moral learning is defined in this scheme as social learning. A norm is learned or internalized when the actor has been sufficiently conditioned by sanctions that his behavior conforms to the norm at a spatial or temporal remove from sanctions. Such learning is, however, never complete; it remains ultimately dependent on subsequent sanctions.

One way to express this is to say that what is internalized about a norm is the expectation that sanctions will be applied to maintain it. If "expectation" refers to some subjective state, some internal cognition of the future, this claim cannot be publicly tested. But that is not the only reference: expectation can be both cognitive, that is, involving discrimination among

---

[3] Allport's important paper, "The Functional Autonomy of Motives" (1937b), has generated a great deal of controversy and research intended to clarify whether motives are indeed functionally autonomous. I think it fair to conclude that most of this has been a waste of time. The research critical of Allport's thesis has been behavioristic, at least in its measurement of "motive," whereas Allport's concept of the functions from which motives are autonomous was narrow and fundamentally phenomenological. This is a case where conceptual clarification, which is cheap, could have obviated much empirical research, which is dear. My general impression is that Allport was conceptually more explicit than his critics, if only because he was a better writer. One embarrassment of reinforcement psychology is that aside from a few exceptions such as Skinner and Homans, its advocates are often inept writers, gracelessly dogmatic and unpersuasive. In contrast, voluntarists usually write with grace, subtlety, and persuasion.

different stimuli, and perfectly objective. In the latter case, "expectation" is the name for the class of discriminative behavior that is based on past events but affecting future responses to them. The cognitive capacities of organisms are important. In the same sense that the pigeon, operantly stretching its neck in a Skinner box, "expects" to be fed even after it has been conditioned to do a lot of stretching for very little food, so the moral man, who conforms to a norm he has internalized, expects that his virtue will be rewarded, even if the prospect is remote.

By this point the theory will already offend not only idealists and the sentiments of moral men but also those empiricists who desire that scientific theory be cleansed of all analyticity, because what has been said so far verges on tautology. We began with the empirical premise that moral activity is an operant (it is empirically possible that it is not). The statement that the maintenance of moral commitment depends on subsequent sanctions follows from this premise and from the behavioristic definitions of normative terms stated in the previous chapter. And insofar as the claim is empirical it is also very general, and therefore risks explaining too much. The statement "behavior is a function of reinforcement" follows closely from the statement "behavior is a function of other variables," because the class of all variables that may be part of a process of reinforcement is not demonstrably separate from the class of variables with which social scientists may be concerned by any criterion of concern. Thus unless one is willing to defend the unlikely claim that behavior is *never* a function of other variables, the claim that there are general reinforcing effects is largely true by definition. Then too the term "behavior" itself is egregiously general, as critics of behaviorism have pointed out (Zener and Gaffron, cited with approval by Koch in his polemic against behaviorism [1964, p. 33]). This is not surprising, since the term originated in a polemical context, and all that the behaviorists wanted to be specific about was what was *not* behavior, i.e., the events presumably reported by introspection.

These logical problems recede in the transition from the general to the specific. I think what is really meant by such claims as "some behavior is not a function of reinforcement" is the more particular assertion that "the rate of activity X is invariant with regard to subsequent stimuli of the class Y." This statement is plainly empirical: its truth or falsity depends not on the definitions of terms but on whether particular stimuli do in fact reinforce and thus change the rate of a particular activity. One empirical task of learning theory, then, is the analysis and classification of reinforcers. Statements of the form "Y is a reinforcer of X" are as empirical as the least formalistic scientist might desire. In the present context, the class of reinforcers Y of morally committed acts X is broad, but it too will prove to be empirical. We shall cite many specific examples in the following chapters.

The opposition to the theory that morality is learned can be analyzed in terms of the statements above. Allport's argument can be approximately translated into: "There are some forms of behavior whose rate of emission cannot be reinforced, and the highest forms of moral behavior provide an example. This is what is meant by moral autonomy." Our own statement approaches this: "Moral behavior is very highly conditioned, and the contingency of its rates of emission on a given quantity of reinforcement is low." But we deny that the contingency disappears altogether. It is the distinctive competence of sociology to provide information on just those contingencies —the relations between sanctions and conduct—that must be demonstrated if this theory is to prevail and the thesis of moral autonomy rejected.

Priorities

The interpretation of "internalization," or its analogs in natural language—"conscience," "moral character," "sense of duty," and "sense of guilt"—as a process of learning or conditioning is by no means original to this work. Acknowledgment of priorities can well begin with the social psychology of Thomas Hobbes. Among his other enduring contributions to contemporary thought, Hobbes stated a theory of human conduct in terms of reward not readily found in writers before him. He widely applied the principle of reinforcement to human behavior long before it was discovered experimentally by Thorndike and Skinner. Most commentators on Hobbes, when not limiting their attention to his political theory, have been so eager to reject his conclusions on ideological or religious grounds that they have either overlooked or obscured the insights into social psychology that run throughout his works. Yet Hobbes must have done something right: his writings remain in print three centuries after they were written, which is more than can be said for the works of most of his critics.

Hobbes had a very simple theory of "conscience," explaining it in terms of negative reinforcement: "The source of conscience, the fear of death" (1651; 1958, Chap. 12).[4] Of religion, whose tenets often provide much of the content of conscience, Hobbes averred that its "natural cause" is "anxiety of the time to come."[5] The only defect in this line of reasoning for our purposes is that it does not go far enough or present sufficient detail: there are more negative reinforcers than the fear of death, and conscience depends on positive as well as negative reinforcers. But Hobbes was right as far as he went. He did not fall into the error of giving an account of

---

[4] See also pp. 93 ff. for an early functional theory of religion.
[5] As paraphrased by Strauss (1952, p. 25) from Hobbes' Latin text in *de Cive*, Ch. 3, art. 27, annot.

morality that was itself morally persuasive. This cost him the approbation of the next dozen or so generations of learned men during an age when religion still tended to monopolize scholarship and the positions of "scholar" and "moral advocate" were not structurally differentiated. But it did enable him to name the factors on which morality depends and which, we have argued, a morally persuasive account must obscure.

Today the monopoly of scholarship by religion is broken, and the explanation of subjective states of morality in terms of objective causes has recently concerned some American psychologists. The first was Gardner Murphy, who wrote a rather neglected paper, "The Internalization of Social Control" (1952). Murphy considered the relations between learning and socialization, and nicely discussed the "decognification" involved in internalization. But his paper appears to have had little direct influence on subsequent publications. The next germane paper was David Ausubel's "Relationships Between Shame and Guilt in the Socializing Process" (1955). Ausubel's immediate concern was to reject the distinction made between "shame" and "guilt" in the anthropological culture-personality literature. According to this distinction, a "shame" society controls by sanctions; a "guilt" society by internalization. Ausubel questions whether the distinction makes any difference. He notes the implausibility of a "shame culture" in which sanctions were never learned, but had constantly to be applied:

> Without the aid rendered by guilt feelings, child rearing would be a difficult matter indeed. If children felt no sense of accountability or moral obligation to curb their hedonistic and irresponsible impulses, to conform to accepted social norms, or to acquire self-control, the socializing process would be slow, arduous, and incomplete. Sheer physical force, threat of pain, deprivation, and punishment, or withholding of love and approval would be the only available methods—combined with constant surveillance—to exact conformity to cultural standards of acceptable behavior. And since it is plainly evident that the maintenance of perpetual vigilance is impractical, that fear alone is never an effective deterrent against anti-social behavior, and that the interests of personal expediency are not always in agreement with prescribed ethical norms, a social order unbuttressed by a sense of moral obligation in its members would enjoy precious little stability [1955, p. 378].

This statement agrees with what we have already said about the ubiquity of moral commitment: a society which through internalization can economize on sanctions in control of activities inimical to its persistence and competitive efficiency has that many more resources to apply to something else. Ausubel argued that the culture-personality writers[6] did not succeed in

---

6 Ausubel bases his discussion of the shame-guilt, external-internal distinction on Benedict (1934, 1946); Leighton and Kluckhohn (1947); and Mead (1949, 1959).

showing that there are any societies that do control solely by shame, and he cites Benedict at length (she having argued that the Japanese showed no guilt) to show that Japanese sometimes behave in a very guilty way indeed (1955, pp. 388–89). Now if what Ausubel calls "guilt" is a part of moral learning, then it is inconceivable that the members of any society would be wholly free of it, since (if guilt follows violation of an internalized or well-learned norm) they would either have internalized none of the society's norms or (even less likely) conformed to all of them.

Most of Ausubel's discussion of shame and guilt is in terms of subjective constructs, but he does tie these to external stimuli in terms of both origin and maintenance. His conclusion on the question of the unavoidability of guilt is that internal commitment and external controls are not opposed but complementary:

> We cannot escape the conclusion, therefore, that both guilt and shame, and internal and external sanctions, can and do exist side by side and mutually reinforce each other. The assertion that "true shame cultures rely on external sanctions for good behavior, not, as true guilt cultures do, on an internalized conviction of sin" (Benedict, 1943, p. 323) is unsupported by available evidence. The presence of the stock, the pillory, and the ducking stool in the public market place offers eloquent refutation to the statement that "the early Puritans who settled in the United States tried to base their whole morality on guilt" (Benedict, 1943, p. 22). Reinforcing most of the moral sanctions that we customarily assign to the domain of conscience is a parallel set of statutes and group pressures enforced by appropriate public reprisals. Even in cultures where moral obligations are highly internalized, we usually find a policeman on the corner giving a friendly nudge to sluggish consciences or a timely warning to impish consciences pondering a brief vacation from duty [1955, p. 389].

Actually, although Ausubel's general point is emiently sound, the stock and the pillory are no evidence at all that the Puritans did not really base their whole morality on guilt. In terms of the theory being presented here, such sanctions are essential to a healthy sense of guilt. Ausubel is using a subjective construction of guilt, with its sense of "freedom from external constraint," even though it was just this sort of construction by Benedict that he was criticizing in the first place.

Mowrer (1960b) advances a theory of internalization in terms of reinforcement (based on his own brand of learning theory) and also thoughtfully reviews some relevant animal studies. Elsewhere (1960a, pp. 300–304) he cites an illustrative study by R. L. Solomon of experimental internalization in puppies. The young dogs were offered as food boiled horsemeat, which they preferred, and commercial dog food. The sanction consisted of swatting the puppies with a newspaper when they tried to get at the horsemeat. Later, as a temptation, horsemeat was made available to the puppies in the trainer's absence, in order to measure how effectively the unpunished response—not eating the horsemeat—had been learned, and how this response varied with other experimental conditions, such as the breed of dog (sheepdogs were guilt-ridden; Basenjis were psychopathic) and antecedent nurturant conditions. Mowrer uses Solomon's experiments to advance a distinction between *temptation* and *guilt*; the former being an awareness of opportunity for deviation prior to any such deviant act, the latter being an awareness of possible punishment occurring after deviation and before punishment (if any). These apparently subjective states are objectively defined with reference to the emotional *behavior,* or lack of it, of Solomon's puppies. Mowrer then suggested that "conscience" is based on both resistance to temptation, and the guilt (whether construed as feeling or as behavior) following upon a deviant act (1960, p. 405). But the basic point, for Mowrer as well as Ausubel (whom Mowrer cites), is whether conscience, though clearly originating in learning, depends on reinforcement later on. He concludes that it does:

> Conscience, then, represents a firm social reality which is always there, in case conscience itself falters; and the manifest social purpose of conscience and value to the individual lie precisely in its ability to supply, in token form, the sanctions which must otherwise be applied, full force, by society. But no assumption of "functional autonomy" or inextinguishability is here implied. Conscience, as the internalized agent of organized society, constantly receives community support and endorsement and is thus normally perpetuated and recurrently strengthened [1960b, p. 408].

About the same time that Mowrer's discussion appeared, Winfred Hill published his article, "Learning Theory and the Acquisition of Values" (1960), broadly agreeing with the theses of Ausubel and Mowrer. Hill's main contribution is his theory of the origins of guilt, which is considered below in that connection and in reference to a subsidiary "theory of hypocrisy."

The most comprehensive discussion of internalization and moral commitment by a psychologist is found in the work of Justin Aronfreed. The author of several research papers, his major statement appears in a recent monograph, *Conduct and Conscience: The Socialization of Internalized Control over Behavior* (1968). Among the writers cited, Aronfreed's work comes closest to the present theory at a number of points. Aronfreed speaks for a number of psychologists, however, in arguing that internalization is not completely dependent on reinforcement, but can come instead to depend on cognitive factors which he views as operating in the absence of reinforcement. Though the language and certainly the emphasis are different, his argument has much in common with Allport's. Allport explains constancy of commitment in terms of emergent and causally efficacious self-concepts (his "proprium"), whereas Aronfreed explains it by "cognitive factors." Aronfreed's theory is clearly an important statement. Our argument in answer to its limitation on an explanation solely in terms of reinforcement, is that cognition, as conceived in Aronfreed's writing and demonstrated in experiments, is itself both subject to reinforcement and part of the process of reinforcement of moral conformity.

These prior statements that moral commitment, though involving behavior at a spatial or temporal remove from sanctions, still ultimately depends on sanctions show that there is little originality in this, the principal claim of the present theory. Such originality as it may claim lies in our more detailed concepts and hypotheses, and in our attempt to interpret sanctions in terms of some variables of macrosociological theory.

An Illustration

Earlier, we cited an example from Talcott Parsons, who illustrated internalization as a process of differential reinforcement through sanctions. We will now use a more detailed illustration, based on the homely process of toilet training. In some societies it is started early, along with the first stages of language learning; and thus it is a human example of learning where the norm cannot be presented in completely symbolic form. And while bladder and sphincter control are not the sort of things that come to mind when discussion seeks an example of high morality, nobody will deny that they come to be very highly internalized.

The process begins with an operant activity. Without elaborate physiological instrumentation of the digestive tract, an observer can do little to predict the time when an untrained infant will empty his bowels or bladder. "You can put the baby on the pot," Homans tells us and mothers generally will confirm, "but you can't make him perform." The training therefore begins with reinforcers, the pairing of an activity, whenever it does occur, with something else that proves to be a reward. This reward may be "coos of approval" which the mother emits while being generally nurturant toward the child. Since all primate infants find nurturant stimuli intrinsically reinforcing (else the helpless and dependent infants, and the order as a whole, would not have survived in evolutionary competition), the sounds the mother emits come to be symbolic conditioners and thus to be reinforcing themselves. The matter is not, of course, simply one whereby every time the child defecates the mother coos with approval, thereby increasing the rate of the defecation. She only coos when he defecates on the pot, thus rendering the pot a distinctive stimulus which the child eventually comes to discriminate. Defecation at other times is either ignored or responded to by maternal behavior that, if still nurturant in a broad sense, still is not likely to reward defecation. In the same way that Skinner's pigeon learns to peck the green target rather than the red one, so the child discriminates between defecation on the pot and defecation elsewhere. So far no "cognition" much removed from stimuli need be invoked; the pot constitutes a readily discriminable bundle of stimuli itself. The infant has his diapers removed, he is picked up and moved to the pot, held or strapped in a particular posture, and so on. Still bladder and sphincter control is not easily acquired; the child, for example, may start to excrete during the unbundling process, or he may learn to emit the vocal patterns associated with defecation before he learns to control it. But the constant reinforcement of defecation at the "correct" time and place, together with the child's capacity make the discriminations on which it depends, gradually produce the specific response that parents desire. At first the probability that he will defecate is increased simply by the approach of the parents. Later it increases only with the unbundling of diapers; and finally the child is likely to defecate when on the pot and only when on the pot. Later still more specific conditions are encountered, requiring even more subtle discriminations by the child. Little boys learn possible postural differences for urination and defecation, little girls learn to maintain a high degree of modesty and privacy during excretion, the child learns to control sphincter and bladder even when asleep, and so on. The subtlety of discriminations and the difficulty of learning such activities are highlighted by the problems of teaching bladder control to the enuretic or "bed-wetting" child, while the dependence of moral learning on the applications of sanctions is shown by the ubiquity of incontinent passing of wind. It is not that there are none who would apply sanctions to suppress flatulence if they could, but because flatulence is the most inconsequential and transitory form of excretion it is the most difficult of all such operants to reinforce or extinguish by pairing with sanctions.

In sum, the child who began by excreting solely according to the exigencies of bowel and bladder pressure learns to wait for the appropriate times and places, entirely in response to the sanctions the social environment supplies and on the basis of his ability to discriminate among them. The advocates of the doctrine that moral behavior stands apart from consequences have not so far claimed that children are born with or invariably acquire a sense of excretory propriety apart from being taught it by a schedule of reinforcement. The literature about child development, as well as the collective experience of parents, testifies abundantly to the original amorality of children on this matter; sometimes they appear to delight in smearing their faces with their own feces. At first, the connection between the sanctions and the proper excretion has to be quite close. But the whole point of the training process is to condition the child so that it will exercise what our voluntaristic natural language calls "self-control"—that is, so that it will emit the appropriate behavior at a temporal remove from the sanctions by which it is learned.

By rewarding excretory control and punishing excretory indulgence, the child is brought round to behave as those who condition him want him to and, for the most part, behave themselves: in Mead's vocabulary, he comes to "take on the attitudes of his significant others." Excretion comes to be associated not solely with bowel and bladder pressure but with the conventional occasions for relieving that pressure, even if the internal pressure gets quite high and the actor consequently reports that he is in pain. The control comes to be exercised even when deviation cannot be detected and sanctions cannot be applied. Excretion may come to be limited to more narrowly discriminated eliciting stimuli than was ever intended by the parents (thereby emphasizing the primacy of behavioral reinforcers and the irrelevance of subjective intent). Counselors at summer camps for youngsters discover that many children cannot defecate in a privy because its stimulus properties differ too much from those more prophylactic urban toilets to which they have grown accustomed; and some adult women find, in their first excursions into wilderness, that they cannot relieve themselves without a toilet seat to sit on. The products of excretion come to be viewed with the conventional disgust, which is extended by generalization to the names for excretion and its products. The rules surrounding the acts evolve further as rules circumscribing the use of the names for them, so that the whole process is referred to by circumlocutions. For these aspects of the process which can occur privately, such as inaudible flatulence, but can still be referred to by name, the prohibition of the name comes to be more effective and more completely learned than the prohibition of the acts, because the name is easier to identify and thus to sanction. Separate reinforcement of the names and reports of the acts, as distinguished from the acts themselves, is part of the phenomenon of obscene words and the basis of the following theory of hypocrisy. The process as a whole, from unconditioned operant to the response of disgust both to the process of excretion and the names for it, provides a paradigm of moral learning generally.

The Argument for Ongoing Reinforcement

In the example just discussed, an originally amoral organism learns to comply with a particular set of norms. The sanctions condition, the behavior is learned, the norms internalized. This accounts for the *origins* of moral commitment. As such, apart from the learning-theoretical vocabulary and the claim that toilet training represents moral learning generally, it is an account to which most social scientists could give a large measure of assent. Even Allport granted that morality, though in his view eventually autonomous, begins with learning: he notes that "the observation of children assures us that the must precedes the ought" as a "necessary first stage," and he therefore prefers an "emergent to an innate theory of moral obligation" (1955, p. 74). Although some commentators will probably want to amend and quality our theory of moral learning in particular details (and especially perhaps to augment it with mentalistic constructions), insofar as it applies to the moralization of the originally amoral actor the theory is not likely to be controversial in its general features.

The discussion and controversy on this theory, and indeed on *any* theory dealing generally with moral behavior, are likely to center on the conditions for the *maintenance* of moral commitment. Although the psychological and psychoanalytic literature contain many theories of moral *development,* both as "learning theories" and otherwise, little beyond what has already been quoted is said about maintenance. The current sociological literature says even less. The present theory, for example, can be generated by an easy and obvious analogy to Mead's theory of self-concept formation, but so far as I know this analogy has not previously been drawn. Parsons does not discuss the issue of the maintenance of moral commitment directly, and certainly the implication of his many published works and countless offhand observations in lectures and symposia is that once the pattern of internal commitment is set up in childhood, it stays that way throughout later life. Parsons is careful to avoid the argument of the largely "biologistic," or only rudimentarily social, determination of behavior that he and others have sensed in Freud's writings, and he stresses the role of complex and variable social conditioners; but he still seems to say that the social contingency occurs only in the early years. The behavior is learned by sanctions, but after a while it comes to be emitted "relatively independently." Yet the principle of reinforcement goes against this. The extinction of learned behavior is slow, but it still eventually occurs. If moral behavior is the operant this theory holds it to be, then some subsequent "maintenance dose" of reinforcement is necessary to sustain the learned rate of activity. Probably no implication of reinforcement theory is more significant and more controversial than this. *Sanctions maintain the learned commitment.*

One interpretation of those existing ideas about moral commitment which do not stress commitment as a function of sanctions is that internalization of a norm continues by inertia as some kind of "steady state" in the absence of external change. Certain evidence on the persistence of learning in animals is sometimes cited in this connection. A pigeon gets reinforced by food for pecking only when it first rotates counterclockwise. Later the rotational contingency is dropped, but by now the response is learned, and the pigeon (which spends its life in the bare environment of a laboratory) is still observed rotating counterclockwise before pecking, thousands of pecks later. Whatever the specific explanation of moral commitment, the implication is common that such commitment (especially when acquired in childhood) is deep and permanent and not normally subject to change during the adult years.

We can account for this sort of behavior through a distinction between the strength of sanctions by which a commitment gets established in the first place and the strength of subsequent reinforcements of alternative or competing responses. Where the establishing sanctions are strong and later sanctions on competing responses are weak, a commitment may be sustained by sanctions so casual and inconsequential as to be readily overlooked, because the reinforcements for a competing response are even weaker. A child who learns through severe sanctions always to tie his right shoe first may continue to do so all his life if he never gets reinforced for doing otherwise. For such responses as these, typically not the concern of strong social institutions, an "inertia principle" of moral commitment seems to make sense.

Commitment to institutionalized norms seldom meets this pattern. Although the sanctions that establish commitment are strong, so are the subsequent reinforcements for deviant responses. Institutionalized norms generally prohibit activities not only inimical to viable or efficient social organization but also rewarding to the individuals whose behavior constitutes that social organization. We often say that the prohibited activities are "expedient" or "tempting" or that they serve "selfish" or amoral interests. Deviant activities are sometimes intrinsically rewarding (that is, subject to unconditioned reinforcers, such as food), sometimes reinforced through elementary social behavior (Homans' level of the "subinstitutional," analyzed in detail in *Social Behavior,* 1961), apart from larger-scale institutional patterns, and sometimes reinforced by larger-scale contra-institutional forces—veritable "negative institutions." This is not to say that some "principle of parity" operates in the moral equilibrium of society and that every norm is balanced by an opposite norm, but only that deviation from major institutional expectations is widely susceptible of reinforcement and that functionally necessary activities thus require institutional support.

To return to the case of institutional control of sexual behavior, it will be noted that such control has evolved over thousands of human generations in which (until very recently) mortality was closely matched with fertility, and the maintenance of reproductive institutions was of primary importance if human life were to continue. Thus norms governing sexual behavior have closely linked it to societally useful and multi-functional groups, and especially to the family, wherein sex comes to symbolize familial ties and reinforces the otherwise fragile bond between parents. But a familial monopoly on sex must compete with simpler arrangements, not bound by multiple social functions, which can much more readily specialize in sexual gratification alone, using as well such additional reinforcing stimuli as "variety,...

perverse gratification, . . . mysterious and provocative surroundings, [and] intercourse free from entangling cares and civilized pretense" (Davis, 1961, pp. 275–76) which familial sexuality cannot readily provide. Contra-institutional sexuality specializes in these kinds of reinforcement, and thus becomes a tangible negative institution in its own right in such forms as prostitution and pornography. The institutional control of economic exchange is made similarly difficult by the reinforcing effect of the advantages of force and fraud; these in turn must be interdicted by further controls. The point is that institutionalized norms will not prevail solely on the basis of a commitment once established and without subsequent sanctions in its defense because, without these sanctions, deviation rather than conformity often brings the greater reward. Virtue generally is *not* its own reward (which is why moral rhetoric claims so strongly that it is), and that is why moral commitment requires sanctions for its maintenance as well as for its origins.

Intervening Psychological Processes: A Question of Evidence

Few psychologists today would deny the relationship of moral commitment—or of most other aspects of human behavior—to environmental and especially to social stimuli. What is likely to be questioned is whether an explanation of commitment in terms of such stimuli is *complete*—or, in the idiom of the machine room, whether social stimuli "account for all the variance." On the basis of the kinds of evidence that psychologists respect, the question is relevant, because the social variables assessed in this evidence do leave much of the variance unexplained. Thus the question may be answered in two ways. One is to defend the adequacy of a social explanation, and hold that the incompleteness occurs in the psychologists' measurement of social factors. This of course is the answer of the present work (expanded in Chapter IV in the discussion of experimental positivism). The other is to hold that various psychological processes intervene in the process of commitment between sanctions and the actor's response. These may be voluntaristic constructs (such as Allport's *proprium* or the varieties of subjective freedom invoked by other humanistic and phenomenological psychologists) or deterministic constructions (such as the well-known constructs and processes of the psychoanalytic theorists, or concepts of motivation, drive strength, drive reduction, tension reduction, consonance, balance, dissonance, or whatever). Since all these processes are inferred from the public behavior that is all psychologists can ever study, their variety is limited only by psychologists' ingenuity in abstraction.

Within the last few years experimental psychologists have begun to write extensively about internalization and moral development. The psychological processes which most of these writers hold to intervene between sanctions and conduct are represented on the cognitive level. Aronfreed's work contains the most complete statement of this position, in terms of both theoretical range and review of research literature. He respects the principle of reinforcement, but finds it an inadequate explanation of the phenomena of commitment. In response to a preliminary statement of our own theory, Aronfreed commented directly:

> [W]hile recognizing the importance of continued extrinsic control, I also have tried to make room for the fact that some forms of conduct become very highly internalized and independent of external outcomes, in part on the basis of value systems which have a remarkable capacity to remain intrinsically sustained. I do not believe that the maintenance of normative controls in the individual can be accounted for entirely by reference to expectations about outcomes of overt conduct. Such expectations undoubtedly do play a large role in internalization. But conduct can also be intrinsically controlled in their absence, because the properties of acts and their consequences can be both represented and evaluated at the cognitive level. There are ways in which cognition can influence action other than the simple representations of external sanctioning processes [personal communication, July 1964; reprinted by permission].

This statement summarizes Aronfreed's theory as he later developed it (1968). But it is characteristic of theories that they run ahead of the data that would confirm or confute them (thus providing a guide in choosing among the infinitude of research that might be performed), and this justifies a scientific division of labor between theory and research. In this regard both Aronfreed's theory and the theory presented here are solidly theoretical: neither can be conclusively tested with the empirical resources now available to the behavioral sciences. Such a test would require longitudinal studies whose delays few academic scientists could endure, for this is the only way that observational methods could effectively measure the dependence of commitment on sanctions in the long run (say ten or twenty years). It would require observation so incredibly detailed (to assess the range of social stimuli) that probably no foundation or federal agency could be persuaded to support it. Experimental tests of the different theories could get around some of the problems that affect observational tests, but they in turn would require controls so complete that only a totalitarian society could impose them.

Relevant if limited evidence, however, could be provided by an experimental procedure which, to my knowledge, has not been carried out. Aronfreed holds that cognitive processes intervene between internalization and subsequent conformity. In contrast, we hold that cognition appears to be an essential factor in many aspects of moral commitment when it really is not (indeed, a hypothesis of the negative association between cognition and commitment follows shortly) because certain cognitive operations (discrimination of stimuli) which may occur together with a morally committed response are independently reinforced. The moral act and its discrimination or recognition, for example, are two different activities, each susceptible to different reinforcers. Often both activities are rewarded together, but it is possible for the application of cognition to a moral act to be punished.

Our hypothetical experiment is built on a typical situation in child rearing. The child who violates a norm is subject to punishment. But if he recognizes or identifies the violation, naming it and stating perhaps that he was "bad" and "naughty," recognizing thereby that the act in question is a member of a class of prohibited acts, his recognition is likely to terminate the punishment or even be followed by verbal approbation, a reward. If the child fails to recognize and identify his act as a violation, he is punished not only for the act but, additionally, for failure to recognize it. Indeed it is possible, among parents who intellectualize child rearing, for the reinforcing contingencies attached to the *recognition* of moral dimensions of activity to be substantially stronger than those attached to the activity itself. Though the moral act and its recognition may often be very closely linked, the immediate point is that they may be separately reinforced. If individuals can be shown to sustain conformity to moral acts in part by applying cognition apart from its reinforcement, then Aronfreed's theory benefits; if not, then the gain is to the present theory. An experiment might thus be carried out in the following way.

Two groups of children—experimental and control—are placed in an experimental situation contrived so as to favor an appealing but conventionally prohibited activity—making a splendid mess, eating ice cream instead of green and yellow vegetables, or whatever. After the activity, all the children are punished. But the children in the experimental group are punished additionally for whatever cognition they subsequently apply to their deviation, such as describing the action as "bad" or attempting (for example, through efforts at reparation) to divine more precisely the relation between the activity and subsequent reward or punishment. In the control group such cognitive efforts would either be ignored or, as is commonly done, rewarded (cognition is highly rewarded generally, but this ubiquitous effect can be controlled by the earlier random assignment of subjects to experimental and control groups and by later comparison between the two). Then, if no differences occurred between experimental and control groups—and of course providing that the experiment used strong enough reinforcers to compete with those of the natural social world by which any children used as experimental subjects will have already been thoroughly conditioned—that would be some evidence for Aronfreed's hypothesis that reinforcement-free cognitive processes are involved in sustaining moral commitment.

But such an experiment is likely to be objected to. It calls for punishing children who admitted their own transgressions, thus reducing the probability that they will give honest accounts of their behavior in the future—the net effect being, to some slight but still objectionable degree, to make hypocrites out of them. Indeed it might, and such results would confirm the following theory of hypocrisy. But the experiment would certainly provide useful data about the independent role of cognition, if some experimental psychologist has the temerity to carry it out.

The more fundamental basis of objection by psychologists to the adequacy of a reinforcement theory of morality which excludes other factors is likely to derive from a narrower view than ours of the possible range of reinforcers. The habit seems widespread among psychologists implicitly to identify the range of all possible behavioral causes and effects with those which can serve, respectively, as manipulated independent and dependent variables in psychological experiments. I call this "experimental positivism" and discuss it more fully in Chapter IV. Thus, at least so far as humans are concerned, the term "reinforcers" connotes to psychologists only those usually feeble stimuli used in experiments in learning and operant conditioning.

In contrast, the theory we are advancing defines reinforcers and reinforcement much more broadly. Sanctions are identical with social interaction and are claimed to be the primary source of morally relevant reinforcements. These constructs may seem far too general for a respectable degree of empirical contingency, and perhaps they would be, were there no social scientists who hold that moral commitment is *independent* of sanctions even broadly conceived as they are here. I believe it is useful to build so broadly in order to present, as evidence for a theory of reinforcement, not only those stimuli which experimentors have license to apply to human subjects but also the stronger, more persistent, and often more sinister and brutal stimuli that operate ubiquitously in the natural social environment. It is to allow for this variety of natural reinforcers that we went to such lengths, in our exposition of concepts in Chapter II, about the conditioned effect of symbolic sanctions, generalizations of meaning, and latent and superempirical sanctions. But it remains at least logically possible that moral commitment is independent of all these sanctions.

Degrees of Moral Learning

Moral learning, like all learning, is a matter of degree. Extinction or termination of a response is slow when learning is relatively complete. But learning varies in its completeness, and this means that moral activity may continue at a variable rate with respect to a given sanction. There is, therefore, a continuum of moral learning, which may be represented as running between two poles: complete calculation and complete commitment. At the first extreme, cognitive behavior is maximized and emotional behavior minimized; at the second, cognition is suppressed and a noncognitive emotional disposition to conform prevails. For convenience, this continuum from unlearned to learned conformity is divided into three categories: (1) complete calculation; (2) partial calculation and partial commitment; and (3) complete commitment.[7]

The terms "cognition" and "emotion" now require definition. Neither, in our discussion, refers primarily to subjective events. They refer instead to the kinds of behavior to which the putatively subjective terms also refer more elliptically. A cognitive-emotional distinction can be built with three variables: (1) the amount of stimulus discrimination; (2) the degree of instrumentality of the behavior; and (3) the amount of gross muscular and glandular activity. The discriminative aspect of cognition was stressed earlier. The idea of "instrumentality" comes from Homans' discussion (following Skinner) of emotional behavior (1961, pp. 26–27). In Homans' usage, an emotional response is one whose rate of emission is not itself subject to variation by reinforcement, although typically it is associated with the reinforcement of some other response. Thus, the pigeon coos when it is fed (feeding being the reinforcement for some other activity) or violently flaps its wings when a previously reinforced activity is not subsequently reinforced. The cooing and flapping are emotional responses. The reference to "gross muscular activity" reflects the common interpretation of behavior as cognitive when the ratio of discrimination to gross muscular activity is high. Behavior, then, is "cognitive" when discrimination and instrumentality are great and gross muscular activity small, and it is "emotional" when discrimination and instrumentality are small and gross muscular activity is great. A cognitive person looks before he leaps; an emotional one leaps first.

The attitude[8] of complete calculation toward a norm is a limiting case involving several empirical impossibilities. The norm is discriminated but not learned. Compliance with the norm thus depends solely on a cognitive

---

[7] Parsons makes a similar distinction between "expediency" and "introjection" (1952b, p. 37).

[8] "Attitude" is used here in its original and still useful sense: as "disposition to act." The old reference is close to "posture," that is, the physical orientation of a person which immediately precedes a given act. This is also its meaning in aeronautics: the "stall attitude" of an aircraft is one it assumes just before stalling. In both the old and the aeronautical sense, "attitude" refers to the probability that a given response will be forthcoming under given conditions. This is not the common reference of the term today. In most sociological and psychological research, of course, "attitude" is thought of as a mental state, operationally defined as "the actor's verbal report of a mental state disposing him to act under given conditions." But the verbal report is a highly imperfect guide to action, because people frequently do not do what they say they will do. More on this matter follows in the text.

assessment of the sanctions which would probably follow compliance, as compared to those which would probably follow deviation. Behavior is geared to the greater short-run reward. All unsocialized infants approach falling into this category, differing from adult psychopaths (who presumably also lack moral learning) solely in their cognitive capacity to identify the norm in question and assess the force of sanctions in its support. This is the condition of the "positivistic actor," as Parsons used that term in *The Structure of Social Action* for the model of conduct where normative factors do not operate (he then identified "normative effects" with "internalized normative effects").

Next in our continuum is the category of partial calculation and partial commitment. Here we find an attenuation but not the extinction of the calculating attitude, and the emergence of learning—an increasing disposition to conform in the absence of immediate sanctions. The effect of the short-run reward resulting from the deviant act is partially checked by a prior learned commitment. The sanctions upon which the norm depends are discriminated to some degree—not to the greatest degree of which the person is capable—but the information provided by such discrimination as does occur affects the maintenance of the learned response. What amounts to an implicit belief that sanctions will follow deviant action has to be reinforced by sufficiently persuasive and present evidence that they do in fact follow. To the extent that such evidence is forthcoming, the commitment is strengthened; to the extent not, the commitment is reduced. Here apply the concepts of empathy and vicarious learning, discussed in Chapter II, whereby a person sees that his status is similar to that of others and learns as a result that what happens to these others can happen to him too.

It is to the situation of other, but similar, individuals that most of the cognition at this stage will be oriented. So rewarding does a social animal find a cognitive orientation toward his fellows that attention to what happens to these others, to the relation between their actions and the consequences thereof, is probably impossible to suppress completely. If it were otherwise—if social animals were really "egocentric"—and if the maintenance of the moral behavior of any one person depended solely on the reinforcement applied directly to him alone—the *analysis* of social control would be very greatly simplified. A vital social component of actual morality would be absent. But, in fact, control of even one person depends on the sanctions applied to others whom, by often very subtle discriminations, that person may classify as in the same situation as himself. The analysis of morality is very greatly complicated as a result.[9] If he observes that others

---

9 That morality is a social phenomenon is a point also made by Cohen (1965). He points out that the individual is not "in a box by himself" and admonishes those studying deviation to look for the impact of group membership on internalized norms.

are punished for deviation, his own learned commitment is thereby reinforced; but if he sees that others are not punished for deviation, or are
rewarded for it, his moral commitment is weakened and what is reinforced
instead is the probability that he will deviate also. The earnest student is
committed to honest and original work in examinations but (as Hartshorne
and May showed in their pioneering studies of moral character, 1932) he
also attends to those who cheat and what happens to them as a result of
their cheating, and how faithfully he conforms to examination rules in the
future is in part a function of the evidence available to him of the relative
costs and benefits of cheating. The young girl of good reputation has learned
to deny precipitate advances of her suitors, and her behavior is reinforced by
symbolic representations of the consequences of assent—pregnancy, abandon-
ment, public condemnation, and so on—but she still attends closely to what
rewards or punishments fall to other girls more compliant than she. The
curiosity of the moral about the immoral is notorious.

The degree of moral behavior which depends on partial commitment,
then, is a function not only of the sanctions applied to a single person, but
also of the sanctions applied to the group of persons who may learn vicari-
ously from each other. Sanction one and you influence all: the good man
is kept good not only because of his own rewards, but also because he sees
the punishment dealt to the evil. This recovers for the reinforcement theory
much behavior that must be lost if it is to be accounted for by direct individual reinforcement. For example, it is difficult to explain by direct reinforcement why casino gamblers persist in giving their money to slot
machines. Although the slot machine presents an ingenious variable-ratio
schedule of reinforcement, over the longer run of a few hours of steady
play it is almost certain to take in more than it pays out, presenting the
gambler with what for most of his repertory of operants is a strong punishment—the loss of his money. But in a casino these are not the only reinforcers: all around him are fellow gamblers whose occasional big wins are
signaled by ringing bells, ritualized personal payoffs of amounts beyond the
"payout" capacity of the machine (eighteen to twenty-two coins), free
drinks brought by pretty girls, and other stratagems of the casino owners.
Since the bells do not toll for the losers, the available evidence tells the
gambler that most players are big winners. This is only one example; in
fact the processes of exemplary reward and punishment are ubiquitous.

The logically possible elements of complete commitment still require a
statement to locate the end of the continuum between calculation and
commitment. Complete moral commitment would depend on a response
so thoroughly learned as to be immune to sanctions following the response.
The commitment would neither be strengthened by subsequent reward nor
weakened by subsequent punishment, and it would also be immune to evidence of the reward and punishment of others. Especially would it have to

be immune to evidence that deviation by others might be rewarded. This would require, in effect, that discrimination would not occur, and that the person would disattend his environment. But cognition itself is too profoundly and generally rewarded, and man is so clever an animal that he responds to slight and subtle rewards: thus, cognition is most unlikely ever to cease completely. Just as men are so susceptible of learning a norm in the technical sense, of becoming committed to it, that they never are completely calculating in their attitude, so are they also so capable of discrimination among sanctions that they never completely abstain from calculation. This, at any rate, is our theory: even when norms are thoroughly learned, when moral commitment is strong, and when a sense of obligation is reported as keenly felt, the maintenance both of conscience and conformity depends on the exercise of sanctions.

Moral Courage and Martyrdom

Men often conform to norms when their commitment is weak and their attitude calculating, simply because they have little information (or wrong information) about the sanctions that in fact follow deviation and those that in fact follow conformity. This is the condition produced by the "moral world-view" of the normatively well-integrated community or society, with its relatively weak arsenal of direct sanctions and its formidable roster of symbolic sanctions, describing omniscient moral watchmen, natural disasters that strike evil men, and the certainty of justice in an imaginary afterlife. Given our previous explication of how such representations function as conditioned reinforcers, they present no difficulty to the theory we are advancing.

The more difficult behavior to explain occurs when moral commitment is maintained in the face of plain evidence that the deviation of others is rewarded—as in acts of conspicuous moral courage, or in the face of extreme punishment of the morally committed person himself, as in cases of martyrdom. These events can be explained by one or more of the following aspects of reinforcement: (1) the distinction between primary (unconditioned) and learned (conditioned) rewards; (2) superempirical sanctions; and (3) the distinction between the strength of individual reinforcers and a strong schedule of reinforcement. These extend the principle of reinforcement to types of behavior often used as examples of what it is unable to explain.

The reinforcing effects of evidence that others are rewarded or punished for their actions may vary according to whether the reward in question is primary or learned. If the reward is learned, the effect varies further, according to whether the person to whom the evidence is presented has learned it himself. Few sanctions are primary reinforcers. The unconditioned effect of most sanctions is slight. So accustomed are we to responding to symbolic sanctions that we commonly fail to distinguish between the potency of symbols themselves and what they may represent. Even so forceful a symbol as a mounted policeman training a drum-fed submachine gun on a hostile mob turns out to be remarkably frail when the mob fails to respond to the policeman as a symbol and attacks him anyway. The policeman represents vastly stronger stimuli than he himself can present: no submachine gun drum carries more than 120 rounds and a few marbles will cause the horse to stumble. What the policeman represents is potent enough (the total police power of the state) but his effect as a symbol depends upon this representation of power being recognized and respected by the mob. If it is not, then extinction of mob behavior requires such massive unconditioned aversive stimuli as those deployed by divisions of tanks and paratroopers. The effect of a symbolic sanction thus depends on learned association with primary rewards. Since the association of symbols with primary stimuli varies among persons and with status, so the capacity of the symbol as a sanction is variable. Thus plain evidence that deviation gains reward will not reduce the moral commitment of a person to whom the evidence is presented if the reward is secondary or learned (most rewards are) *and* if the commited person has not been conditioned to value it himself. The general issue is that of the relativity of reward and punishment, as discussed in Chapter II, and it is worth the space to repeat that discussion's major point: *a reward or punishment is defined in terms of its effects.* This complements what W. I. Thomas meant when he spoke of "the definition of the situation." The thesis that "when men define situations as real, they are real in their consequences" finds one expression in the fact that when men learn to respond to originally impotent effects as punishing, they *are* punishing. When a particular stimulus, which a sanctioning agent imagines to be universally punishing, actually rewards a deviant for a given act although the same stimulus would be punishing to a conformer, then the apparent immunity of much moral commitment to evidence of rewarded deviation is no evidence against the claim that moral commitment always depends on reinforcement. The major concrete differences in the learned effect of sanctions probably lie along the major axes of differentiation of ascribed status—age, sex, social class, ethnicity. Thus as regards the effect of class differences discussed in Chapter II, the disreputable poor have no status to lose and enjoy their vice because its consequences are not punishing to them; and middle classes, for whom the consequences of vice would be status-degrading and therefore punishing, remain indignant, sanctimonious, and committed. All are explainable in terms of a reinforcement theory of moral commitment.[10]

Superempirical sanctions may reinforce where merely possible ones cannot. By definition, nobody can ever be stimulated by superempirical sanctions as direct reinforcers, but everybody is likely to encounter symbolic representations of them which, if believed (i.e., adequately learned), can serve as strong secondary reinforcers (the general characteristics of superempirical sanctions were reviewed in Chapter II). Skinner is one among many who have observed that the events alleged to occur in worlds and times to come are made up of reinforcers whose effects can be adequately learned in this world now:

> Traditional descriptions of Heaven and Hell epitomize positive and negative reinforcement. The features vary from culture to culture, but it is doubtful whether any well-known positive or negative reinforcer has not been used. To a primitive people who depend upon forest and field for their food, Heaven is a happy hunting ground. To a poverty-stricken people primarily concerned with the source of the next meal, it is a perpetual fish fry. To the unhappy it is relief from pain and sorrow or reunion with departed friends and loved ones. Hell, on the other hand, is an assemblage of aversive stimuli, which has often been imaginatively portrayed. In Dante's *Inferno,* for example, we find most of the negative reinforcers characteristic of social and non-social environments. Only the electric shock of the psychological laboratory is missing [1953, pp. 352–53].

That belief in superempirical sanctions does in fact maintain particular types of moral behavior is illustrated by common religious beliefs which associate behavior in this world with sanctions in another: empirical virtue brings a superempirical reward; empirical vice brings superempirical punishment. The chosen people shall sit at the right hand of God; men rich in worldly wealth have little chance to enter heaven, Mormon spinsters have none at all, and Hindu spinsters go straight to hell.

Superempirical sanctions work because a purely symbolic reinforcer is still a reinforcer. They work in the same manner as merely empirical sanctions, differing from them only in the probability that what they represent will be directly encountered. There has never been any good evidence that what superempirical sanctions represent will ever be encountered, and

---

10 Cf. with the fascinating theory of moral posture of Ranulf (1938, especially pp. 1–8, 198). Ranulf argues that the lower middle classes are morally repressive toward others, pursuing a policy of "disinterested punishment" which offers them no direct gain, because their precarious status permits them no chance to indulge in the "institutionalized evasions" of institutionalized norms available to those of secure status, that is, the aristocrats and the disreputable poor. Ranulf marshals a truly Weberian spread of comparative evidence for his thesis.

this limitation on their effectiveness is only partly offset by their reputed power. But this is only a limiting case of a situation that applies to most all symbolic control of behavior: even when the consequences represented are empirical, many are never encountered or are encountered infrequently and perhaps fortuitously. Jean Piaget cites (together with his own worldly asides on the matter) the case of the naive child who believed that a bridge collapsed at a particular time in order to punish an evil man who was walking over it (1929, pp. 257, 261–62). The collapse of the bridge is not social interaction; it follows an action but is not a social response to it. But the *belief* that bridges collapse according to the worthiness of their traffic certainly depends on social interaction, and such beliefs widely reinforce conformity and moral commitment.

Empirical symbolic sanctions often refer to primary sanctions which would be applied through interaction if they were given at all, but which are in fact either not applied or, when they are, occur fortuitously and not as a response to morally relevant acts. Such "moralization" of fortuitous reinforcement is typical of the symbolic "moral world-view" that is so important in the socialization of the young (and which is therefore discussed in Chapters IV and V). Examples are allegations that one can go to jail for civil liability, or that promiscuous women are invariably despised and never marry well.

If a sanction has powerful effects when it is used, but is difficult or expensive to use or leads to various other complications when it is used on a large scale, then it is economical to have the maintenance of morality depend as much as possible upon the symbolic representation of this sanction and as little as possible on its direct application. There is the risk that the mob may challenge one mounted policeman, but he is cheaper to maintain than a standing army for internal social control. A society is not as safe from mob violence as it would be if it marshaled an army against the mob, but it is not as poor as it would be if it had to support such an army. Social control, in practice, is a compromise between cost and effectiveness, and the symbolic representation of sanctions does much to make the compromise workable.

The strength of symbolic sanctions depends mainly on what amounts to faith in the symbol rather than on evidence of its application: men believe that they will be punished for wrongdoing because a moral tradition tells them they will; but, precisely because they have learned the meaning of the symbol and are committed in some degree to the norm it represents, they do not discriminate as sharply as they might between the symbol and its putative referent. Few men study the law closely and learn the distinction between civil and criminal liability, between innocent overspending and intent to defraud, nor use the defense of bankruptcy: they simply believe in vague sanctions represented in portentous tones by creditors, collection agencies, and moral commentators—and, for the most part, they pay their bills. Symbolic sanctions contribute fundamentally to the learning of norms by blurring the discrimination between the actual and the reported application of sanctions. The function of the admonition "Crime does not pay!"—a symbolic sanction—is to dissuade people from any close analysis of conditions under which it might pay quite well.

Since viability and competitive advantage in social organization benefit from economical social control, much is to be gained by the society that obfuscates normative elements and, especially, sanctions. We argued in Chapter I that this obfuscation has been produced in Western societies (noted for their relative economy in internal control) through their institutionalization of a voluntaristic psychology and a belief in free will, because these disincline men to calculate about sanctions. Indeed the sociological mind reels at the cost of social controls which would have to cope with the unrestrained exercise of amoral human intelligence. Symbolic sanctions, which represent primary reinforcers in place of their actual use, and which therefore can represent primary sanctions that are never actually applied, are vital to human social organization. Superempirical sanctions are simply the most extreme form of symbolic reinforcement. While the *cognitive* capacity of men has always led some proportion of them to doubt the truth of superempirical references, at the same time their *moral* capacity, the extreme degree to which they learn from symbolic sanctions, has guaranteed a place for the symbolic representation of primary effects far beyond anything that could be based on primary effects alone. Symbolic representations are susceptible of test, but only infrequently is the test—the reduction to primary reinforcement—carried to much length. The circumstances under which they *are* tested, however, are crucial to the understanding of rates of conformity to and deviation from particular norms. Yet they pose no exception to the interpretation of morality in terms of reinforcement: rather they prove it by showing the ultimate impotence of pure symbols.

Finally, the distinction between the *strength of individual reinforcers* and a *strong schedule of reinforcement* explains other seeming exceptions to the principle of reinforcement. It is one form of a distinction often made between frequency and intensity. One can multiply frequencies by a measure of intensity, varying one inversely as the other, and produce a constant. When this is done for reinforcers, however, constant products of frequency and conventional measures of intensity do not always produce a constant effect. A similar case is the behavior of photosensitive materials, where not all combinations of light intensity and exposure time which multiply to a constant value produce a constant density of silver halide crystals in the developed image. This is called the "failure of the law of reciprocity," and the term may be used in reinforcement theory as well.

For an example, let us return to the animal laboratory of the comparative psychologist, with its learning experiments and electric shocks. Suppose we are trying to train a hungry dog to abandon a dish of horsemeat and jump a barrier into another pen where there is no horsemeat and his hunger will go unrelieved. Suppose, further, that our only aversive stimulus is. an electric shock. We find that some shocks are too weak to affect the dog at all, no matter how frequently we apply them. As we gradually increase the voltage, however, there will be a point at which the reinforcement tends to be constant for a constant combination of the frequency and intensity of shock—that is, the dog stops eating and jumps the barrier after, say (we assume a large dog with a thick and highly dielectric hide), ten shocks of 30 volts each, or five shocks of 60 volts, two shocks of 150 volts, and so forth. There will come a point at which the frequency-intensity reciprocity breaks down. It might prove impossible to train the dog by one shock alone: it might require 300 volts, which at any reasonable amperage might prove lethal, and dead animals cannot learn. The point is that a strong schedule of reinforcement cannot always be composed of the application, for a short period of time, of the strongest possible reinforcers. It may be necessary to use weaker reinforcers over a longer period of time. The implication for moral commitment in humans is clear.

Those who argue against the dependence of morality on the social environment and its reinforcers often cite situations in which a particular pattern of behavior was maintained against the application of severe sanctions. The Maccabees were dismembered in a few hours, but refused to the death to worship false gods. European resistance fighters did not name their associates even though subjected overnight to savage torture and eventual death. But these brutal reinforcements were all applied briefly—perhaps too briefly—to produce much change in behavior. The subjects soon died; they had no time to learn. We attend to such examples as these not because they are effective, but because they are brutal. Yet they are often cited to show the independence of morality from the conditions of learning.

Examples of moral stamina are harder to find, however, when they are opposed by sanctions which are less than lethal and are applied consistently for a longer period. The man who, short of death, cannot be broken on the rack may yet yield to two weeks of solitary confinement. Isolation is a weak negative reinforcer over short periods of time; the respite from interaction after long exposure to it may be a positive reinforcer. But those who are concerned to produce massive changes in behavior, using nearly any means available and with the time to apply them, have learned that isolation for long periods of time, together with periodic evidence of the rewards available upon a change in behavior, can be built into a schedule of reinforcement that has been resisted by few if any of the persons to whom it has been applied (a widely cited source on this process as used to secure the profession of previously repugnant ideologies is Schein, Schneier, and Barker [1961]; see also Schein [1964]).

Similarly, support from a person's primary groups may enable him to resist pressures to change, even when composed of extreme primary reinforcers. Interaction with kith and kin can present strong conditioned reinforcement. Symbols characteristic of primary groups are strong through association with prior conditioning. Brutality and torture, on the other hand, are usually uncommon and are thus relatively meaningless: the strength of torture as primary aversive stimulation obscures its relative ineffectiveness as a secondary punishment. Some of the social reinforcers are strong primary reinforcers, but their main effect derives from the long time over which they operate.

"Total institutions"—agencies such as prisons, mental hospitals, concentration camps, and monasteries, where the environment of "inmates" can be completely controlled by "staff" so as to produce a specific kind of subsequent behavior—are the best places to study the effects produced by the enduring application of relatively mild sanctions. The literature on them is therefore reviewed in Chapter V, and most of the evidence supports our theory.

What men call moral courage is perfectly real. Its scientific interpretation is what occasions debate. That moral commitment can be maintained in the face of adversity does not mean that it is autonomous from the insults of society. It means that it was learned well. It was learned through sanctions and can also be unlearned through them. The fact that heroes have resisted some sanctions to the death does not mean they could have resisted other less lethal ones, applied with less anger but more patience and artful intent to control.

Theory of Hypocrisy

The distinction between "words and deeds" (in Irwin Deutscher's phrase) or between an activity and its verbal self-report (in our language) has been made from time to time for many years. It was made in incisive terms by LaPiere (1934). He argued among other points that some verbal professions (as measured by standard interrogatory research, that is, interviews and questionnaires), such as religious beliefs, could be taken reliably at face value so long as there were no other events to which the profession was assumed to refer and with which it could in principle be compared. In this sense such a profession of belief (for example, the messiahship of Christ) is a "logical primitive." But as a report of real or possible behavior (for example, whether he who assents to Christian divinity will punish Moslems or Jews) the profession cannot be taken at face value. Too many other factors intervene. LaPiere reported a study in which professed policies excluding nonwhites from travelers' accommodations proved to be very much at variance from the policies he later observed to be actually followed. Such discrepancies, he argued, might greatly attenuate the accuracy of rates of frequency of behavior inferred from tallies of verbal reports. Although LaPiere acknowledged that other risks are involved, he concluded that "it would seem far more worthwhile to make a shrewd guess regarding what is essential than to accurately measure that which is likely to prove quite irrelevant" (1934, p. 237). The laboring mountains often bring forth a ridiculous mouse, who is also a chronic liar.

The distinction between activities and self-reports that LaPiere and Deutscher make in general terms is especially important in the case of norms and values. In our analysis of these concepts in Chapter II we distinguished at length between profession and practice. Values are predicable of reward; how much a person values a reward is a function of how much activity he will put out to get it. Norms are not defined as the practice of particular persons, who may still conform or deviate, but rather as the reinforcing practice of their social environment, the sanctions to which they are exposed. The sanctions that define the norm are among the important variables that determine particular conforming or deviant acts, but they are not all of them. This is why it is necessary to distinguish the norm from the activity to which it applies.

Many morally relevant acts are difficult for others to observe. But the *report* of an act is inherently a public event, involving by definition both the reporter and an audience. Since the more public an activity the greater its audience, those who are disposed to sanction others will find it easier to sanction relatively public events, including reports of activity, than events which are relatively private.[11] The result is that verbal reports of an activity are, on the whole, easier to sanction than the activity itself. This implies that verbal reports of activities will be more elaborately conditioned than the activities themselves, and thus that norms will be more thoroughly learned with regard to verbal reports of morally relevant acts than with regard to the acts reported. We are more moral in what we say than in what we do.

That acts and their verbal self-report are separate events, and thus subject to different sanctions, may in turn be discriminated by the reporter.

---

11 If an activity is necessarily and essentially private—that is, one which can be observed by (or is a stimulus for) only one person—it is a "subjective" event. By definition it cannot figure in interaction, and so sociologists may professionally ignore it. We are speaking here, however, not of methodologically private events but of events which are private in some degree and in some respect, even though they have public and social consequences.

Moreover, much morally relevant behavior is virtually if not methodologically private, becoming subject to sanctions only when the individual reports his acts or intention: that is, probably no one will know what he is up to if he simply says nothing. And often, when the result of an act is public, determining just who did it is often difficult or not worth the trouble. Under these circumstances the person may well learn that the sanctioning of an activity is mainly contingent not on the activity itself, but on a verbal report of it; this strongly reinforces that particular verbal report which is followed by the greatest reward. When an activity is subject to reward, the actor will be rewarded for reporting that he did it or that he intends to do it; when the activity is subject to punishment, he will find it least punishing to say nothing.

Further, the *cost* of verbal behavior is low. Talk is cheap. The cost of an activity is the value of other activities that had to be foregone in order for it to be performed. Non-verbal activities vary greatly in intrinsic costs (costs attached to the acts apart from the associated sanctions): some are easy to perform, taking little time or energy and leaving much available for other activities; others are difficult, drawing heavily on the store of time and resources that might have been applied elsewhere. But the unique human capacity for free and easy emission of speech makes its intrinsic cost generally quite low: we seldom talk till we become bored or hoarse. Further, because most conversation and much written language is extremely topical in content and selective in audience, it is widely possible to say one thing at one time and something else later, without encountering any significant penalty for inconsistency. The cost of verbal behavior is therefore almost wholly a function of the sanctions applied to one remark as compared to those applicable to others that might at the same moment have been made in its place. Thus purely verbal conformity costs little, and this too results in verbal behavior being much more moral than non-verbal behavior.

Thus is explained the prevalence of hypocrisy, of which the dictionary definition is "simulation of virtue or piety," the opposite of moral candor. Since different rewards are applied to verbal reports than to the activity reported, since the reward due an activity can often be claimed simply by reporting that it has been or will be done, and since the intrinsic costs of emitting the report are low, the aphorist La Rochefoucauld was eminently correct to remark (1665–1678; 1959, p. 218n) that "hypocrisy is the homage vice pays to virtue" (although the homage is purely verbal). Hypocrisy occurs because men are intelligent enough to discriminate between an activity and its description; it illustrates once again the problems that cognitive capacities present in social control.

If it may be granted that activities and their verbal report are independently variable to a great extent, the range of variation of each may still set some limit on the range of variation of the other. I have not found reports of research that bear directly on the matter, but it seems a plausible hypothesis that, other things being equal, the performance of an activity (or a gain in the rate of performance) increases the probability that the activity will be reported; and conversely, that the report of an activity increases the probability that it will be performed. When we work hard on something for a long time we are likely to tell somebody else about it. The man who, on awakening in the morning, shouts "Rise and shine! Greet the new day!" is probably more likely to get up than the man who awakens and just lies quietly in bed. The problem, of course, about the verbal profession of morally relevant acts is that it is in the nature of social life for other things not to be equal. While acts may constrain reports and *vice versa,* so that hypocrisy is not without limit, the independence of acts and reports is still great enough to have a strong effect on much of the conformity and deviation which concern social scientists. Hence techniques of research that use verbal behavior as a measure of nonverbal behavior often account for little of the variance in the dependent variable, and instead only confirm Pareto's suspicion that the range of things people are prepared to say is much greater than the range of things they are prepared to do.

It is also true that hypocrisy is itself prescribed: this is one of the morally important conditions of natural social life that violates the criterion of "other things being equal." The problem with the normative control of hypocrisy is that it is so difficult to distinguish from moral candor. Sometimes there is enough interest in the truth of a verbal report to compare it, or to launch an attempt to compare it, with the behavior reported, and when this obtains the hypocrite is liable to be punished. But often either interest in or the means for comparison are lacking, and on these occasions hypocrisy is more rewarded than candor: the hypocrite gets the intrinsic rewards of prohibited activity and the extrinsic rewards of the profession of morality. Small wonder then that norms prescribing honesty and sincerity (that is, some degree of correspondence between action and its verbal representation) are ubiquitous and strong; small wonder too that they are ubiquitously violated.[12] Sinners claim to be saints, and when the pattern of group esteem, itself a potent reinforcement, is reversed in deviant subcultures, saints claim to be sinners, illustrating again the close relation between moral profession and reward. Contrition may sometimes share the insincerity of hypocrisy: just as the hypocrite falsely claims virtue so the contrite person may falsely confess to a vicious habit. Contrition may often be followed by

---

[12] For a parallel analysis see Staats and Staats (1963, p. 390) on "rationalization." The same behavior is differently reinforced according to the reasons or motives reported to account for it.

strong rewards, as in interviews with parole officers, ideological coercion of prisoners-of-war, and election to the papacy.

Although hypocrisy is regarded as a vice, it is also useful in social control. We saw in Chapter I that a societal advantage inheres in the use of internal moral commitment because of its efficiency in social control. A society whose basic norms are well learned by its members gets more conformity for a given sanction and thus has more resources to deploy elsewhere. Because human society makes so much use of symbolic representation, however, the social control that sustains learned commitment has many symbolic properties itself. Not only are prohibited acts punished and encouraged acts rewarded, the names of acts themselves become subject to norms. The names of virtuous activities become sanctified; those of vicious acts deprecated. The explanation of hypocrisy involves the same variables as the explanation of obscene words: these words are prohibited precisely because *they facilitate the cognitive discrimination of certain actions and objects which efficient maintenance of a normative order requires to be suppressed.* In this connection the attachment of the stigma of obscenity to certain words is merely the extreme expression of a general pattern: to avoid candid and disinterested reference to interdicted acts and to rely instead on obfuscatory euphemism and circumlocution, which better maintain moral emotions. Indeed the main moral concerns of a society can be largely inferred from the roster of activities to which its morally committed members cannot refer in unambiguous and economical terms. Thus orthodox Jews cannot utter the name of God, ordinary prostitution becomes "the social disease," Irish coroners diagnose cirrhosis as hepatitis, and much judicial exegesis is required to learn that "the detestible and abominable crime against nature" is nothing more deadly than homosexual anal intercourse. In Mead's terms the name of an interdicted act becomes a significant symbol, an epithet that produces the same moral attitude as the act itself might elicit. Interdiction renders the meaning more emotional than cognitive.

Insofar, therefore, as the hypocrite deviates in his private conduct, but pays public homage to virtue verbally and in public, he serves the interests of social control better (as well as his own) than if he were to advertise his deviation. The result is that private deviation is likely to go undetected, not only by those who would apply sanctions but also by those who are themselves tempted to deviate and who would be tempted more were they to discover that others discreetly deviate with relative impunity. For the same reason slight but conspicuous deviation often draws stronger punishment than severe but inconspicuous deviation. Wealthy bohemians find it difficult to cash checks because their exotic or ragamuffin attire conspicuously deviates from sumptuary conventions, which systematic check forgers are careful to observe these conventions (cf. with Lemert, 1958, p. 115). The hypocrite also is likely to conform in conspicuous and superficial ways, the better to deceive those who would punish him. But he also contributes to the vital pretense that conformity is frequent and deviation, because inconspicuous and infrequently reported, infrequent. Both hypocrisy and superficial conformity are therefore basic parts of the moral order of society. They give norms a reputation of widespread conformity that a more disinterested assessment of rates of conformity and deviation would not give them, and thereby extend the efficiency of social control (that is, the amount of conformity produced by a given sanction).

If it seems paradoxical that hypocrisy and superficial conformity are useful to society, it is because we see them in the perspective of moral men, in terms of the rhetoric that moral men both use and believe in, rather than in terms of a scientific analysis. Just as prostitution sustains the family, and rules calling for solidarity among kinsmen are also a precondition to illegitimate birth, so here too an "immoral" cause has "moral" effects. In moral rhetoric good must cause only good, and evil cause only evil, but in the natural world that rule of causation is often violated.

Moral philosophers (themselves usually very moral men) often cite "honesty" as a concrete example of goodness. The example is not well chosen, for honesty is valued in society only with substantial qualifications. In fact a social order made up of completely honest men would be intolerable to its members. Societies must extract some degree of conformity, and since some men know of rewards for deviant acts they will conform only reluctantly. Marital roles often call for a high degree of sexual fidelity to and emotional priority of wives, but few marriages could survive a complete and candid account of husbands' interests in other women. Little could be accomplished in any heirarchical organization—a classroom, a business enterprise, a warship—where each rank in the heirarchy regularly vented its hostility toward the others. It is of course true that men do not remain completely silent about the inevitable incongruence between what is expected of them and their own attitudes, but it is also true that they are strongly rewarded for much less than complete candor in accounting for the incongruence.

Moral Commitment and Putatively Subjective States

The traditional discussion of moral commitment has not conceived it as conformity of methodologically public acts at some remove from sanctions, but rather as various methodologically private events, for example, subjective mental states. The names for some of these—"duty," "obligation," "conscience," and "guilt"—are laden with connotations, and they are the core of the vocabulary by which moral commitment is usually discussed. So far as the vagaries of natural language permit, we are attempting here to ignore methodologically private events. But much continuity with other discussions of morality would be lost, however, if these central terms in the moral vocabulary were to be omitted altogether. Then too most sociologists and many psychologists take little offense at introspection and fail to understand the paradox contained in the idea of a public science of veritably private events. Many of them would rather read about private guilt and sanctimony than public conformity and deviation, and this essay must come to terms with its audience.

The traditional vocabulary of morality does not, however, refer *solely* to private events. The behavioristic movement in psychology became most persuasive not when it ruled all putatively subjective terms outside the court of science (as Watson did), but when it took the more diplomatic course of Tolman and later of Skinner and showed that these terms had a very substantial public reference and were eminently relevant to a public science. Here we shall use the method of Tolman and Skinner and attempt to define the traditional moral vocabulary in public terms. A person who feels guilty is not, after all, limited solely to his own methodologically private sensations. He can, and very well may, produce verbal reports whose conventional public meaning is that he "privately feels guilty." In truth he may so feel or he may not, and only he will know, but publicly he is imputed to feel guilty, and that is enough for guilt to be a factor in interaction. But in the process it comes to rest on a public label rather than a private event. Then too the person may "act guilty," quite apart from his verbal claims, in a manner which also imputes his guilt; for if the reports of psychotherapists and others are to be believed there often is some association between verbal reports of private guilt and public "guilty" actions. The method is to look for the public evidence that underlies the private reference.

The term most intimately associated with internal commitment is probably "obligation." Obligation can be described as public behavior, however, if we recall the idea of the generalization of a stimulus or a response. Persons can generalize their response to an internalized or learned norm, through its symbolic representation, in the same way they can generalize their response to other parts of their symbolically represented world. If there is anything distinctive of the learned response to a norm, then it is reasonable to expect that it can be generalized. Thus, obligation can be interpreted as the response which the actor makes to all sufficiently well learned norms, and it is a perfectly public response. Obligation is the general name for learned conformity to norms.

Durkheim (1903, and subsequently) stresses a distinction which commentators who celebrate the subjective have made much of. They say that obligation is not gross conformity but rather an "inner urge" to conform which resists temptations to deviate, and so on. This conflict between commitment and temptation Durkheim represented thus:

> Something in the nature of duty is found in the desirability of morality. If it is true that the content of the [moral] act appeals to us, nevertheless its nature is such that it cannot be accomplished without effort and self-constraint. The *élan,* even the enthusiasm, with which we perform a moral act takes us outside ourselves and above our nature, and this is not achieved without difficulty and inner conflict [1903, p. 45].

Perhaps this is true only of the phenomenology of a very moral man—and by all accounts Durkheim was a very moral man. At any rate, this passage can be interpreted so as to advance in public terms the distinction that subjectivists have stressed. If it is true that it is in some respects rewarding to conform to a norm ("if it is true that the content of the [moral] act appeals to us")—and it is, because conformity is rewarded—it is also true that the actor, in conforming, must usually incur costs. If the prohibited activity were not itself rewarded one way or another, no norm would have evolved to counter it with alternate rewards. In claiming the latter, the moral man foregoes the value of the prohibited act. Conformity thus requires time and energy that might have gained other rewards ("it cannot be accomplished without effort and self-constraint"). Further, the person may calculate the cost. He may in fact strain to discern which of two paths of action (conformity or deviation) will produce the greater satisfaction because of the greater reward (the moral act "is not achieved without difficulty and inner conflict"). Thus Durkheim's dutiful actor is visited not only by moral obligation but also by amoral desire, greed, or other emotion. Add to this the possibility that the actor may in turn discriminate this conflict, and even give a verbal report of the discrimination—in short, he is conscious[13] of the conflict—and we have in hand a useful definition of *duty*: it is the response of obligation in those cases where the actor is aware that the completion of the moral act will be costly; that is, that it will be punishing in some aspect or that alternate rewards will have to be foregone. Duty is obligation when it hurts.

----

13 A variety of methodologically public conceptions of consciousness have been advanced by behavioristic psychologists. One is that a psychological state is conscious when it is available for verbal report. The behavioristic notion implied in the notes of G. H. Mead's lectures parallels this; consciousness is better conceived as a process of access to certain contents rather than (as with Wundt) those contents themselves. For the lecture notes see Mead (1936, p. 30); also his more formal statement in "The Definition of the Psychical" (1903, pp. 77–93). A more recondite and general definition is given in Tolman (1927). Tolman wanted to refer to conscious rats and this posed problems. Consciousness became a variation of "readiness to discriminate"; for example, the rat is conscious of the maze when he discriminates between the paths that lead to food and the dead end.

Similar attention to consciousness defines *conscience*: it is the availability for verbal report of the dutiful condition or of the more general one of obligation. Internal commitment, though always involving some cognitive orientation toward sanctions, "however small the voice of calculation," can be either conscious or unconscious. Indeed, internalization has been defined by Guy Swanson as a type of learning in which the circumstances of learning cannot be consciously recalled.[14] There are perhaps good reasons for this conception, especially for those who respect the psychoanalytic emphasis on repression and other movements toward the unconscious. Swanson's requirement that internalization entails a lack of awareness of the conditions under which it was acquired, however, differs from the present theory in two respects. First, it is narrower, since the present theory considers commitment simply as conformity at a remove from sanctions, whether the individual is aware of the original conditions or not. Second, Swanson emphasizes an obfuscation of *past* conditioners, whereas we stress the interaction between commitment and the sanctioning environment, posing an opposition between cognition and the maintenance of commitment. Thus, we emphasize the effect of commitment on the obfuscation of *future* conditioners—the sanctions the person might still expect to be applied even though he may have forgotten earlier ones. This difference between past and future reference separates the Freudian and Skinnerian perspectives more generally. The Freudian looks back to events in the early history of the person; the Skinnerian looks forward to the reinforcement the actor has yet to encounter.

"Anxiety" and "guilt" can be defined similarly, in terms of Durkheim's distinction between the mechanical and synthetic consequences of an act. "Anxiety" can be viewed as the general expectation of negative reinforcement, whether social or not; "guilt," as the more specific expectation of social punishment of deviation, that is, through sanctions. Guilt is the expectation of punishment when the individual is aware that he has violated a norm to which he has a learned commitment. It is because he has internalized the norm that he expects sanctions to be applied. For some theorists, the sense of guilt has been irreducible evidence of the autonomy of internal commitment; if morality were reduced to self-interest, they argue, why would men "punish themselves with guilt" when in all likelihood no one else could punish them in any manner? The hypothesis that moral learning entails the *expectation* of sanctions broadly answers this question. Guilt is a special case of the general expectation. The self-punishing aspects of guilt, like those of anxiety, derive from external punishment.

---

14 "It seems desirable to reserve *internalization* for the...psychoanalytic...usage [as distinguished from learning and symbolization], i.e., learning (or the state of having learned) in cases where the learner is unaware of the conditions which have impelled, influenced, or motivated him" (Swanson, 1960, p. 345).

A more detailed theory of "guilt" has been developed by Hill (1960). Hill shares our ambition to explain moral behavior in terms of reinforcement. Guilt seems to him to be the hardest aspect of "conscience" to explain. The striking thing about it, he writes:

> ...which has seemed to some students to set it apart from the ordinary laws of learning, is that it often involves the seeking of punishment. The person who has transgressed, rather than trying to avoid punishment, or even waiting passively for it to come, actively seeks out the authorities, confesses, and receives his punishment with apparent relief. He may also, or instead, go to great lengths to make restitution. Were it not for these phenomena of punishment-seeking and self-sacrificing restitution, it would be easy to dismiss guilt as merely the kind of fear associated with anticipation of certain sorts of punishment. As it is, the existence of guilt serves as an argument for regarding conscience as something more than the sum of all those avoidances which have moral significance in one's culture [p. 325].

Aronfreed (1968) has dealt similarly with what appears to be self-punishment by an "anxiety theory." The transgressor knows he has done something for which he is liable to be punished. He is therefore in some fear of punishment, which he has learned will probably come. This fear is anxiety, the expectation of punishment, which is itself punishing and is therefore something the individual tries to avoid. There may be less punishment in confessing a transgression and relieving the anxiety, since the transgression would be punished anyway when it was discovered by others. Anxiety, in short, reinforces confession.

Hill's explanation complements Aronfreed's. He reviews studies of child rearing and distinguishes "disciplinary" from "love-oriented" modes of socialization. The former relies on physical punishment, which "is likely to occur all at once and be all over quickly." "On the other hand," he writes:

> Discipline by withdrawal of love...probably much more often lasts until the child makes some symbolic renunciation of his wrongdoing, as by apologizing, making restitution, or promising not to do it again. The child is deprived of his parents' love (or, the parents would claim, of the outward manifestations of it!) for as much or as little time as is necessary to get him to make such a symbolic renunciation. When he has made it, he is restored to his parents' favor. If the normal relation between the parents and child is one of warmth, such discipline strongly motivates the child to make the renunciation quickly. On repeated occasions of transgression, punishment by withdrawal of love, and symbolic renunciation, the child may be expected not only to learn the renunciation response as an escape from parental disfavor but eventually to use it as an avoidance rather than merely an escape response. Thus if the wrongdoing is not immediately discovered, the child may antici-

pate his parents' impending disfavor by confessing in advance and making the symbolic renunciation [1960, p. 325].

Guilt and confession, then, are public acts, performed because they terminate or avert a punishment.

Such a pattern of training as Hill describes early teaches children to discriminate between transgressions and their report, and thus risks making hypocrites out of them at an early age. Hill recognizes this and speculates on the moral future of children whose parents' wrath is invariably stayed when the child says "I'm sorry." In fact, however, few punishments applied to adult statuses are entirely averted by a profession of guilt. A show of contrition for commission of a felony may produce a lighter sentence than would a show of proud contempt for the law or the court, but it seldom produces a suspended sentence.

Conclusion

The preceding statement of a reinforcement theory of moral commitment has many faults. It is discursive but also abstract and analytical. In attempting to develop some implications of the premise that moral behavior and moral commitment are operant activities it offers hypotheses of greater scope than are easily tested by available data. But if these hypotheses prove fruitful or interesting then that seems reason enough for presenting the theory in its present form even though it might prove eventually to be badly reasoned or empirically wrong. The next two chapters offer more empirical materials which support the hypothesis that moral behavior is an operant and which suggest—at least to me—that the theory is correct.

CHAPTER IV

Application of the Theory

to Socialization

The process of learning can be divided roughly into two parts: "shaping," which begins with an unconditioned operant and is characterized by a high but decreasing ratio of reinforcements to acts emitted; and "maintenance," where the ratio is low and the response is learned, and is continued after reinforcement is reduced. This distinction separates the next two chapters. In this chapter we deal with "moral training" or "socialization," the process whereby persons (usually as children) learn norms to which they did not previously conform. In the next chapter we discuss and review research on the maintenance of moral commitments that are already learned, mainly in terms of the pattern of sanctions involved in adult statuses.

The association of "shaping" and "maintenance" with age-graded statuses is somewhat misleading, because many responses get learned so well and so early that they reach the "maintenance" level during childhood, and because "shaping" of responses through novel schedules of reinforcement is by no means infrequent among adults. The association gains unwarranted support through the hypothesis, implicit in much of the literature in social and developmental psychology, that operant or other principles of learning are useful in the analysis of the socialization of children and, perhaps, youth, but are not useful in studying adult behavior. To be sure it is helpful to set off the relatively unconditioned and plastic situation of children and the relatively conditioned and fixed situation of adults. But this does not necessarily reflect a difference in the extent to which behavior in the two age-grades is an operant. An alternate hypothesis offered here is that childish behavior is plastic because the subordinate status of children exposes them to strong and changing schedules of reinforcement, and that adult behavior is stable because the superordinate status of adults limits the relative strength and degree of change of the reinforcers that can be applied to them.

This chapter offers first a criticism of research in order to account for the relative lack of data—at least in the conventional forms that behavioral scientists respect—which the argument of the preceding chapter requires if it is to be either confirmed or confuted: data of the effect of social reinforcement on the moralization of children. Although some recent studies by psychologists have begun to fill this gap,[1] the accumulated evidence is hardly sufficient to convince the critics of a reinforcement theory of morality of its adequacy, especially if they respect evidence from introspection on subjective aspects of moral commitment.[2] But it does provide a start. Some data are already available in sociological materials (though variable in quality), but less available in the experimental form that research workers in psychology and child development are presently more disposed to accept.

Much evidence of the effect of social reinforcement has been overlooked, in my judgment, as a result of two broad perspectives, which I call respectively "experimental positivism" and "the psychoanalytic fallacy." These are discussed below. Further, those research workers not limited by either of these perspectives still must contend with the scarcity of longitudinal studies done by others and the difficulty of doing their own. Next the concept of "identification" is discussed. We argue that this vague and protean concept offers a name rather than an explanation and that its presumed effects are better explained in terms of learning a role through differential reinforcement. Finally we review an alternate theory of moralization, the neo-Piagetian theory of Kohlberg, and show how his notion of "parasocial" unilineal development of "moral character," seemingly opposed to a theory of social reinforcement, can be explained in its terms. We stress throughout the role of the main sociological forms of status ascription—age, sex, social class, and "ethnicity," or inheritance group membership—and attempt to show how they organize the reinforcements of social interaction.

---

1 Two volumes in particular cover this topic well enough for the burden of the present chapter to be greatly reduced. These are Bandura and Walters (1963) and Aronfreed (1968).

2 See in this connection the review by Daniel Miller (1966) of Bandura and Walters (1963). Bandura and Walters show high fidelity to traditional behavioristic idiom and gesture; Miller clearly sees behaviorism as largely misapplied in the study of humans.

Criticism of Research

Published reviews of research in every field of the social sciences invariably despair at how little has been done and how much remains to be done. This pessimism is especially strong in the literature on child development. Yet few subfields of social science have had more research, researchers, or publications. The problem is that the study of children, like the study of the family, has a strong popular appeal, and much of it is therefore designed for immediate application rather than for disinterested scientific interpretation. More important, both fields study strong social institutions, with the result that the scientists involved, being moral and well-socialized men themselves, tend to respect the institutional taboos and to exclude from their analysis the norms defining the institutions. This practice systematically favors the moral over the scientific perspective. Kingsley Davis, after a decade of writing on the family for a scientific audience that was slow to gather, remarked wearily that "the subject has a reputation for being either moralistic or pornographic, and reputable scientists therefore shy away from it" (1949, p. 393).

The situation with respect to the study of children is even worse. Moral accounts of the family do give a rough idea of the norms involved, and pornography suggests some of the propensities that norms have evolved to control. By combining the two a rough but useful beginning can be made toward a scientific account—an account too well informed to take moral claims as scientific fact, but not so sophomoric as to ignore normative aspects altogether. But the original, pre-verbal amorality of the child has no such literary representative as pornography provides for sex and the family. The great bulk of putatively scientific material in this field is only incidentally scientific in substance: it is only a slight exaggeration to say that the main concern is a sophisticated defense of morality whose function (of which its writers are not always aware) is to reinforce motherhood.[3] So strong are the institutional controls in this field that few investigators would care to phrase their conclusions in terms which, if judged from a lay point of view, would seem to mock the commitments of parents: not much less than politicians are scientists expected to be in favor of motherhood. Indeed, a

---

[3] Thus even the widely discussed and influential book by Sears, Maccoby, and Levin (1957) is a mixture of psychological prose and the evocative style characteristic of female journalists who write to praise traditional femininity, while the text is interlaced with drawings of affectionate interaction between parents and children. The discussion of "conscience" and other moral phenomena stays closer to lay conceptions than might have been expected from its senior author, a past president of the American Psychological Association with a reputation as a tough-minded learning theorist.

dispassionate analysis of child development would have the same moral defect as pornography, for it would facilitate precisely that recognition and analysis of sanctions sustaining parenthood that it is in the interests of society (with its need for reproductive institutions) to suppress.

Experimental Positivism

Experimental procedures have a long history in psychology. A century ago they served to set off psychology from philosophy, and today they set it off from sociology and anthropology. Even when experimentalists use examples from everyday life their heart is still in laboratory work. The impact of Freud and psychotherapy tended to split psychology into "clinical" and "experimental" camps, and experimental procedure has long served to separate the "hard science" psychologists from what they judge to be the uncritical dialogs and speculations of the clinicians and therapists. Then too the theory of randomization and statistical inference developed by Sir Ronald A. Fisher greatly extended the power of psychological experimentation. It also allowed psychologists to use mathematical terminology and gather thereby some of the prestige attached to the more traditionally quantitative sciences. The dominance of experimental method is as a result firmly entrenched in psychology today and the terms "experimentation" and "research" are casually used there as if they were synonyms.[4]

The basic idea of an experiment is simple. Either control all the variables that affect a given dependent variable—what you want to explain—or control what you can and randomize the rest. Manipulate one variable at a time and observe its effect on the dependent variable, preferably using "randomized" experimental and control groups—that is, groups into one or the other of which the subjects or units of the experiment all have an equal likelihood of being assigned. There is no better way to establish conclusively the other variables of which any given variable is a function, and all sciences profit by using experimental procedures wherever they can. Especially do the behavioral sciences profit, because experimentation gives them a sim-

---

4 For examples of psychologists' emphasis on experimentation, see Staats and Staats (1963, pp. 3, 7). They stress the power of experimental methods, but say nothing about their limits. Yet their book could hardly have been written solely on the basis of experimental evidence. See also a reputable text in child psychology: Mussen, Conger, and Kagan (1963, p. 20).

The non-Fisherian method of experimentation preferred by the operant conditioners is ably presented by Sidman in *The Tactics of Scientific Research* (1960)— more accurately subtitled *Evaluating Experimental Data in Psychology* (to which one might add "according to operant principles"). Sidman allows that other disciplines use "ingenious [non-experimental] techniques for investigating their own spheres of interest" (p. 31), but the general connotation of his text is that he who says science says experimentation.

plifying starting point for analysis of their apparently complex subject. The concept of reinforcement probably could not have become widely accepted had it lacked a definition in terms of isolated and repeatable effects produced by Thorndike, Skinner, and others in laboratory experiments.

Benefits, however, seldom are gained free of costs. The power of the experiment in determining the relationship among a few variables at a time, and perhaps especially in the power of randomization in attenuating the effects of extraneous variables, seems to have inclined many psychologists to overlook the fact that experimentation in itself offers no special economies with regard to access to and manipulation of variables. More often it leads to special diseconomies. Many sciences cannot afford to use experimental methods, because the magnitude of the variables which it is their fate to study is simply so great that the discipline has not the resources to manipulate them. This is the lot of many behavioral sciences, but it affects other sciences too. Then champions of experimental method who celebrate it as the *sine qua non* of science fail to note that until very recently there have been no experiments in gravitational astronomy, which somehow has muddled through to become the theoretically most complete and perfect science of all. Many other sciences deal with variables which they can afford to manipulate, but which cannot be studied experimentally because such research would trespass on certain moral rights invested in the objects of the experiment.

These moral rights strongly limit the sciences of human behavior. Especially do they limit the study of the effects of reinforcement on the moralization of children. Purely as an exercise in experimental logic it would be a fairly simple matter to design a series of experiments that would resolve to everybody's satisfaction the question of the extent to which moral behavior is a function of reinforcement, cognition, "innate" patterns of development, or anything else. Such a project might cover several decades and require thousands of subjects and scores of experimentors, but its cost, though high, would not be beyond the range of recent research support.

It would not be so easy, however, to design the society in which such experiments could be carried out. It would scarcely resemble the Western democracies, which are distinctive both for the favorable environment they provide for the growth of science and for the limits they impose on the strength of reinforcers that may generally be applied in social interaction. Considerations of economics and morality limit the utility of experimentation in the sciences of human behavior: effective reinforcers of humans are often very expensive, and their application is narrowly delimited by norms. Indeed, these norms often constrain the scientist more than the layman, who, in influencing his fellows in daily activities, is more free to use the potent reinforcers of amoral incentives and others stratagems of everyday life.[5] The scientist, on the other hand, because of his past connection with established religion and continuing role as teacher of the young, is expected to be a moral exemplar.

Textbooks on experimental methods in the behavioral sciences generally stress the logical problems in experimental design, especially those involved in the sound application of statistics. Yet the real problems are usually not logical but practical—the troublesome combination mentioned above of morals and economics. One may constrain an experiment even if the other does not. The limitation of cost, for example, usually applies only to manipulation of the independent variables. Moral limitations, however, can apply both to independent and dependent variables. The complex of norms that define a status limits not only what its occupants can do, but—and this is often overlooked—also what other people can do to them, regardless of whether doing it is cheap or dear. It may be cheap and easy to teach young persons to be pickpockets or hypocrites, but we are not permitted to do it just the same. The proscription is rather strong for academic scientists: parents, for example, are freer than psychologists to use extreme sanctions on children and even to produce offensive habits. The advantage to experimentation in being a parent and the disadvantage in being a psychologist have led more than one person who is both to merge his roles and study his own children as subjects. Despite the ingenuity of many research workers, the constraints of economy and morality combine to restrict seriously the number and range of variables that can be studied experimentally, including many that are widely believed on theoretical grounds to affect moral commitment. They restrict the study of variables relevant to *this* theory, at any rate, and that is one reason it rests much of its case on non-experimental materials.

There are, broadly, two ways to get round the limitations on experimentation. One is to make observational studies. The other, much more the

---

5 Controversy over experiments conducted by Stanley Milgram illustrates this point well. His subjects were instructed to administer controls which (they had been told) applied electric shock to another human subject. In the course of the elaborately contrived experiment, the subjects were asked to inflict what appeared to be damaging or lethal shocks (see, for example, Milgram, 1963). Milgram was thought by many to have gone beyond his scientific license, and many statements of "experimental ethics" have appeared in response to his work.

My own view is that Milgram erred in misjudging the practical limits (the "constraints of morality" discussed in the text) of experimentation on humans. He exhausted far more than his share of the limited supply of public good will toward research in the human behavioral sciences (and also more than his topic warranted, since "obedience" is far more problematic ideologically than theoretically).

The result at this writing of draining down public good will (to be sure, by many others besides Milgram) has been strong restrictions imposed by universities and funding agencies on research on humans. Review committees that evaluate research proposals (the author is currently a member of one) often require removal of all of the guts from experimental proposals that usually were pretty gutless to begin with.

choice of psychologists, is to adapt research topics to the limitations. This is done in two ways: by studying only those variables not ruled out by excessive cost or moral objection or by limiting the range of variation of the variables studied. This latter resort is particularly useful when either cost or moral objection is a matter of degree. If "natural society" uses money or food as powerful rewards, then experimentors "sample" money and food as variables, using such small magnitudes of them as the research budget can afford. Nobody gets filthy rich or starves in psychological experiments: college sophomores get paid off in two-bit pieces and grade-school children receive candy-coated chocolate drops.

As a sociologist who has reviewed the psychological literature on child development, I get the impression that many psychologists are *enthusiastic* about experimentation, in the original and depreciatory sense of that word. Rather than adapting their methods to their subject, they have adapted the subject to the method, and have celebrated its potential to the point where they have largely forgotten its limitations. I call this adaptation *experimental positivism,* and define it as the view that scientific interest is exhausted by what can be studied experimentally. As practiced in the behavioral sciences, experimental positivism usually reduces to one or more of the following more specific beliefs: (1) samples that are available for experimental control are sufficiently representative of all populations of scientific interest; (2) variables which can be experimentally manipulated are sufficiently representative of all variables; and (3) the range of the variables that is available for experimental manipulation is sufficiently representative of their total range. Carried to its logical conclusion, experimental positivism denies extra-experimental sciences, and few psychologists would formally or consciously assent to such a restrictive doctrine. Yet they often carry out research and advance theories as if they did agree with it. If they do not preach it truth it still describes very well much of their practice.[6]

A preference for experimental research is not the same as experimental positivism, although the two often occur together. The former is a habit of research work; the latter a habit in making inferences. The emphasis on experimentation alone does not produce experimental positivism, but rather, it seems, its combination with a cautious and somewhat anti-theoretical (or at least anti-deductive) empiricism. If experimentalists were to contemplate a model or theory of a natural process (for example, "personality," "eco-system," "society") they might then select by abstraction subprocesses operat-

---

[6] At least one psychologist has made a similar point: in recommending the "non-experimental behaviorism" of animal ethologists, William Verplanck writes that "the psychologists' fixation on a few easily manipulated and already identified variables may seriously limit the power of their generalizations" (1955, p. 144). Harry Harlow also suggests that many "principles of learning" are atomistic (and unpersuasive) simply because the experiments on which they rest are too simple and too brief (1949, pp. 51–52).

ing within the model which they have the means and license to study experimentally. In this way, the model and the processes selected from it for experimentation are kept distinct; and the corollaries—that there are other processes operating in the model which are not amenable to experimental study, and that those which are so amenable are no kind of "representative sample" of the model as a whole—could not be readily suppressed. But this is not how experimental positivists work. A well-formed "grand theory" of a process antecedent to research on it offends their desire to stay close to the facts. For them the research must be antecedent to the theory, which in turn must be built by cautious induction. Insofar as their experiments are a biased sample of a natural process, then to that degree will the model inferred from the experiments misrepresent the natural process.[7]

It is therefore in the inferences to which it leads that experimental positivism is defective. It does not lead psychologists to do bad experiments but it does lead them to neglect the question of whether the experiments inform us about a process beyond the experiment—what has been called "external validity." They tend not to dwell on the matter of external validity but to concentrate instead on the more clearly defined and statistically manipulable problems of "internal validity." Thus they gradually lose sight of the social world that extends beyond what their experiments can capture from it. Now if the subjects for experimentation were representative samples from populations of theoretical interest (who were then randomly assigned to experimental and control groups) the first premise of experimental positivism (as stated above) could be readily granted. Then the major problem of external validity—whether an experimentally demonstrated relation obtains beyond the experiment—would be reduced to the technical and easily solved questions of sampling statistics. But in fact human experimental subjects are not selected in this way, and it is inherent in the nature of experimental work in human society that they cannot be.

---

[7] A consistent experimental positivist might grant that there are processes that experimentation cannot study, but he would still recommend, in view of the other virtues of experimental work, that scientists simply ignore them as not worth studying, in somewhat the same manner that we recommend they ignore methodologically private events. Often in this connection invidious distinctions are made between experimental and observational research as methods of abstraction, as in Morris Zelditch's distinction of observers as interested in "topography" and experimentors as interested in "principles." The problem with this simple and appealing dichotomy is that one man's topography is another man's principle: thus (to invert the invidious comparison) the goal of observation of norms may be, metaphorically speaking, to prepare a map of isobars of conformity and deviation, whereby the experimentor becomes a mere stratigrapher, content to drill for beds of water-bearing gravel. In any event, just as the concern with private events has seemed too important for many psychologists to be given up, so a restriction to experimental research will seem too severe for many sociologists. Moral commitment is widely viewed by them as a process many of whose aspects cannot be studied experimentally given present practical restrictions.

A status in a social system (both experimentors and human subjects always occupy such a status) prescribes not only what its occupant is expected to do, but also, as we observed above, what others can do to him. The occupants of statuses high in the hierarchy of statuses can apply strong reinforcers to the many who hold statuses below them, but can only be reached by strong reinforcers from the few statuses above them. Low-ranked statuses, on the other hand, are exposed to reinforcement from the many statuses above them. The relative strength of stimuli that can be applied in interaction is thus a function of the position of persons involved in a status hierarchy. This inheres not in the historically conditioned vicissitudes of particular societies, but in the hierarchy itself. If persons of low rank succeed in applying strong stimuli to persons of high rank over any period of time, this simply changes positions in the hierarchy (as in revolution).

Because it involves the application of stimuli by one person to another, the right to perform experiments involves the relative status of the experimentor and subject. The more subordinate the subject, the stronger the stimuli that can be applied. If the abstract concept of a hierarchy of status be extended to interspecific interaction, it will be noted that common experimental animals, such as rats, pigs, pigeons, and fruit flies, have a very low status relative to that of humans. To borrow a phrase from Mr. Justice Taney, they have no rights that humans are bound to respect (except those extended through the grace of other humans, such as the antivivisectionists, who have hindered research on dogs and other household pets).

But status differences among experimentors and human subjects are seldom sufficiently great to give the experimentor much freedom in the selection of stimuli. Nazi concentration camps provided such a difference, but that in itself was the object of extreme moral objection from scientists. Medical experimentation generally proceeds as far as possible on experimental animals, and then, when it moves to human subjects, uses those with degraded statuses, such as prisoners and mental hospital inmates. The "operant conditioners," who follow Skinner with a strong sense of mission, tend to apply relatively strong schedules of reinforcement. But like medical experimentors they tend to work with "institutionalized" subjects (in mental hospitals and reformatories) because only here can they get the authority to apply fairly strong schedules of reinforcement that run to periods of days and weeks. The authority of the teacher over the student is used frequently to gain access to experimental subjects, as in introductory courses in psychology where a common part of the course requirement is that the student submit to experimentation (usually by graduate students). But this authority is limited (the student, who often takes undergraduate psychology because it is an easy way to meet a "science requirement," may choose to drop the course and take physical anthropology instead), and so too is the strength of applicable stimuli. As a general rule, psychologists and other behavioral scientists do not stand very high in the status hierarchy of the societies in which they work, and this substantially restricts the strength and duration of stimuli they may present in experimentation with human subjects. Here lies a dilemma. The more representative of a general population is the group from which experimental subjects are drawn (and many theoretically relevant populations are dispersed throughout a society) the weaker and briefer are the stimuli that the experimentor has the license to apply; the more subordinate the group (and thus the stronger and more persistent stimuli that may be applied) the less likely it is to represent populations of general interest. The situation is not likely to change until psychologists become kings (or tyrants), when all become subordinate to them and strong stimuli can be applied to widely dispersed and representative samples.

The problem of sampling the full range of a variable rather than a population of interest is less difficult. In principle, the failure to utilize the entire range of a variable should not be a serious shortcoming. But it becomes a serious shortcoming in research on humans for three reasons.

First, the variables in this field tend to be ill-defined. It is often quite difficult to determine whether the theoretical conception of a variable is adequately represented by measurements in concrete research: what is claimed to be only a difference in degree may really be a difference in kind, and *vice versa*. Defects in definition are often alleged to result from a lack of empiricist fervor and resulting incompleteness in "operational definition." More often they result from a shortage of research funds. It is really rather easy, once you get the hang of imagining an unlimited budget, to think up well operationalized and testable yet theoretically adequate definitions of concepts; yet pretty close to impossible actually to get the funds to measure the massive complexes of behavior to which they refer. We therefore make do with feeble indicators and egregiously crude approximations. And we do not cut down theory to match the poverty of our research because even modestly funded disciplines benefit from elegant theories.

Second, even when concepts are well defined in terms of research operations, behavioral science measurements are still quite crude—again largely because thorough research is expensive. The range of "instrument error" is often greater than the small variations produced in economically and morally constrained experiments.

The third and probably the most serious difficulty in studying small increments of a variable is that these indicate the effect of large increments only when the effect is linear or at least monotonic. Yet the emission of a response is seldom a linear function of variables of reinforcement even in the simplest cases.[8] Most of these functions appear to be exponential, and

---

[8] Few of the response-reinforcement graphs that make up most of Skinner and Ferster (1957) are linear; many (especially interval schedules) are non-monotonic as well.

these of course can easily be reduced to linearity. But the problems of linearity and monotonicity are made worse when experimental reinforcers are not primary but conditioned, and given the lack of genuinely naive human subjects, most of the reinforcers which can be used in experiments depend on prior conditioning for their effect. Money reinforces because it is a complex symbol of status (thus large payments can reward, but smaller ones punish, because they demean the subject's status; while no monetary reward at all is "neutral") and the response is not a monotonic function of the exchange value of the money. Food reinforces not because the organism has been reduced to 80 per cent of normal body weight (as Skinner is able to do with his pigeons) but because even to a satiated organism it has become a symbol of primary group solidarity or some other complex of strong and abiding rewards. The relation between such secondary or learned reinforcers and any particular activity is itself a function of other stimuli with which they have been associated through prior conditioning (as a past generation of sociologists would say, "The meaning of the symbol is a function of the situation"), and in practice it is truly difficult to show that this relationship can be reduced to combinations of linear functions.

To be sure, there are quantitative specialists who will admit that if life is not linear, at least it is monotonic, and this is all that many quantitative analyses require. But this brings to mind Harlow's accusation that simple-minded experiments are what make simple-minded theories of learning credible. If all social life were interconnected by a simple network of non-monotonic functions, there is an excellent chance that the behavioral scientists of this era who are fond of "hard data and large N's" would never discover them, simply because their preferred statistical techniques, based on the venerable Pearsonian r, decompose determinate non-monotonic functions to a residue of "variance unexplained."[9]

The tandem problems of sampling relevant populations and measuring small increments of large variables are not, of course, limited to experiments, and they do not imply that experimental research cannot play an important and perhaps vital role in the study of human affairs. But they do tend to constrain experimental more than observational research. The natural social world abounds with events relevant to reinforcement theories (and to others as well) whose full range of effect over a large and heterogeneous population are relatively easy to observe, but difficult or impossible to replicate or

---

9 The theoretical possibilities for non-monotonic functions are enormous. Psychoanalytic theory is one rich source. Now it could be that all non-monotonic functions can, through analytical reduction of their variables into simpler ones, be expressed as a network of monotonic functions. Something like this seems to be what experimentalists hypothesize in their claims that experimentation gets at "fundamental processes." But this hypothesis can only be proved inductively, that is, by actually reducing all functions to monotonic functions. Meanwhile, various disciplines and specialties are consigned to study "complex" variables and non-monotonic functions.

apply to the same group under conditions of experimentation. This is why the habit of experimental positivism is not heuristic but obfuscatory, and why observational rather than experimental data will better test a reinforcement theory of moral commitment. In practice the problems involved in operational definition and measurement adequate to a wide range of theories have been overlooked because of a preoccupation with experimental procedure.[10]

The work of B. F. Skinner himself reflects clearly the heuristic risk of experimental positivism. Skinner's advocacy of experimental methods is almost as strong as his disavowal of subjective interpretations. Yet he cannot limit his scientific curiosity to what he can afford to study experimentally, with the result that he moves from the narrowly experimental results of *Schedules of Reinforcement* to astute but utterly anecdotal observations in his *Science and Human Behavior* and *Verbal Behavior* and, in his most directly sociological (and most popular) work, *Walden Two,* across the river and into the trees of fiction. Most of Skinner's students respond to his experimental emphasis rather than to his intellectual achievement of a comprehensive and consistently behavioristic method of explanation, and so far none of them have been able to match his scientific impact.

Perhaps one reason why psychologists have relied so much on experimentation has been the rather peculiar record of non-experimental research on children. Early excursions of psychologists into the natural social world— as in studies published between 1937 and 1949 by Miller, Davis, and Dollard—used anthropological field methods, a problem-oriented sociology, and many psychoanalytical concepts.[11] In combination these produced results whose reliability and validity were questionable: research of this sort seemed to be able to prove anything and therefore gave rise to the suspicion that it really proved nothing. Ethnographic reliability looked especially weak after 1951, when Oscar Lewis restudied the Mexican town of Tepoztlan that Robert Redfield had studied earlier and came to quite different conclusions (Lewis, 1951; Redfield, 1930).[12]

Somewhat later (1953 and continuing) came another wave of "cross-

---

10 The hazards of limiting psychological research to experiments has not been completely unnoticed. Barker and Wright (1954) advocate field studies which they call "psychological ecology," and which they have carried out in their own work. It is surprising that their approach has been little noted by sociologists, for the psychological ecology of humans is nothing more or less than the subject matter of sociology.

11 Dollard (1949); Davis and Dollard (1940); Miller and Dollard (1941).

12 Redfield was apparently out to vindicate the happy *gemeinschaft* of his folk-urban dichotomy and found what he wanted to find: Lewis had other suspicions and reached different conclusions. For a comparison of the two studies, see Lewis (1951, pp. 427–42).

cultural" studies (see, for example, Whiting and Child [1953]; B. Whiting [1963]; and Minturn and Lambert [1964]). These still relied methodologically on ethnography and conceptually on Freud, and the net result was not much more likely than the earlier work to convince psychologists of the need for more "naturalistic" data.[13]

Between experimentation and ethnography lies the interrogatory survey. Less flexible and exploratory than ethnography, it also allows better statistical controls: less rigorous than experimentation, it is a far more efficient way to assess the end result of a long process in time and (in some cases) can measure more completely the effects of strong social reinforcers, if not the reinforcers themselves. Surveys have their own shortcomings: they are subject to many of the same constraints of cost as experiments, and they sometimes attempt to operationalize and measure complex processes and concepts through inadequate or even trivial interrogations. Surveys are poor tools for investigating deviant behavior because, relying as they do on verbal reports, they are easily put off course by the frequent discrepancy between actual rates of conforming and verbal reports of these rates. Yet modern survey analysis can still produce useful explanations, especially in the study of macrosociological variables (such as those involved in the field of political sociology) which operate on too large a scale to be studied cheaply in any other way.[14] Eventually survey research may throw considerable light on the hypotheses of the present theory. Survey interviews only indirectly measure most forms of reinforcement, but they show its effects and are especially useful in identifying factors that differentiate reinforcement schedules.

The psychologist Urie Bronfenbrenner has called psychologists' attention in several publications to the amount of variation in conventional psychological variables that can be explained by age, sex, and social class. These staple variables in demographic and survey research (and sociological theory) have been traditionally neglected in psychology precisely because they cannot readily be manipulated as independent variables in experiments. They are basic to status ascription, however, and thus define important schedules of social reinforcements. In his paper "The Role of Age, Sex, Class, and Culture in Studies of Moral Development," Bronfenbrenner reports what happened when child psychologists began to look at the social environment:

---

[13] Somewhat less ethnographic is the survey study of Sears, Maccoby, and Levin (1957). But the object in that work is to delineate patterns of child rearing not by observing interaction between mothers and children, but by interviews of mothers— who often are egregious hypocrites. The sample leaves something to be desired and often the gap between "concept" (an elaborate pattern of reinforcement or psychodynamic process) and "indicator" (interrogations) is so great as to make much of the book quite unpersuasive.

[14] A widely cited (and controversial) article in this regard is Lipset (1959).

...Until relatively recently, psychologists were much preoccupied with documenting observable changes with age in practically every variable that they had succeeded in measuring. The result was an impressive array of apparently highly consistent variations as a function of the developmental level of the child. But then, with the growth of the interdisciplinary approach in the behavioral sciences, investigators of developmental trends began to look for possible variation as a function of the child's role in society—his sex, his ordinal position, and the social status, ethnicity, and religious background of his parents. With the introduction of these social factors, the seeming generality, simplicity, and regularity of developmental age trends were challenged first from one quarter, then another. As a result, the notion underlying much of American child psychology as late as the 1940's of a normal maturational sequence that could be expected of all children everywhere was cast into serious doubt. In its place there emerged a social-situational conception of development in which maturational conditions were accorded only a vague and somewhat secondary importance [1964].

This statement probably overemphasizes the dominance of the social perspective. The notion of environment-free development (especially moral development) is still very much alive, and the studies which Bronfenbrenner cites in support of his view of increasing appreciation by psychologists of social effects tend either to be neglected or quite recent. That psychologists ever believed in a "normal maturational sequence" shows how experimental procedures can obscure strong environmental variables: putting all their faith in the power of the experiment, psychologists studied what they could experiment on easily. This turned out to be a remarkably homogeneous group (sometimes their own children).

The variables that Bronfenbrenner discusses are also powerful in explaining the behavior of adults. Although as components of familial status ascription they are not the only variables of which social organization may be composed, they are the only ones that can be used to distinguish among children at the time of their birth and thus to organize specialized training early in life. Yet for both economic and moral reasons they cannot be manipulated to any significant degree as independent variables in an experiment. If these variables are important, two conclusions follow: first, experimental and quasi-experimental procedures are especially ill-suited for the study of their effect on children; second, if the definitions of "status" and "interaction" that were advanced in Chapter III are accepted, training of children in terms of these ascribed statuses is a process of social reinforcement.

Longitudinal Studies

In what psychologists call a "longitudinal study" (and survey research specialists a "panel study") the same persons are observed at two or more points in time. There are few such studies in the literature on child development (one is Kagan and Moss, 1962). In part this probably reflects the special difficulty of longitudinal experiments, but the fact is that all longitudinal research with humans tends to be difficult and thus infrequent. There is little more of it in sociology than in psychology.

It is possible to train a pigeon or a rat in a hurry, and if this is done in a psychological experiment the results can be published in time to accelerate a promotion for the author, thereby rewarding him and increasing the probability that he will do more such quick and timely studies in the future. The journals of psychology therefore contain many studies which, whatever else they have to recommend them, are at least quick and timely. But it takes longer to train human children, even in some of the simpler skills that their complex social environment requires and even though the domination of infants by parents and the power of the reinforcers at their command is not too much less than the experimenter has over his animal subjects.

One broad theme of Freudian psychology—perhaps the one with which non-Freudians can most readily agree—is the claim that childhood events affect adult life. A theory of reinforcement does not deny this at all, although it is likely to amend it by postulating intermediate reinforcements in the intervening period. A sociological reinforcement theory would go further and postulate interrelations among the reinforcers. The particular type of toilet training that a mother uses, for example, is not likely to be idiosyncratic. It will have much in common with the parent's sanctions of other areas of the child's behavior, and much in common also with those used by other mothers in the same situation—that is, others of the same age, social class, education, and ethnic affiliation, who are dealing with children of the same age, sex, birth order, and so forth. Thus "anal compulsiveness," as that term is used among educated laymen, refers not just to excretory habits (whose details are seldom very public) but rather to a broad and public disposition toward orderliness, routinization of activity, and so forth, of which some aspects of toilet training are only the imputed primordial event. Just as adults come to discriminate such a pattern in the behavior of others, so children can too (although they probably will not give it the same name), and that much better when what they are discriminating is also a pattern of sanctions to which they are subject. Discrimination in such a case leads to the avoidance of punishment and thus is highly reinforced, whether verbally reported or not. "Anal compulsiveness" may thus result not from premature toilet training but because orderliness and routinization are rewarded in themselves, starting at an early age and continuing later, especially in school and other bureaucratic settings that the young widely encounter.

But learning to be orderly is likely to take time, even without any repressed Freudian effects. The process of anticipatory socialization involves a considerable passage of time between learning a status and actually performing in it. Little girls learn to flirt long before they are nubile, and to act maternal long before they become mothers. Any such process—especially, perhaps, that of toilet training in westernized societies—very likely starts with discrimination that long antedates verbal labels. When the behavior in question is highly moral, its verbal representation will be rewarded when it obscures discrimination and punished when it facilitates it, for the reasons advanced in Chapter III. Thus areas of behavior subject to strong institutional controls, such as sex and excretion, are themselves first referred to, especially when addressing the young, in special terms that evoke strong emotions but only vaguely identify details of behavior.

The result is that the interrogatory methods which sociology uses as a substitute for longitudinal observations of behavior are quite severely disadvantaged. Suppose we ask our respondent to describe his first experience on excretory conditioning. The responses are worse than useless: the experience preceded verbal representation, and the names he learned for describing his own excretory behavior were selected not to identify but to obscure. When Swanson chose to define "internalization" as learning whose circumstances the person cannot verbally report, he certainly indicated why retrospective interrogation may not be a good way to study it. When commitment is strong, emotion is strong and cognition weak, and this precludes most interrogatory study of moral commitment and other emotional processes. In principle this difficulty can be got round by "projective" techniques, in which a particular response denotes past events by a meaning the respondent cannot fathom. The trouble, of course, is that most of the time the investigator can't really fathom their meaning either, although he usually professes earnestly that he does. The actual determination of the significance or meaning of the projective response would require just that kind of detailed comparison to the behavioral history of the respondent whose unavailability, paradoxically, inspires some psychologists to invent projective techniques.

Both sociologists and psychologists sometimes attempt to offset the lack of longitudinal data by observing a class of adults, and then studying a contemporary group of children whose present situation is presumed to be similar to what the adults in question went through when they were children. But this use of "cross-sectional" data in place of longitudinal data involves great risks in rapidly changing societies, and most textbooks in research methods routinely condemn it. In societies which are changing rapidly the span of a generation, "ordinarily but a mere moment in the life of a social system," includes a great deal of structurally significant change itself, and we do not know whether we are measuring the changing effects of constant reinforcement or changes in the reinforcement. This risk is greatest not in industrial societies but in pre-literate societies, which anthropologists study with "one-shot" ethnographic methods. It is probably fair to say that anthropologists have tended much more than sociologists to underestimate the massive changes in all aspects of these societies which follow from contact with economically and militarily dominant western societies. In sum, the shortcomings of cross-sectional studies, together with the scarcity of genuinely longitudinal ones, and the long time involved in the process of human moralization, all combine with the emphasis on experimentation to exclude from the literature the data needed either to confirm or to confute a reinforcement theory of morality.

The Psychoanalytic Fallacy

The doctrines of Sigmund Freud have long been debated from a variety of points of view, and their substantial impact on research on children shows once again the role of theory as a guide to selection among the infinite variety of topics available for research. In their original formulations, Freud's theories were analogs of a reinforcement theory. How a child was toilet trained, for example, was held to determine a broad and diffuse "personality structure" later on. In such an interpretation, both the independent and dependent variables are behavioral events.

Although the development of Freud's thought is a topic best left to specialists in that field, one transition that stands out clearly for psychoanalytic doctrine as a whole is the movement away from external events to interrelations among "internal" processes. Originally the constructs of "id," "ego," and "superego" were invoked to explain relations between childhood conditioners and adult behavior, but increasingly the first and last parts of the sequence were slighted while the middle internal psychodynamics were emphasized. It is in this connection that the psychoanalytic approach is discussed here—that is, in terms of what it has inspired research workers *not* to study. Preoccupation with psychoanalytic constructs in psychology and elsewhere has produced a learned incapacity to deal with the plain facts of commonplace behavior, to avoid the obvious in an effort to deal with the obscure. I call this "the psychoanalytic fallacy." More formally, it is the assumption that the *explanations of behavior by obvious and simple factors, especially those implicit in lay folklore or "common sense," are illegitimate or false; and that only explanations in terms of complex and obscure factors, especially those which are esoteric and unconscious, are legitimate and true.* A particular esoteric theory may, of course, prove to be true, and an exoteric one false. The error of the psychoanalytic fallacy consists in the conclusion that an exoteric theory *must* be false, not because the data confute it but because the data are obvious. Such reasoning usually goes: "This explanation is superficial, for it does not take into account the profound effect of hidden psychodynamic factors," and so forth and on.[15]

The psychoanalytic fallacy is widely committed in interpretations of research in child development. Explanations in terms of plain facts are avoided in favor of attempts, almost necessarily unsuccessful, to investigate childish psychodynamics. The best examples are found in research on identification, where what gets studied often seems very remote from the original concept.

The psychoanalytic fallacy derives in part from the placement of psychoanalytic constructs on the subjective or methodologically private level, where they partake liberally of the defects of such constructs outlined in Chapter I. The psychoanalytic concern with unconscious mechanisms means further, however, that these mechanisms are not available for verbal report. And since these reports constitute the only possible evidence of subjective states, this makes the direct verification of the operation of these constructs inherently impossible. Scientific commentators are thus disposed to criticize psychoanalytic theory because its theories depend on many hypothetical constructs whose presence or absence is difficult to verify. Correspondingly the advocates of psychoanalysis—which is vastly more than just a scientific theory—become impatient and critical of scientific attention to evidence and verification. Murdock, even while acknowledging the heuristic value of Freudian ideas, put the matter well when he averred that "the theoretical system of psychoanalysis is in the highest degree obscure, that its hypotheses are frequently overlapping and even contradictory, and that it fulfills few of the requisites of a rigorous, testable, and progressive body of scientific knowledge (1948, p. xvii).

Indeed, it is probably fair to say that the main appeal of psychoanalytic ideas is literary or religious, rather than scientific. The connection of Freudian ideas to literature has often been noted; less often the connection to religion. Yet psychoanalytic lore has many structural and functional similarities to ordinary religious doctrine. Religious doctrines are unverifiable because of their reference to superempirical states; psychoanalytic ones are unverifiable because of their systematic emphasis on the subjective. Both are inherently unprovable and therefore also not disprovable, making possible claims of certainty and a dogmatic attitude that are not always respected in the empirical sciences. Yet the popular quest for certainty is a persistent one which science cannot easily satisfy, and as religious belief is eroded by competing scientific explanation, psychoanalytic doctrine (whose antagonism

---

15 For examples see Dollard (1949, p. 143) and the second thoughts on psychoanalytic explanation by Spiro (1965, p. xiii). But at the same time Spiro is still tempted by the obscure depths: "Much of social science research seemed to me to be ...superficial, if not wrong, because of its neglect of the unconscious determinants of

to scientific explanation is less clearly understood) acquires a special appeal. It becomes a functional alternative to religion, and this gives it an intellectual vitality which is the despair of its critics.

The viewpoint of the sociology of knowledge suggests perhaps another reason for the popularity of psychoanalytic ideas and the unpopularity of some competitive views. Different social classes use different "models of man" and invoke different "rhetorics of motive." The model of man held by lower classes in Anglo-American society stresses the strength of primary drives, the ubiquity of simplistic calculation of objective consequences, and the fragility of a system of morality that depends solely on symbols to control primordial animal drives. It is the theory of the cracker-barrel philosopher of the country store, the predatory "psychology" of the shrewd but unlettered salesman, the theme that underlies the folklore and commercial diversions of disadvantaged groups, and the emphasis that lends the plays of Bertold Brecht so much of their verisimilitude and pungency. It has some points in common with the "model of man" implied by the present theory.

Class mobility, the movement from membership in one social class to another within a single lifetime, has a lively symbolic aspect, as shown in "reference group" behavior. This involves not only the acceptance, which is widely recognized in the sociological literature, of symbolic forms believed to be characteristic of higher strata, but also a less well recognized rejection of those of lower strata. This includes the rejection of the model of man held by the lower classes. The socially mobile person is disposed to assent to doctrines which confute this lower-class model, and thus to believe in models which stress the strength of secondary drives or the transformation of primary ones, which replace simplistic calculation of external effects with complex internal dialectics, and which stress the force of symbolic morality, especially the power of pure symbols to modify animal appetites. Thus psychoanalytic doctrines may have prospered not only because they are functional alternates to religion but also because they refute the lower-class model. If so, then learning these doctrines is reinforced by social mobility. This may partly explain the popularity of psychoanalytic ideas first in psychology and then in sociology, for these fields have served in that sequence as popular routes of upward mobility in the academic professions. The incomprehensibility and unreality of psychoanalytic explanations to the working class, who have a much keener sense of parsimony in explanation than do their social betters, may render them especially appealing to mobile

---

behavior." Such research will be neither superficial nor wrong if it *explains* the "unconscious determinants." The "level of personality" may be a viable level of analysis, but if so it still is subject in principle to explanation by variables not on that level.

intellectuals. To recite the psychoanalytical lexicon is one way to sanskritize in the West.[16]

The psychoanalytic fallacy occurs not only in research in child development but also in studies of moral commitment and conformity. Often data on public conformity are overlooked in favor of speculations about private guilt. In other cases, the plain facts of behavior are used as dependent variables (as, for example, among the vast literature on juvenile delinquency) but are explained in terms of psychodynamic constructs whose existence always has to be inferred. The method of inference is introspective, relying on extrapolation from "the phenomenology of the moral man." The research worker—a moral man and usually middle-class as well—reflects on his own subjective experience and infers that what he discovers in this way also occurs in the persons whose behavior he is trying to explain. Now if objective rather then subjective explanatory factors were being sought, the great difference in the reinforcements to which the research worker and his subjects have been exposed would become apparent and the assumption of similar phenomenological content would be rendered dubious. But this objective difference resides precisely in those obvious plain facts which commission of the psychoanalytic fallacy leads the research worker to avoid. And those research workers who avoid the psychoanalytic fallacy often tend instead to be constrained in their perspective by experimental positivism. Between these two constraints, little research gets done that is really suitable for testing a reinforcement theory of morality.

Identification

Probably no concept is invoked more frequently in discussion of moral development or "character formation" than that of *identification*. Probably,

---

16 This is illustrated in a "negative case" in the remarkable similarity of the conclusions of Homans (1961) to the apothegms of the cracker-barrel philosopher. Indeed, Homans cites many of these apothegms which he later derives from more elementary propositions about reinforcement and the forms of social interaction. Homans' book is unique both in its mixture of learning theory and sociology and, as a sociological work, in the extent to which it corresponds to the lower-class model of man. Homans himself can afford to do this, however, with an immunity to his own position that few sociologists can match. He does not need to sanskritize (to affect Brahmin status by imitating the language and manners of Brahmins) for he is a Brahmin (Boston) by birth, wealthy by inheritance, and a professor at Harvard. See the valuable and remarkably candid "Autobiographical Introduction" in his *Sentiments and Activities* (1962, p. 4). The hazard we run in presenting a cracker-barrel theory of moral commitment to a socially mobile audience with a propensity for sanskritizing must be fearfully acknowledged. For further discussion of the impact of sanskritizing on sociological theory and the origin of the "Bunthorne syndrome" (the ascription of great profundity to bad grammar) see my review of Parsons (1968, especially pp. 455–56).

too, no other term has a broader range of meanings, not all of which are consistent with all the others.[17] That the term is so popular, and that its meanings are so confused, testifies once again to the influence of Freud and psychoanalytic thought. Freud's *charisma* has extended to the concepts he advanced: lesser men note that their own poor work will be judged more wise the more they make use of the wise Freud's words. This worsens confusion about a term which (as several commentators have mentioned) was not used very consistently by Freud himself. Observing this process elsewhere, Boring justified the inclusion of much biographical material in the *History of Experimental Psychology* (1950) by calling attention to the importance in psychology—even, hard, tough, data-bound, experimental psychology—of the argument by authority, as compared to the appeal to evidence. "Men," he reminds us, "have mattered much" (1950, p. x). Often we lack evidence in science, but never authorities.

The process to which the term "identification" is assumed to refer can be explained more economically in terms of reinforcement. Here as elsewhere the data are inadequate, but the need for data can be greatly reduced by an exposition of the logical difficulties that result if we assume a theory of identification to be true. We need assume only that (1) parents are the principal objects of identification, or "models," for children, and (2) some of what children learn varies by sex and age.

The concept of identification already has many critics, but few of them have gone so far as to recommend that it be abandoned as a lost cause. Most have tried instead to rescue the term by modification or qualification of its definition. Such rescue missions testify to the influence of the psychoanalytic persuasion, even on its critics. Defenders of the concept of identification have also argued that it is necessary in explaining moral development precisely because the mechanism of reinforcement is inadequate for this task.

Theories of identification also draw support from experimental positivism. Note this remarkable discussion of identification by Sears, Maccoby, and Levin:

---

[17] See, for example, Slater (1961). Slater offers a "minimal" and general definition of identification as "any tendency for an individual to seek to maximize his similarity to another person in one or more respects"; his two types of identification, "personal" and "positional," involve respectively identification with a concrete individual, "motivated primarily by ego's love and admiration for [a concrete and individual] alter," and identification "with the situation or role of alter...motivated not by love but by envy and fear" (p. 113).

See also the monograph by Winch (1962); especially the "semantic morass sketched in the foregoing paragraphs" (pp. 12–28 of his work). In escaping from the morass, Winch is led to conceive of identification as "the more or less lasting influence of one person on another" and of his monograph as an attempt to "arrive at a sociological explanation of interpersonal influence" (pp. 2–3). But if this is his mission, one may well ask why he retained the term "identification" at all.

If one wants to speculate quite beyond the bounds of any testable hypotheses, one can imagine that the human capacity for identification may be one of the major factors accounting for the extraordinary pre-eminence of our species. No more than a few thousand years ago, man was but a superior kind of ape. Now he is the intellectual master of his universe. The years are too few for biological evolution to have accounted for the change. Of course, the accretion of culture is in part responsible, but human culture is now so complex that each new generation could not possibly learn it all if each tiny element had to be taught through laboriously arranged rewards and punishments. The child's spontaneous tendency to "try on" the roles he observes around him, and thus learn the actions implied in these roles, makes for enormous efficiency in this learning [1957, pp. 392–93].

What a limited view of the effects of social structure is expressed here! In the laboratory to be sure, rewards and punishments are "laboriously arranged." But the admittedly complex schedule of reinforcements required for a growing child to learn what he does outside the laboratory (always vastly less than "all the culture") has long been the result of social structure, that is, the organization of interaction and the division of labor and learning, which, with all their complexities, are no less likely to have evolved than is the human constitution that is able to learn from it. The limited perspective of the social environment produced by experimental positivism inspires a quest for explanations in which social processes play a subsidiary part, and the concept of identification offers both an appealing psychodynamic obscurity and an instant convenience of application.

Sanford (1955) quoted E. C. Tolman on the rather general meaning the term had acquired by then. Identification "refers to the process (a) wherein an individual tries to copy—to take as his pattern or model—some other older (or in some other way looked-up-to or envied) individual; (b) of the adherence of the individual to any group of which he feels himself a part; and (c) the acceptance by an individual of a cause" (Tolman, 1943; cited in Sanford, 1955). Our concern is with Tolman's first usage, since the other two would appear to be explainable as some sort of generalization from whatever mechanism accounts for the first. Hill offers a still more general summary: in his view, the three related terms, *identification, introjection,* and *internalization,*

    ...all involve some relation between an·individual...(or) subject (S), and another person or personalized entity, the model or M, such that S's behavior is in some way patterned after M's. However, these terms may refer either to a state of affairs or to the process which brought it about; the process may be a person, a group, or an idea; and the relation may involve specific responses, broad meanings, or emotional reactions [1960, p. 317].

This emphasis on some process of modeling wherein one person's behavior comes to be like another's is notable because Hill's more general concern is to advance the explanation in terms of reinforcement, rather than any concept of modeling that goes on apart from reinforcement.

Sanford concludes his paper by arguing against using "identification" in a narrow sense and remarks, as we have already, that internalization need not be necessarily unconscious:

> Accepting parental standards as a means for pleasing [the parents] and as a means for controlling impulse does not require the operation of any peculiarly psychoanalytic mechanism. The acceptance is by and into the ego system, the whole process may be largely conscious; standards accepted in this way may contribute heavily to the more or less mature conscience.

He then recommends more attention to reinforcement:

> I propose, in conclusion, that we do two things. First, we should give more attention to those superego elements that have been based upon introjection. Second, we should consider that normal character development can be largely explained without benefit of either identification or introjection on the basis of common forms of learning. A child learns which of his actions please, and which displease, his parents, which win him love, which disapproval; he learns what reactions are effective in inhibiting those impulses which if allowed free rein would lead to catastrophe; he learns how to regard himself from the way others regard him; and in building his ego system and his self-conception he learns what to keep and what to discard [1955, p. 117].

The most comprehensive discussion of identification is in Bronfenbrenner (1960). This excellent paper gets into some of the sociological issues involved in identification, especially in Parsons' formulation of the concept. Bronfenbrenner discusses these further in his related chapter (1961). Although Bronfenbrenner criticizes the way the concept of identification gets used, he does not reject it. But his analysis of what Freud and others meant by "identification" provides a good beginning for the argument that it really refers to a process of operant conditioning: less the modeling of persons, more the learning of roles. Role learning may often resemble modeling, and such resemblance as there is gives some plausibility to the idea that "identification" is somehow a distinct process by which behavior changes, or (as is often said in the case of age-linked changes among humans) "develops." More plausibility is added by extrapolation from the socially enforced bond between parents and their children. This bond is a major part of the norms defining parental roles and guarantees that each infant born into an ongoing society is first physically nourished and protected and later trained to perform in a more-or-less specialized position in that society. Societies identify parents with children in order to reinforce the necessary functions of child care and status ascription (for a fuller statement of this point, see Davis [1940, 1949, pp. 97 ff.]). *What has happened in theories of child development is that the sociological bond is mistaken for a psychological process.*

The main problem with identification as an explanation of moral learning is this: the relationship between "subject" (or "identificand") and "model" is always in many ways very much less than any precise modeling and it is at the same time in other ways always very much more. This has not gone unnoticed. But in the absence (as Bronfenbrenner notes) of detailed studies of what gets called "identification," it is also plausible to assert that the similarities at the same point in time between the model and the subject, or between parent and child, are superficial in comparison to the differences. The similarities and differences can be classified roughly in terms of the differentiation of statuses by sex and age.

Differentiation of status by age and sex exists in all societies. The normative prescriptions of which these are composed vary: they may be precisely or imprecisely associated with a particular age or sex (while age may be defined broadly or narrowly), and transitions from one broad age group to another may be made continuously and gradually, or discontinuously and marked by rites of passage. But insofar as such differentiations do occur, they complicate greatly the acquisition or change of behavior by the process of identification.

If we assume that identification is a process that shapes behavior, and that statuses are differentiated by age and sex, then we reach one of the following alternative conclusions: (1) identification shapes only those aspects of behavior that are invariant with respect to age and sex; (2) models present to identificands only behavior appropriate for the age- and sex-status of the latter (for example, a six-year-old girl, or a mother who systematically acts like a six-year-old girl, is the only model for a six-year-old girl); or (3) some selective mechanism must operate whereby the identificand "acquires" from the model only those activities appropriate to the identificand's age and sex. Conclusions (1) and (2) presume socializing institutions and groups (families, schools, peers) organized in radically different ways from those actually found in extant human societies. Indeed, the more differentiated by age and sex the status structure of a society, the less identification can be attributed to families and the more it can be linked to homogeneous peer groups. Yet it is within the family—homogeneous as to class and inheritance group and heterogeneous with regard to age and sex—where most discussions assume that identification typically occurs. Further, in terms of frequency (and, possibly, intensity) of interaction, most young boys in the West associate with their mothers more than with their fathers, yet it is with the father that identification is supposed to occur. This problem exercised Freud and caused him to postulate a number of psychodynamic constructs. Condition (3) is not impossible, but is certainly a highly unparsimonious assumption if its sole purpose is to rescue the concept of identification.

Since youthful behavior is differentiated by age and sex, the mechanism of identification is not logically sufficient to account either for internalization or more generally for what we call "socialization." Some other mechanism is necessary also, and if it be the mechanism of reinforcement, then identification may not even be a necessary mechanism. Whatever the mechanism (or mechanisms) may prove to be, it must square with the fact that the agencies of socialization do not correspond in sequence or in frequency of interaction to the age and sex differentiations of status to which children are subject and to whose prescriptions they generally conform.

These differentiations are, of course, obvious once mentioned. In my view it is the disdain of the obvious and commonplace and pursuit of the esoteric and obscure—the psychoanalytic fallacy—that causes them to be overlooked. But there is possibly a more general reason why the discrepancy between models and identificands is neglected. Much of the discussion of socialization has a rather "middle-class" bias. The socializing group is typically assumed to be a complete nuclear family, operating efficiently as a going concern, with both parents taking an active if perhaps unequal part in the process. Thus Freud, Mowrer, and Parsons all use as an example the learning of the man's role by the young male child. They presume that the presence of the father as a model is required for the child to acquire male habits. Yet this overlooks abundant evidence that many male children grow up, especially among the "disreputable poor," in families where fathers are absent, yet still acquire an adult repertory that (however reprehensible it may be on other grounds) is certainly conspicuously masculine. Sons grow up to exhibit the same reprobate amalgam of sexual adventurism, indecision, idleness, brutishness, and petty criminality as their absent fathers. How did they acquire these habits? The plausible answer is not through identification but through differential reinforcement from their mothers, their peers, and other adults.

Even if we grant that reinforcement is not the only factor in behavioral change but merely one among several, it still has several characteristics that render it ubiquitous in the natural social world. It is possible for a reinforcing agent to instill patterns of conduct that the agent does not present in his (or her) own conduct. A devout and timorous Mexican mother can, by selective application of reward and punishment, raise her son to be a secular and courageous adult—a process that evidently does go on, from what we are told of the absence of fathers and the cult of "machismo" among males in Mexico's lower classes (Lewis, 1961, pp. 175 ff. and *passim*). These examples do not prove that identification never operates. But they do show that it does not operate everywhere. At the least some explanation of why it operates in some settings and not in others is required. The advantage of greater economy in explanation falls to the process of reinforcement.

In view of the relevance of father-absence to the test of theories of identification, it is notable that it has been little studied. One such study is that of Lynn and Sawrey (1959). The Norwegian case affords a good test (free from the lower-class factors of Latin America and elsewhere) because many sailors in that country's labor force work away from home, often for years at a time. The research and interpretation by Lynn and Sawrey are worth reviewing in some detail because they show how the effects of social reinforcement can get obscured in the field of child development.

Two issues are present in their study: the *effects* of absence, however produced; and the *mechanism* that produces them. There are several reasons why father-absence can be expected to produce effects. The father is not present to reinforce the child, nor is he present to interact with the mother, which interaction can both reinforce children and also shape the pattern of reinforcement provided solely by the mother during short periods when the father is not present. The absence of the father may also affect interaction with outsiders. The amount of interaction between husband and wife is in general negatively associated with the wife's amount of interaction with kin in her own line of descent—her sisters, for example, or especially her mother. Since the two sexes often disagree about child rearing, a boy raised by a mother who meanwhile interacts with her husband may well behave differently than one raised solely by a company of women. But this need not result from a process of identification and from different models. It may well derive from a different schedule of reinforcement. Lynn and Sawrey review studies that show, with varying degrees of persuasiveness, that there is indeed a difference in children's behavior, especially for boys, according to whether the father is present or absent. But the authors' hypothesis is that this difference is produced by the process of identification.

Lynn and Sawrey's set of hypotheses is interesting in itself.

The following predictions were made as to the direct effects of father-absence: (1) More father-absent boys would show immaturity than father-present boys; (2) Being insecure in their identification with the father, the father-absent boys would show stronger strivings toward father-identification than father-present boys; (3) The father-absent boys would react to their insecure masculine-identification with compensatory masculinity; and (4) The father-absent boys would demonstrate poorer peer adjustment than father-present boys and than father-absent girls. (5) It was also predicted that father-absent girls, perhaps threatened by the absence of one parent, would become more dependent on the mother than would father-present girls [pp. 258–59].

Several comments can be made on these hypotheses. Hypotheses 2 and 3 give the whole set a rather tautological character. The general logic of father-identification is that the boy behaves like his father because his father is present to serve him as a model. No father, no identification. But here we are asked to believe that "father-absent boys...show stronger strivings toward father-identification," resulting in "compensatory masculinity." No father, *more* identification. Obviously, this won't do.

A look at the data themselves renders them unpersuasive. The research is reported as if it were an experiment, with all of the "experimental" and "control" terminology and conventional tests of significance of results. Yet the independent variable, the presence or absence of a father, was not manipulated. The data themselves are not records of observation of ordinary social behavior that identification might affect, or even verbal reports of such behavior. They are, instead, results of doll-play "projective tests" and conceptually uneconomical and rather tenuous interpretations of interviews. That the child "identifies" with the doll, and that placing the doll in either a bed or a crib reflects the extent of his identification with a parental model, is highly problematic to say the least. Neither the interview schedule nor selected relevant questions are reported, and what is reported on the determination of "compensatory masculinity" is unpersuasive in the extreme. The key problem here, however, is not methodological but conceptual. "Identification" is vaguely construed, and the dominant reference is not to any kind of behavior but to private and unconscious events, fundamentally untestable, and which no amount of research, good or bad, will ever illuminate.

It may be possible to distinguish empirically between behavior acquired through identification and behavior acquired through reinforcement. If so, then we could not reject "identification" as an explanatory concept simply because it is uneconomical and replace it with a concept of reinforcement, for explanations solely in terms of reinforcement, though economical, would then be incomplete. Suppose a child is placed in a situation in which, first, he is presented with a model; second, the model performs a number of activities, some rewarded and some punished (these rewards and punishments previously having been established as effective with this particular child, to permit vicarious reinforcement); third, the child is observed to determine whether he does what he saw the model do; but fourth, these acts are rigorously protected from any nonvicarious reinforcement. If the child does what the model was rewarded for, but does not do what the model was punished for, the process is vicarious learning as defined in Chapter II. The child has learned that what rewards others may well reward him too, so he is more likely do what the model did preceding the reward. But if the child performs not only activities for which the model has been rewarded but also those for which the model was punished, then the process is something other than vicarious reinforcement and may involve identification.

Bandura and Walters (1963) cite a study that relates to this hypothetical example. A "model" (a young woman) interacted with children in a laboratory game, performing as well "relatively novel verbal, motor, and aggressive responses that were totally irrelevant [or so we are told] to the game to which the child[ren]'s attention was directed." The model was "rewarding and nurturant" toward one group of children, whereas toward another she was "distant and nonrewarding. The authors observed that children who experienced the rewarding interaction with the model imitated her behavior to a substantially greater extent than did children with whom the same model had reacted in a distant and nonrewarding way (Bandura and Walters, pp. 95–96, citing Bandura and Huston, 1961). This study, and related ones which Bandura and Walters review, give a new twist to the discussion. Children appear likely to behave like a model not only according to how the model is rewarded but also according to how the model rewards them. The separation of these two effects would require assessment of imitative behavior under conditions wherein some agency other than the model supplies the reinforcements, which was not the case in the study cited. But the varieties of social reinforcement demonstrated in such experiments suggest increasingly that the concept of identification is unnecessary in explaining changes in the behavior of children.

The Sequence of Events in the Moral Process:
A View of Anticipatory Socialization

The events involved in the process of moral commitment and social control can be viewed as a sequence and may be outlined as follows: first, an *act*, a part of the behavioral repertoire of persons and usually amenable to operant conditioning; second, *reinforcements*, mainly as sanctions (social reinforcements) but often including nonsocial primary reinforcers; third, *consequences* in interaction, so that the act is a stimulus and reinforcer to others, whose subsequent activity in turn stimulates the original actor. This last aspect of the process has usually been singled out in most discussions of social morality as its distinctively moral aspect.

In what order to these events occur? Since consequences, by definition, always have to follow the act, the only "degree of freedom" attaches to the reinforcement, which, by definition, always follows some particular act but which, with respect to a *class* of acts more generally, may precede any other act after that act defining the reinforcement. Further, only in abstraction do most acts occupy a single point in time; most concrete activities take a measurable span of time, and reinforcement may precede this span of time, follow it, or occur at some point within it. The effect of differences in the sequence is our present concern. It is quite possible that the effect of the reinforcement—and especially its *efficiency* (the ratio of the frequency or magnitudes of reinforcers to those of operants) may vary as a function of the time when it is applied. In this connection I first review some evidence and discussion of this variation in efficiency by Bandura and Walters. Then I consider the neo-Piagetian theory of Lawrence Kohlberg, and criticize the failure of his theory to consider the effects of symbolic anticipatory socialization—a case where symbolic reinforcement is supplied years in advance of the emission of the activities to which it relates.

Bandura and Walters review several experiments in which children are presented with the opportunity to commit a deviant act and are then subjected to punishment at various times during its commission.[18] The general conclusion is that the earlier the onset of punishment, the more effective the extinction of the deviant act in the future. A child who is punished when he reaches for an attractive but prohibited toy is less likely to reach for it in future settings (where playing with the toy is neither rewarded nor punished) than a child who is punished only after he has actually begun to play with the toy.

That these results should obtain is not surprising, especially in view of Homans' analysis of "cost" in social reward and punishment (1961, pp. 24 ff.). Assume that the prohibited act is either intrinsically rewarding or extrinsically rewarded (most immoral acts are one or the other, else there would be no need to sanction them). The child punished at the outset of transgression is punished before he gets the amoral reward of the transgression itself. But the child who gets punished after transgression receives both the punishment and the amoral reward.

"Cost," the reader will recall, is the punishment endured or reward foregone in connection with reception of a particular reward. In a "profitable" activity the reinforcing effect of the associated punishment or the reward foregone is less than that of the reward; otherwise there would be no net reward at all and no "profit." By reversing the valences one can equally well speak of "loss," which suggests in turn that cost can also have a negative value. I propose to call this negative value of cost "windfall," and to define it as the reward gained or other punishment avoided in connection

---

[18] Priority in the theoretical statement of effects of timing goes to Mowrer, in his *Learning Theory and Behavior* and *Learning Theory and Symbolic Processes* (both 1960), which were discussed in Chapter III of this work. Bandura and Walters review research of Aronfreed and Reber (1963); Aronfreed (1963); and Walters and Demkow (1963).

with receiving a particular punishment. The child who gets punished after he plays with a prohibited toy does at least have the fun of playing with it, and this is a windfall reward; while the child who is punished before his play or early in it gets little or no windfall reward. If the punishment is the same in both situations, it is reasonable to presume that windfall reward reduces the net reinforcing effect of a given punishment.

Hill's theory of guilt (1960) can also be examined in connection with timing of punishment. Hill's object is to account for the human propensity to confront oneself with *prima facie* punitive stimuli—especially such stimuli as are only symbolic. He suggests that this habit may come about through the following schedule of reinforcement. The child encounters an opportunity for transgression and commits a deviant act. It subsequently comes to the attention of his parents, who punish him. Hill points out that the punishment itself often takes the form of "withdrawal of love," that is, the cessation for (so far as the child can tell) an indefinite period of those parental symbolic gestures which the child has learned to associate with primary reinforcement. Punishment, in other words, is often not "short and swift," especially perhaps in the middle classes. But Hill suggests that there is one operant in the repertory of the child which will renew the valued flow of love: a *verbal* show of contrition. After the child makes some statement that convinces his parents that he is contrite—that is, that he has "internalized the norm" governing the transgression—love (symbolic reward) is once again extended.

There is some reason to believe that the "withdrawal of love" technique is indeed a very efficient schedule of reinforcement (Bandura and Walters, 1963, pp. 196–97). But its efficiency in reducing the probability of future transgression—as distinguished from its effect on verbal reports about the transgression—depends on the ability of the parents to assess the accuracy of verbal reports better than the child can do himself. Here the child has a great advantage over even the subtlest and most perceptive parents. He alone knows, if anybody knows at all, his "subjective intent"— what he really "plans to do" in the way of future transgression at the very time he confesses guilt and claims a desire never to transgress in the future. His parents simply cannot know what is going on in another organism's private mind, no matter how much they flatter themselves that they "know what their child is really thinking." If they knew, their child's mind would not be private. For information about what their child will probably do in the future, the parents rely, as in the nature of the case they must rely, solely on their child's public behavior (including his symbolic behavior, that is, his talk): all parents are practicing behaviorists no matter how devoutly they preach psychodynamics. The parents may attend, of course, to useful cues of which their child is unaware—to the impressions, in Goffman's terms, that he "gives off," rather than those he consciously "gives." Such cues may serve the parents as better predictors of what the child will do than the child's subjective states serve him as predictors of what he will do, but this is not always the case. The child is likely to learn early to discriminate between his own behavior and his verbal report of it. When he is subjected to a schedule of reinforcement in which sanctions not only follow the deviant act but are further contingent upon what he says about it, he is in effect reinforced for distinguishing not only between the "windfall" reward that comes with deviation and the subsequent punishment, but also among the various operants in his own repertory whose emission will terminate or attenuate that punishment. If the operant is a verbal profession, it has the further advantage of economy, for talk is cheap. The argument of Hill (and others) on this point is that emission of the verbal operant (confession of guilt) that terminates punishment leads in time to internalization of the norm which is defined by the sanctions thus terminated. But if our earlier hypotheses on hypocrisy are accepted, then the effect that this propensity to confess guilt following transgression will have on the propensity to transgress in the future depends on cognitive suppression of the distinctions among confession, a verbal report, and the behavior reported. Otherwise the child may easily calculate the following strategy for maximization of net reward: transgress, obtaining thereby the "windfall" reward, and, when discovered by sanctioners, emit a suitable confession of guilt. In the future, transgress only when the risk of discovery or punishment is low.

To be sure, the child who confesses his guilt and then is discovered transgressing again by the same sanctioning agents is liable to punishment not only for repetition of the act (which punishment may be more severe than in the first instance) but also for making an "insincere confession"—that is, one which failed to predict his future behavior. In such a case, the capacity of confession to terminate a given punishment may well be more than offset by the further punishment that often follows a proven false confession. The child then learns to make yet another distinction: for each combination of transgression (or class of transgression) and sanctioning agent, confession only terminates punishment once. To maximize probable net reward, each new transgression should risk discovery only before a *new* sanctioning agent. One thinks of students who use the same persuasive excuse for late or missing assignments over and over again, but never more than once on the same professor.

Thus we return to the ubiquity of hypocrisy. Hypocrisy is reinforced because sincerity, though normatively reinforced itself, requires for that reinforcement a comparison between an individual's verbal report of behavior and his subsequent behavior—a comparison that is often hard to make. The child is reinforced for hypocritical confession when he learns to confess only before those who are unlikely to observe his subsequent behavior. Perhaps this partly explains why parents so often regard their own children as more moral and more sincere than do other people. Because the parents are in a better position than other people to observe and sanction both transgression and sincerity, the child will be in fact more moral and sincere toward the parents than he is toward others.

The capacity of the transgressor to analyze the conditions of punishment, and subsequently to combine his acts and his verbal reports of them so as to "work the system" for maximum amoral reward depends on the sanction always being applied (when it is applied at all) after the act. One way to constrain this capacity, and keep people from working the moral system, would be to apply the sanction before the act. Formally, of course, this is impossible. But in practice the sanction in effect can come first, because symbolic sanctions can be applied before a *particular* act (not the same act which by definition must precede their application) by representing the act symbolically before it is actually performed by the person to whom the sanction is liable to be applied. A statement of the form, "If you do X, sanction Y [reward or punishment] will subsequently be applied to you," both identifies an act and can serve as its symbolic sanction. The sanctioning of one person can, through symbolic generalization to all persons in the same class and through vicarious reinforcement, also serve as a sanction of another person who may not himself have yet emitted the act that preceded the sanction. Although it is not possible for reinforcement effectively to precede the operant for organisms whose capacity for symbolic behavior or vicarious reinforcement is weak, it is possible in the case of humans for sanctions to precede actions in highly significant and practical ways. This is why anticipatory sanctions, and thus anticipatory socialization, loom so large in moral learning.

There is some reason to believe that anticipatory sanctions are generally quite efficient. The studies cited by Bandura and Walters (1963) all deal with the efficiency of reinforcement that *follows* an act by varying intervals. The shorter the interval, the greater the efficiency. By extrapolation from this empirical relation, we would expect efficiency to be even greater when the interval is negative—that is, when the sanction, represented symbolically, precedes the act. Anticipatory sanctions have another advantage: by inclusion in elaborate systems of moral belief, such as those based on religion, they can even deny that any windfall reward will accrue. Such systems take a long time to learn, and hence lend themselves especially well to anticipatory socialization.

Anticipatory socialization is not very precise. Its effects are broad and general rather than narrow and particular. But precision in reinforcement is not always necessary, either for the narrow interests of one individual who reinforces another, or for the broad interests of an ongoing society. A folk saying expresses the idea well: "Beat a child every day; if you don't know what he's done to deserve it, he will." Such a schedule of reinforcement, whatever its other consequences, will at least be general in its effects. And a general pattern of behavior, whether shaped by daily beatings or by other schedules, may be adaptable to social organization despite its lack of precision. In fact it may be more adaptable just because it *is* imprecise. If a society is to teach its children a broad and general pattern of behavior— such as the tendency to work hard, regardless of the object of work, as in the "Puritan ethic" of industrial societies—then that society may profitably adopt a pattern of highly anticipatory and very general socialization.

This emphasizes a key feature of age-graded statuses, perhaps especially in advanced societies. Persons in a particular age grade are not pre-scribed to limit their behavior solely to what is characteristic of their present age, although they are always so prescribed to some degree. They are also taught a great deal about what they will be doing in the future, through an often elaborate and complex symbolic rehearsal of acts and sanctions— acts which they will not perform, and sanctions which will not be applied, for several years to come. If there are any distinctive aspects of moral behavior that are produced by anticipatory socialization, theories of moral learning or development certainly need to take account of them.

Anticipatory socialization has probably evolved as a feature of advanced societies because it is highly efficient. Consider once again the universal normative problem of the regulation of sexual activity, variously expressed in rules on incest, premarital celibacy, marital priority, and so on. Sexual behavior is difficult to control. The reward value of many prohibited acts is high. The acts themselves tend to be performed in relative privacy (partly as a result of other norms), and thus are hard to discover and sanction. A society that would apply sanctions relatively late, after sexually mature operant behavior has already emerged, would face a task of nearly unmanageable proportions. In order to offset a powerful and recurring windfall reward, it must apply sanctions strong enough to overcome its reinforcing effects. Then too the sanctions would not only be costly because severe, but also because expensive investigation would be required to discover the transgressors. In contrast, the early application of sanctions trains a large undifferentiated population, without attending to the variable prob-ability of deviation for each member of the population. Not just those children who will later prove to be promiscuous, but almost all children, are taught the value of chastity and sexual constraint, by a program of symbolic anticipatory socialization which, though based on an elaborate ideology of myth and fact, still partakes of the economy and adaptability of all sym-bolic representations.[19] It is economical because it is cheaper to tell children that chastity will be rewarded and deviation punished in the future than it

---

[19] This is not to say that norms of sexual restraint are constant throughout societies or that conformity rates are constant even when the sanctions defining the norms are constant. But neither is symbolic anticipatory socialization constant. Both sexual amorality and weak or inconsistent symbolic anticipatory socialization are more frequent in lower strata.

is to apply actual rewards and punishments to the acts themselves. It is adaptable because the actual reinforcements can be symbolically represented as if *moral conformity were in fact the behavior more strongly rewarded overall.* The possibility of windfall reward is denied. Such a representation can be highly effective in the sexual moralization of pre-pubescent children, for they are able to learn well by symbolic representation the rewards of chastity and the punishment of carnality long before they can be directly reinforced by post-pubescent genital excitation. To be sure, symbolic anticipatory reinforcement must be followed by some amount of subsequent reinforcement, but it can be the smaller "maintenance" reinforcement rather than the larger "training" one.

Of course, a broad pattern of anticipatory socialization leads through incidental learning to many "side effects": not only do most young boys and girls restrain themselves before marriage (or at least more so than they would otherwise), but some women remain sexually unresponsive after marriage; and some young men, strongly conditioned to associate sex with matrimony, blurt out a hasty proposal of marriage to the first girl they manage to seduce. These side effects may seem unnecessary to the main tasks of socialization, and indeed are often criticized, especially by spokesmen for the diverse ideologies that pass for disinterested science under the name of "mental hygiene." But however poignant the "pathologies" of many persons who have been so conditioned, we know that modern complex societies can endure these personal effects of incidental learning. We do not know that they could do without the broad pattern of anticipatory socialization that produced them. Probably they could not, for without anticipatory socialization, moral learning and social control would come to assume so much of the society's resources as to be inconsistent with essential aspects of a complex organization.

The neglect of anticipatory socialization seems to me to be the main defect of studies of moral development in the tradition of Piaget (1928). The leading contemporary research psychologist in this tradition is Lawrence Kohlberg. In a series of studies beginning in 1958, Kohlberg has continued and elaborated Piaget's ideas, and, in some respects, subtly become *plus royaux que le roi.*[20] Kohlberg's work concentrates on moral *judgment,* evaluations of cases as measured by the verbal responses of children. Only incidentally do they refer to moral behavior apart from verbal references.

---

[20] I draw mainly from two long essays by Kohlberg: "Development of Moral Character and Moral Ideology" (1964); and "Moral Development and Identification" (1963). For a fairly complete bibliography of Kohlberg's writing until 1966, see his references to it (1966). Kohlberg's approach is well summarized by Brown (1965, pp. 404–7).

Yet his theories of moral judgment certainly have many implications for the analysis of behavior, which he does not fail to make explicit. They are interesting to the sociologist in many contexts besides the age-grading of anticipatory socialization.

Kohlberg holds that moral development is development in a truly genetic sense—that is, it proceeds from an "infantile" to a "mature" condition not as a function of schedules of reinforcement (age-graded or otherwise) but as a function of physiological growth and the passage of time, with social factors serving, if at all, only as "catalytic agents." More than once Kohlberg stresses the independence of moral development in his theory from sociological factors, and by "moral" he definitely means more than "in accord with social norms" (see, for example, 1964, p. 417). In some respects Kohlberg has presented a conception of an innate moral faculty analogous to Chomsky's conception of an innate linguistic faculty. The cautionary remarks we addressed to Chomsky's conception in Chapter II hence apply directly to Kohlberg's.

Indeed the whole Piagetian tradition seems studiously ambivalent as to the extent to which moral development is *determinate,* not only in relation to environmental but also to physiological factors. Often it suggests the possibility of what Parsons called voluntaristic acts, not completely determined by heredity or environment. This possible "free will" bias in Kohlberg's work is not the present concern, but it does suggest that followers of Piaget would be critical of a reinforcement theory and hence indisposed to look for reinforcements relevant to their field of study. Since Kohlberg has probably published more on the moralization of children in the last decade than any other author, this critical indisposition may prove important in the growth of the field of research.

In support of his various theses, Kohlberg offers a very substantial review of psychological literature. Some of the evidence presented might be objected to on the ground, outlined above, that it reflects the shortcomings of experimental positivism. Justin Aronfreed, himself disposed to believe that the role of cognition may intervene in crucial ways between reinforcement and moral commitment, criticizes Kohlberg's work for its seeming assumption that

> ...patterns of conscience necessarily evolve, through a fixed sequence of qualitative transformations, in the direction of what is considered socially desirable or "mature," provided only that certain common forms of social experience are available to the child. Failure of the sequence to reach its terminal point must be regarded as an arrest of the natural order of development. . . . The undertone of these conceptions is unmistakably that of Rousseau's *Emile* [Aronfreed, 1968].

Aronfreed also points out that Kohlberg's postulation of an invariable sequence is at odds with studies which show other patterns of change in moral judgment in different social classes and societies.

From our point of view, Kohlberg's interpretation is important because it is based on the verbal behavior of a small and usually homogeneous sample of children. For this reason we are not necessarily at odds with it.[21] This is because the kind of moral development that Kohlberg claims is a psychological process is also an age-graded institutionalized expectation, at least in the northern European and American societies where his type of studies is carried out. The theory of hypocrisy stated above explains why verbal reports of behavior (generalized and abstracted as professions of moral judgment) differ from the behavior reported, and why the report is usually more moral than the activity reported. Kohlberg's and the present theory are therefore offering explanations of the same data (verbal professions of American youth) and a choice between them may be made on a number of grounds. Criteria of generality and conceptual economy favor the reinforcement theory, since it uses fewer concepts to explain more variation in verbal professions among age groups, social strata, and societies. But in fact such a choice is more likely to be made on philosophical grounds or preferences for institutionalized "models of man." A belief in idealism or voluntarism, or respect for the phenomenology of the moral man, will probably cause the reader to favor Kohlberg's theory.

The difference between Kohlberg's and the present theory can be illustrated by comparing two "models of man": the model of Rousseau and the model of Hobbes. For Rousseau's "noble savage," morality is either inherent or at least a strong latent possibility, which society can only frustrate. Evil in this model is a social product, but goodness is pre-social (and therefore by implication invariant among societies). The Hobbesian model of man is one of a wholly amoral actor, made moral, if at all, entirely by social processes—usually, in Hobbes's terms, through constraints or negative sanctions. Both good and evil are social products in this view and thus vary as societies vary. Rousseau's model is far more popular among moral men; Hobbes's work, as we noted above, has long been singled out by them for special criticism. The present theory builds on the Hobbesian model and risks being fixed with its stigma. It is Kohlberg's work in the tradition of Rousseau that enjoys the bulk of institutional and intellectual support—and probably more so with the recent rise of subjectivism and romanticism among the educated young.

---

21 Although Kohlberg claims that his conclusions disagree with a reinforcement theory (1963, p. 332). He also depreciates psychoanalytic models, which lends weight to the notion that what he is really against is *any* deterministic theory. The adjective "autonomous" frequently appears in his work to modify the nouns "value," "values," and "moral judgment."

That Kohlberg's theory is consonant with the model of Rousseau is illustrated in his list of six dimensions of "genuine moral development" (1964, pp. 396–98). In these Kohlberg follows Piaget, stressing a decline in attention to sanctions and an increase in rationality as the main aspects of moral development. The dimensions are (1) "intentionality in judgment," or attention to the motive for action rather than to its effects; (2) "relativism in judgment," or recognition of the possibility of diverse opinion; (3) "independence of sanctions," or attention to the goodness or badness of an act apart from its liability to reward or punishment; (4) "use of reciprocity," or do unto others as they do (or as you would have them do) unto you; (5) "use of punishment as restitution" rather than as vengeance; and (6) "naturalistic views of misfortune," the distinction between sanctions and fortuitous natural events which may also punish or reward, that is, Durkheim's distinction between mechanical and synthetic consequences. All these add up to a highly ratiocinative concept of morality. It is in many respects sharply opposed to a view of morality as a property of social interaction.

Consider "intentionality." The role of intent in morality has long been debated by obviously mature and presumably intelligent adults. In the concept of *means rea* it is the basis of ancient arguments in jurisprudence; and while black-letter law varies in the respect it accords intent, its main interest has always been in consequences. Good intentions not only pave the road to hell but also give no defense to a charge of legal wrongdoing, although they may mitigate the punishment (for example, there are various degrees of murder, distinguished by relative "malice," or badness of intent).

It is also possible to question Kohlberg's implication that an emphasis of intention is somehow contrary to an emphasis on consequences. Intent is made known by a statement of future action. "I intend to help my mother" means that in the future I shall in fact provide such help. Ultimately, intent is made known through a comparison of professions of intention with the acts performed. To use, as the criterion of intent, solely a verbal profession is to subject the concept to the same problem which arises when we make verbal profession the sole criterion of value—that is, an incorrigible drunk must be allowed to value sobriety so long as he says he does. When someone says over and over again that he intends to help his mother but in fact never helps her, we ultimately conclude either that he is mentally defective and does not know what constitutes help, or that he is a liar and a hypocrite. Legal statements of intent, as in contracts, provide for penalties for nonperformance of the intended act.

To stress intention is to move away from consequences in the short run, but not in the long run. Murder is distinguished from manslaughter by an assessment of whether the circumstances wherein human actions cause death provide grounds for belief that the person whose actions are involved will cause more deaths in the future. Here "malice" (bad intent) is an elliptical reference to a high probability of future interdicted acts. Statements of intent symbolically represent consequences and like all such representations they lose in reliability as they gain in abstraction.

Kohlberg studies "intention" by adapting a vignette from Piaget. Two children are to be compared in terms of relative virtue: one child breaks one cup while attempting to steal cookies, while another breaks six cups while trying to help his mother. Among Kohlberg's subjects, four-year-olds regard the latter breakage as more culpable; nine-year-olds, the former. This is not surprising, but it is not all that might be done in studying the process. Kohlberg limits his concern to judgments or verbal professions. But were one to go beyond this and attend to the reinforcement of behavior the matter might well grow more complex. One might first ask mothers about the relative offensiveness to them of this pair of acts; and second, observe their behavior (since mothers must often be hypocrites) in order to determine which child in such a situation would actually receive the greater punishment. My own prediction is that mothers would *say* they would punish the cookie thief more but that in fact they would behave so as to present (not perhaps "intentionally") the greater punishment to the multiple cup-breaker. Mothers must of course respect conventionally good intentions but they also desire not to have their household inventory destroyed by youthful *shlemiels*. The relevance of "intent" in this connection may be that it is a criterion which nine-year-olds respect better than four-year-olds in their verbal presentations to others. The children may be learning that distinctions as to kinds of "intent" are good predictors of the sanctions to which their verbal reports are liable (as we pointed out in the discussion of confession and contrition) at the same time that "consequences" are more important in predicting sanctions following the acts themselves.

As children grow and move into the ambivalent status of adolescence they are exposed more and more to the world of adults. This world is morally less perfect in fact than it is represented to be in the symbolic instruction of children. As youth enter this world they encounter one of its moral imperfections, that is, that results rather than unconfirmed professions of good intentions usually command the important rewards. The Yiddish epithet of *shlemiel,* denoting a well-intentioned blunderer, describes adults who confuse good intentions with good results and fail to heed the primacy of the latter. Yet it would appear in Kohlberg's terms that the *shlemiel* is not defective or "arrested" in his moral development.

Kohlberg's third point, "independence of sanctions," is on the face of the matter directly contrary to this theory. But in detail his notion of independence turns out not to be a question of whether behavior is shaped by sanctions, but of whether behavior so shaped will be so reported. If, as we argued in Chapter III, moral learning is facilitated by a "turning off of cognition," an obfuscation of the sanctions of which a norm is composed, then an efficient pattern of general morality will include the norm that actors should not attend to morality's reinforcements—that is, discrimination or awareness of sanctions is itself punished. Kohlberg's older subjects may have learned to avoid this discrimination (or at least to avoid reporting it) better than the younger ones. This should occasion no surprise. The primary issue for the analysis of social organization is not what the child *says* about why he does what he does—although this may be an important secondary issue—but just what he *does,* whether he says anything about it or not. Kohlberg found that children, in response to a story of the reward and punishment of various kinds of children, will describe a conventionally virtuous child's act as "good" even though it is punished; Aronfreed (1968) and Bandura and Walters (1963) found that children tend to emit "bad" acts which they observed were rewarded for others. The discrepancy is only apparent and is easily explained. We need only assume that children learn to discriminate their own behavior and their verbal report of it, and, when suitably reinforced, to say one thing and do another. Thus, what appears superficially to be an independence from sanctions is actually a more subtle discrimination of sanctions by the child than by the developmental psychologist.

Perhaps the most interesting part of Kohlberg's approach is his association of maturity, cognition, and morality. He holds that an increase in cognitive capacity leads to an increase in "moral maturity" at the same time that the child is maturing in a strictly chronological sense. Kohlberg sometimes has trouble squaring this view even with his own data. The relationship does hold in his data from the beginning of verbal facility till about age fourteen, the period covered by most of his studies, but after that it apparently starts to break down. I think this can be explained by combining the reinforcement theory of morality with the changes in status that come with age and with anticipatory socialization, drawing on the antithesis between cognition and morality presented in Chapter III and on the persistent tendency for anticipatory socialization to misrepresent the future.

Kohlberg's "stages of development" follow those of Piaget. They are defined, in connection with "Motivation for Rule Obedience or Moral Action," as:

Stage 1. Obey rules to avoid punishment.
Stage 2. Conform to obtain rewards, have favors returned, and so on.
Stage 3. Conform to avoid disapproval, dislike by others.
Stage 4. Conform to avoid censure by legitimate authorities and resultant guilt.

Stage 5. Conform to maintain the respect of the impartial spectator judging in terms of community welfare.

Stage 6. Conform to avoid self-condemnation [1964, p. 400].[22]

Kohlberg then lists some responses as illustrations of judgments at each stage:

Aspect 3: Basis of Moral Worth of a Human Life

Stage 1: *Life's Value Based on Physical and Status Aspects*

A ten-year-old respondent:

a. (Why should the druggist give the drug to the dying woman when her husband couldn't pay for it?)
   "If someone important is in a plane and is allergic to heights and the stewardess won't give him medicine because she's only got enough for one and she's got a sick one, a friend, in back, they'd probably put the stewardess in a lady's jail because she didn't help the important one."

b. (Is it better to save the life of one important person or a lot of unimportant people?)
   "All the people that aren't important because one man just has one house, maybe a lot of furniture, but a whole bunch of people have an awful lot of furniture and some of these poor people might have a lot of money and it doesn't look it."

Stage 2: *Life's Value as Instrumental to Need-Satisfaction*

A thirteen-year-old respondent:

a. (Should the doctor "mercy-kill" a fatally ill woman requesting death because of her pain?)
   "Maybe it would be good to put her out of her pain, she'd be better off that way. But the husband wouldn't want it, it's not like an animal. If a pet dies you can get along without it—it isn't something you really need. Well, you can get a new wife, but it's not really the same."

Stage 4: *Life Sacred Because of a Social and Religious Order*

A sixteen-year-old respondent:

a. (Should the doctor "mercy-kill" the woman?)
   "The doctor wouldn't have the right to take a life, no human has the right. He can't create life, he shouldn't destroy it."

Stage 6: *Life's Value as Expressing the Sacredness of the Individual*

Another sixteen-year-old respondent:

a. (Should the husband steal the expensive drug to save his wife?)
   "By the law of society he was wrong but by the law of nature or of God the druggist was wrong and the husband was justified. Human life is

---

22 This sequence of development is similar to that outlined by Allport in a late statement of his argument for "functional autonomy" (1955, pp. 72–73).

above financial gain. Regardless of who was dying, if it was a total stranger, man has a duty to save him from dying.[23]

There is indeed a difference between stages one and six. The ten-year-old's blunt attention to V.I.P.'s contrasts sharply with the older youth's carefully wrought rationalization. The second sixteen-year-old is not necessarily a conscious hypocrite, carefully telling the interviewer only what he presumes the interviewer wants to hear. Perhaps his respect for a natural law higher than society's may by now have been proved sincere by his involvement in a student demonstration or some other dramatic rejection of the Philistine proprieties of the social establishment. The general point is that *these moral judgments refer to types of situations in which none of the respondents are at all likely to have been involved.* This is so partly because the respondents are young, and the situations they are asked to judge involve adults. But in another sense nobody, not even adults, could really get involved in such situations. As Brown (1965, p. 405) comments in his discussion of Kohlberg, these dilemmas consistently force us away from everyday routine to "admit of a morality by which the conventional morality can itself be judged."[24] The problem is that the resultant "moral judgments" are highly abstract and general verbalizations which prove to be inapplicable to the concrete and particular details of human action in real societies. As verbal operants, the events reinforcing the judgments are themselves largely symbolic, consisting of references to events that are yet to occur. Their relation to what persons really in the situation will do—or even to what the respondents would do were they actually in the situation —is problematic.

Symbolic representations are always abstract and therefore selective: not every aspect of what is represented is transmitted in the symbol. A response to a symbolic representation of a situation will not likely be the same as the response to the situation itself. The comments of Kohlberg's second sixteen-year-old, for example, reflect his ignorance of the host of regulations that in all advanced societies control the dispensation of drugs, the responsibility of professionals rather than patients or relatives for

---

23 Kohlberg (1964, pp. 401–2). Quoted with the permission of Martin L. Hoffman on behalf of the Russell Sage Foundation.

24 The idea of a moral canon prior to and legislative for those of particular societies figures in all kinds of non-relativistic ethical theories, such as those of the ethical intuitionists (whom Kohlberg cites with approval [1964, p. 405], on the character of a "genuinely moral judgment"; cf. with Ross' [1930] criticism of Durkheim, quoted in Chapter I of this work). But there is no end to the number of such prior canons that may be postulated. The hierarchy of such canons (each legislative for all less general than itself) is also endless, giving rise to an infinite and vicious regression of judgment, whose results become increasingly remote from any possible application to human affairs.

their use, and so on, all of which bear heavily on what is regarded in practice as a "responsible" decision.[25]

There is good reason to believe that Kohlberg's research has not revealed a cumulative sequence of development, which can be extrapolated monotonically to adult judgment and behavior, but instead has captured nothing more than what is commonly called the 'idealism of youth." This idealism results from intensive anticipatory socialization and a cognitive belief in a world (yet to be experienced) where good men are generally respected and evil ones generally despised. Their ideals and beliefs are yet to be compromised by much evidence ten of shortcomings in the schedule of moral reinforcement or by experience of windfall reward.

That the young are often more moral than the old is hardly a new observation. The explanation of their superior virtue in terms of an early-sanction schedule of reinforcement is perhaps more recent. Kingsley Davis offered a similar point in his paper, "The Sociology of Parent-Youth Conflict" (1940). The young are receptive to symbolic antipatory socialization "because they have little social experience—experience being largely kept from them." Also kept from them is realistic symbolic representation of the ubiquity of windfall reward (often through systematic censorship of entertainment, textbooks, teachers, and so on). Thus unchecked, youthful ideals "soar to the sky" (1940, p. 527). Seymour Martin Lipset has also applied the similar and earlier observations of Max Weber to the analysis of student political action—itself an expression of generational conflict. Weber observed that youth tend to follow "a pure ethic of absolute ends" (as do Kohlberg's sixteen-year-olds) rather than an "ethic of responsibility" which

---

[25] Thus the dilemma, which Kohlberg composed in order to force attention to very general standards, contains both impossibilities and implausibilities. Here it is in full (as reprinted in Brown, 1965, p. 405, from an earlier publication of Kohlberg's):

In Europe, a woman was near death from a special kind of cancer. There was one drug that the doctors thought might save her. It was a form of radium that a druggist in the same town had recently discovered. The drug was expensive to make, but the druggist was charging ten times what the drug cost him to make. He paid $200 for the radium and charged $2,000 for a small dose of the drug. The sick woman's husband, Heinz, went to everyone he knew to borrow the money, but he could only get together about $1,000 which is half of what it cost. He told the druggist that his wife was dying, and asked him to sell it cheaper or let him pay later. But the druggist said, "No, I discovered the drug and I'm going to make money from it." So Heinz got desperate and broke into the man's store to steal the drug for his wife. Should the husband have done that? Why?

Anyone familiar with the medical complexities of radiotherapy, pricing policies which amortize research and development costs, the hazards of handling radioactive materials, and a host of other technical details, will probably find this vignette too unrealistic to pass judgment upon (one wonders whether some stubbornly concrete pragmatist among Kohlberg's respondents ever suggested to him that the vignette was ineptly drawn). The point is that teen-agers are often ignorant of crucial technical and practical contingencies and to that extent their moral judgment is not so much exemplary as sophomoric.

attends to consequences; the young, after all, are not constrained by responsibility for what actually happens. Though Lipset refers only to university students, the naive objective morality of student demonstrators is a good example of the socialization of the young in complex societies generally:

> University students, though well educated, have generally not established a sense of close involvement with adult institutions: experience has not hardened them to imperfection. Their libidos are unanchored; their capacity for identification with categories of universal scope, with mankind, the oppressed, the poor and miserable, is greater than it was earlier or than it will be later in life. Their contact with the articulated moral and political standards of their society is abstract; they encounter them as principles promulgated by older persons, as imposed by authority, rather than as maxims incorporated into and blurred by their own experience. Increasingly in the modern world, which includes the highly educated sector of the emerging nations, equality, efficiency, justice, and economic well-being are represented as the values of the good society. Poverty, racial discrimination, caste systems, social inequality, administrative and political corruption, and cultural backwardness are all violations of such principles. In all countries, of course, reality is usually at variance with principles, and young persons feel this strongly. Educated young people everywhere thus tend to support idealistic movements which take the ideologies and values of the adult world more seriously than does the adult world itself [Lipset, 1965, pp. 3–4].[26]

Words and Deeds in Moral Careers

The combined effect of anticipatory socialization, the distinction between action and its verbal report, and changes in moral commitment over time can be represented as a function of chronological age, using for examples the moral progressions of Anglo-American societies. These societies are characterized by nuclear families and low fertility, long adolescence, specialized extrafamilial education in massive groups of age-peers, and high levels of moral learning. To illustrate the effect of age we refer to a hypothetical norm, one which meets two restrictive conditions: (1) the norm is not sharply graded by age, sex, or social class, but rests on sanctions applied to all alike, and (2) the norm is commonplace, relating to activities frequently performed, recognized, named, and sanctioned in everyday life so that behavioral and verbal conformity can readily be compared. That few concrete norms meet the first criterion attests to the importance of the sociological variables to which it refers.

---

26 See also the thoughtful discussion of the "institutionalization of hypocrisy" and its relation to social change in Keniston (1968, p. 237).

Pre-verbal infancy may be taken to be the first moral stage. The behavior of infants is reinforced by parents in various ways, including verbal (that is, secondary or learned) reinforcers. Though the parents cannot converse with the child except in a very rudimentary way, they talk to him anyway in anticipation of the time when a more reciprocal flow of communication will occur (indeed it is difficult to overstress the element of anticipation in this stage of moralization). At the same time, the child is learning to discriminate among the verbalizations of his parents and to respond differentially to them, long before he can verbalize on anything like an equal footing. This advantage in symbolization gives a profound advantage in the ability of the parents to control the child, and here familial socialization operates at its most totalitarian level. At this moral stage the infant probably cannot very well conform to our hypothetical norm, not so much because of an inefficient schedule of reinforcement by parents (though that may be important) as because conformity lies beyond the range of the infant's repertory of operants. Toilet training at six weeks, for example, is a waste of time. And since the child has not yet learned to talk, there is no discrepancy between his behavior and his own verbal report of it. There is no verbal report.

Verbal childhood may be taken as the second stage. Here language skills proliferate, and the child learns not only to differentiate among pitch, volume, and frequency and to sort out word order and other elements of syntax, but also to incorporate these skills into his own verbal emissions. In time the child speaks with ease and facility. Since the cost of talk is low, he can usually afford to produce more of it for a given reward than he can of the nonverbal activity to which the talk may refer. His talk is therefore more throughly shaped by conditioning than is his action. We see this in the trend of statements by young children reported by Kohlberg. The verbal professions of the youngest children are but little abstracted from sanctions they have experienced, but the older children move rapidly to highly abstract examples. Within this stage the child's rate of conformity as assessed on his verbal reports gains rapidly on his rate of conformity as assessed on his nonverbal behavior. As his verbal professions grow more abstract, they become less constrained by any possible comparison with his nonverbal acts, so that his moral aspirations are "free to soar to the sky."

Youth or adolescence represents the third moral stage. With certain exceptions, involving specialized adult occupations (discussed below), this will be the most moral age of man, insofar as morality is measured by verbal profession. Here the young person rehearses roles whose actual performance still lies in the future. He does this as a result of symbolic anticipatory socialization and as a result of separate schedules of reinforcement for verbal professions (of which rehearsals for adult roles are mainly composed) and for the routine activities of adolescent life. The young person is therefore likely to learn—at least at this time of his life—that the more crucial sanctions attach not to what he does but to what he says he will do, for this is thought to imply more for his adult life. And since by now the young person's verbal skills are close to their full development, his moral professions can reflect a sophisticated and subtle assessment of what is rewarded ("good") and punished ("bad") in the society's abstract moral order. He has also learned the important tacit rule that evil must not be equated with punishment nor goodness with reward, since such an equation calls intelligent attention to sanctions and thus is in the interest of an efficient moral order to suppress. Whatever else they show, Kohlberg's data record a regular increase in verbal professions of morality from childhood till adolescence. The well-socialized teenager "talks a scrupulous life," and we should not be surprised that he does so: it is easy for him, he is well-rewarded for it, and he has been largely denied knowledge and experience of immoral temptation. The adolescent is a hypocrite, but generally an unwilling one: the discrepancy between his professions and actual human conduct (including, in time, his own) in the situations to which his profession refer results more from simple ignorance of what lies ahead than from any conscious intention to deceive.[27]

The young adult represents the next moral stage. This age-grade is not set off very sharply by visible indications or rites of passage from those below it, but instead involves an ambiguous and inconsistent movement. Gainful employment (usually outside the family) is more or less necessary but is not always sufficient (as in the disadvantage of legal minority). The young-adult status of "student" is one of exceptional ambivalence: the student is at one time rewarded for docility and deference, at another for assuming "mature" authority (cf. with Matza, 1964, pp. 192 ff., in "position"). The ambivalence is well illustrated in student radical movements. Gradually the young adult moves toward a more consistently adult position and thus participates more and more directly in the events that he knew before only symbolically. Rewards for deviation from previously learned norms now become available to him. Even student radicals, for example, get involved in organized movements and thus learn of the unavoidable evils and tactical benefits of organization. Commitment acquired through symbolic rehearsal is now tested in the absence of strong symbolic admonition (not as legitimately applied to the old as to the young) and in the

---

[27] For a related analysis of the varieties of youthful "overmoralization" see the excellent review and suggestive argument by Matza (1964, pp. 194–97, especially pp. 201–3, 208–13), on scrupulosity, studiousness, radicalism, and bohemianism. "Scrupulosity" is a distinctive risk of (American) Roman Catholic parochial education, which concretely exemplifies to a remarkable degree the process outlined above of symbolic anticipatory socialization and insulation of the young from worldly experience.

presence of temptation. Variations in resultant conformity are accounted for by the degree of prior learned commitment, the strength of present sanctions, and the presence of rewards for deviation, the combinations of which depend on the differentiation of statuses within the age-grade.

Here an interesting shift occurs in the rate of verbally reported conformity. We observed earlier that behavior and its verbal report, being differentially reinforced, often diverge. But we also observed that the differentiated reinforcements do not vary completely independently of each other; what one says affects the reinforcements for what one does, and *vice versa*. Hence rates of behavioral conformity and of its verbal report may not vary completely independently either. Then too an adult, increasingly free from the morally disciplined control of information given to the young, simply has more information. The intelligent use of information is intrinsically rewarding, and it is also so useful to human society in its contests with other species and the inanimate environment that it receives general social reinforcement also: intelligence is rewarded, stupidity punished. The *amoral* exercise of intelligence is of course a critical problem of social control, resolved to varying degrees by strong moral learning, ongoing suppression of a calculating attitude toward institutionalized norms, and withholding of information that would erode conformity. Still persons tend to behave intelligently (to make fine discriminations among stimuli) on the basis of such information as they can gain, and tend also to avoid those verbal professions which, however otherwise morally commendable, would make them appear ignorant or stupid. The sense of this is nicely captured in the very contemporary dichotomy of "hip" and "square"; but the distinction is an ancient one and has been expressed in various ways in the literature of all complex societies.

The possession of what we commonly call worldly wisdom is therefore reinforcing for adults because it signals their (by this time) creditable discretion and discernment and because it is more or less appropriate for their age-grade to have the information on which it is based. Worldly wisdom is not socially reinforced for youth, but it would still be intrinsically reinforcing for them: youth therefore notoriously aspire to study the adult mysteries but generally learn of them only in a highly inaccurate and institutionally biased way. Through their programs of mass education, industrial societies create large age-peer groups, and thus increase the importance of age-homogeneous as compared to age-heterogeneous interaction (such as occurs within the family). Since school-age youth are alike in their ignorance and unworldliness, socialization in age-peer groups is often a case of the blind leading the blind.

Eventually the adult comes to be reinforced for denying the same professions of moral commitment he made in his youth, and whose plausibility at that time depended on his morally sustained unworldliness. Thus in our own society youth may profess that love conquers all: being good and true all its expressions are sanctified, and so forth. In a society with no corporate descent groups, weak rules of endogamy, and highly imperfect mechanisms for arranged marriage, such a profession is useful because, together with other norms regulating sex and reproduction, it recruits young people to marriage and new families. Thus adults tend to commend such a profession by adolescents even when they themselves do not believe it, because it shows that the younger person is as properly committed and innocent as he is supposed to be. We judge a young girl's view of love to be inaccurate to the point of foolishness and also think it a good thing that she holds that view. The same profession by a male adult is viewed quite differently and is liable to different sanctions. It suggests that he may impetuously abandon responsibilities to his family and also that he may lack the worldly wisdom he ought to have at his age; that is, the knowledge that what persons in love profess to be eternal devotion is often a mask for ephemeral lust, and that in fact it very definitely does not conquer all, being inimical to all sorts of other occupational and familial commitments which are backed up with strong sanctions. This exemplifies an important shift in the moral stages of man: the shift from "youthful idealism" to "adult realism."

Such a nonmonotonic shift in the moral career—from childish realism to youthful idealism and back to adult realism—sharply limits any theory (such as Kohlberg's) of unilinear stages of moral development. If anything like the progression outlined above does in fact occur, then the "higher stages of moral development" that Kohlberg finds revealed in the verbal professions of adolescents are not generally superceded by higher stages or even sustained at the same level in adult life. Rather the adult's views about what ought to be done in this world will be tempered by his worldly wisdom about what *is* done and what *can* be done. This clearly would be "immature" in terms of Kohlberg's stages.

In the "airline stewardess" vignette, the ten-year-old respondent pays close attention to status. In another several years, he probably will be more egalitarian in his judgment. Yet the discovery by a worldly adult that indiviously discriminated statuses in human society, rather than any abstract moral principle of distribution, really are profound determinants of who gets scarce and highly valued rewards, eventually influences his actions with regard to who does get them. Ultimately it conditions his view of who *ought* to get them. Even today, when expressions of youthful and radical egalitarianism are widespread and many profess democratic ideals or some rule of distributive justice, only a few spend much time fighting the stratification system in a really disinterested way. Most criticism of inequality eventually repairs to the "injustice" of the critics' own place in that system; and even the critics admit the inequality is real. Thus adults really agree with much of our ten-year-old's naive moral realism about the importance of persons who are, in cold fact, important. To be sure, stewardesses are not put in a "lady's jail," but the sanctions that would follow if they favored those in the narrow seats in back over those who paid more to sit in front and receive preferential treatment are clear enough to those in the transportation business.

Kohlberg mentions some data that bear on this point: "Recent unpublished reports [probably his own] of longitudinal findings in later adolescence suggest the relatively frequent occurrence of marked changes in moral character from high school to college years" (1964, p. 393). Yet he is unable to explain such findings in terms of his theory of unilinear development. He is thus led to the paradoxical concept of moral maturity suggested in the following passage: "The writer has found teachers telling thirteen-year-old children not to cheat 'because the person you copied it from might have it wrong and so it won't do you any good.' Most of these children were capable of advancing much more mature reasons for not cheating" (p. 425). Perhaps Kohlberg's notion of maturity makes sense in terms of the straightforwardly ethical concept of moral maturity held by the philosophers whom he cites with approval. But in the more disinterested terms of science, "maturity" signifies the condition of older organisms whose rate of change is slow relative to younger ones. If old people have persistently evil habits, then such habits are characteristic of genuine maturity. If what has been said above about the decline of youthful idealism is correct, Kohlberg's concept of maturity is invidious.

Even less than they predict the *verbal* professions of adolescents are Kohlberg's interpretations likely to predict behavior, either of adolescents or adults. Although it is a reasonable speculation that conformity generally will decline with age, particular situations may reinforce it strongly enough to produce an increase. The possible variation that different norms may introduce is great. Adult conformity to the norm of intelligence will generally increase so long as an occupational or other advantage can be gained thereby, and in some cases conformity to this norm can reach the point where the person is deviating sharply from other institutionalized expectations. This point is illustrated by the conspicuous iconoclasm and superficial cynicism of persons who are socially mobile because of their ability to manipulate symbols, such as playwrights, journalists, advertising copywriters, and political organizers. Such people can gain special rewards for not respecting precisely those norms which are reinforced by more conventional groups, for in order to manipulate these norms symbolically it is necessary first to analyze them. To manipulate symbolic norms requires a cognitive attitude toward them, and thereby corrodes commitment to them.

Not all adults, however, are rewarded for analyzing norms. In those who deal with the young (teachers, textbook writers, ministers, mothers), a high level of verbal conformity is rewarded, a level often higher than that expected of adolescents. The extreme virtuousness of these positions (at least in their performance before an audience of children, to use Goffman's metaphor of the stage) is unconvincing to other adults, however, and those who hold them are therefore liable to a mild and humorous disrespect because of it. Indeed, many persons who are rewarded for pretending a childish virtuousness in their work often use their leisure to exhibit a mild but conspicuously deviant personal style, by *outré* dress or demimondaine activities, the better to proclaim that, despite their work, they too are respectably wise in the ways of the world. Schoolteachers on vacation, as Willard Waller observed, are often aggressively free spirits.

It complicates matters that many persons who move from youthful idealism to adult realism then find, when they become parents or teachers, that once again they are constrained to profess childish virtue. A youth may tell his mother that he likes green and yellow vegetables because, although he still has to eat them, this at least avoids the further punishment of a tedious maternal discourse on nutrition. Later, as a young adult, he may tell his friends that he still detests the green and yellow vegetables his mother made him eat as a youth. Still later, as a father, he conspires with his wife to feed his own children green and yellow vegetables, hypocritically telling them that he is very fond of such vegetables and eating them with feigned enthusiasm.

These examples hardly display the profound soul searching that is supposed to be associated with moral change, but they do outline the way in which the social reinforcements directed at people of different ages and statuses cause them to modify their words and deeds. No undirectional or developmental concept of moral change can hope to explain this. A developmental account has the moral virtue of reinforcing moral commitment by associating it with abstract ratiocination. But it may have the scientific vice of failing to explain variations in time and space, both in moral behavior and in verbal professions of morality.

Conclusion

In this chapter we have not marshaled much research in direct support of the claims made in the preceding one. Instead, we have mainly criticized existing concepts and approaches. Such criticism we believe to be warranted because these ideas and points of view have strongly indisposed most researchers working on child development to design studies which would either confirm or confute a reinforcement theory of moral commitment. Too often the relevant reinforcers simply have not been assessed.

However, the alienation of theory from research is being relieved. Among the voluminous research in the field of child development, the few studies of the moralization of children are recent, and the direct study of social reinforcement of moralization is even more recent. Within a few years the literature will probably tell us much more about the strengths and weaknesses of the ideas we have been advancing here than we can know about them now. As it is, our discussion has already approached the moral conditions of adult life. We can therefore move from the acquisition of morality to its maintenance.

CHAPTER V

The Maintenance of Moral Commitment in Adults

The doctrine that the child is father of the man, held both by the followers of Freud and by "developmental sequence" psychologists, leads directly to the conclusion that the important events to study in order to explain adult behavior are not those contemporary with it, but rather those which preceded it in childhood. The contemporary environment thus becomes a set of dependent variables. Though adults of course interact with the nonsocial environment and with their fellows, the independent variables that account for this are not seen as found in the interaction itself, but in the personal histories of its participants: in patterns of love, rivalry, nurturance and hostility, which characterize the first few years of life.

Quite apart from any respect for the theoretical positions from which it derives, the childhood-determinant hypothesis has much to recommend it. Much evidence supports it. Ever since community studies have been carried out in sociology, the variables represented by childhood events have proved to be powerful predictors of adult behavior. This is true in all forms of status ascription, of which the variables of "father's occupation," "father's education," or "father's income" are clear examples. The events to which ascription refers are contemporary not so much with the adult behavior which is to be explained as with the adult's childhood. Nor is the hypothesis of childhood determination necessarily at odds with a reinforcement theory. "When learning is established, extinction of the response by termination of the reinforcement is slow." What the child learns to do well enough he may continue to do throughout all his adult years. Skinner has observed pigeons still emitting learned behavior years after the last reinforcement: cannot man, with his greater capacity for learning, do better?

This sort of defense of childhood determination sometimes inclines toward logic-chopping. The statement "If the child learns it well enough, the behavior will be forthcoming without any further reinforcement" is a practical tautology; for if the behavior is *not* produced it is generally taken to mean that it was not well enough learned. A better empirical question is this: how well has any specific activity been learned? Logically it is possible for behavior to be determined in childhood; empirically it is problematic.

This leads us to two reasons for questioning the hypothesis of childhood determination. The first is practical and empirical. Events predicable of childhood are good predictors of adult life, but not perfect ones. Then too, some of the more powerful predictors from the days of childhood, such as the various ascribed statuses, are by no means predicable solely of childhood events. Ascribed statuses generally depend on those few distinctions which can be made about a child or about his family of orientation at his birth, but the distinctions do not disappear afterward. Later they determine which schedule of reinforcement among a plurality of such schedules (for example, those differentiated by age, sex, class, and ethnicity) the child will be exposed to for a long period of time. The reinforcement based on the distinctions only begins with youth; it may continue indefinitely. Later reinforcements may be sharply different from earlier ones, but they are still very much contingent on the earlier ones and on the learned response to them.

Consider a working-class boy who is rewarded by his kith and kin for fighting but not for reading. He learns to fight well and to read poorly, and is subsequently classified in school as a slow learner and a disciplinary problem. Thus classified he gets placed in classes that concentrate on time-serving custody and do little to encourage gains in literacy. As a relatively illiterate adult, he is employable only as unskilled labor, and is firmly fixed at the bottom of the stratification system. His class position is clearly an ascribed status, because the schedule of reinforcement on which his occupancy of it depends starts with the accident of his birth into a lower-class family. Had he been born into a middle-class family he would have been reinforced more for reading than for fighting and the whole subsequent pattern would have been changed. What is true of an ascribed class position is also true of other ascribed statuses such as sex and inheritance group membership (for example, ethnic and religious groups).

That ascription prevails as the crucial starting point in subsequent schedules of reinforcement is not however a good argument for the traditional doctrines of childhood determination. Ascription *is* important in human affairs, and many social scientists are prone to overlook it (partly because they are moral men conditioned by norms that prescribe achievement and condemn ascription). But its effect depends on subsequent reinforcement which may involve processes other than ascription. One fundamental characteristic of industrial societies, as compared to pre-industrial ones, is that they make more use of nonascriptive mechanisms of status placement. Industrial societies also change relatively rapidly, and each new generation has available to it positions which did not exist for an older group (there is also the disappearance of other positions). These new positions cannot be readily filled by ascription, because it stresses continuity and stability between generations. Industrial and other forms of social change are therefore important limitations on the extent to which the events of childhood can predict adult behavior, through ascription or any other mechanism. Orthodox psychoanalytic "genetics" presuppose a static society.

The second reason to question the principle of childhood determination is more abstract, involving some basic aspects of the process of conditioning and reinforcement. In the absence of reinforcement the extinction of a learned response is slow. But it still does get extinguished. If a stable rate of the learned response is to be maintained, some level of subsequent reinforcement—the "maintenance dose"—must be applied. No matter how well established in childhood, moral learning requires some degree of reinforcement in later life. So we said in Chapter III, and this chapter is therefore a quest for evidence of the reinforcers that apply to adults.

We first report some exploratory interviews on a shift in adult behavior from learned commitment to a norm to deviation from it. Then follows a brief analysis of variables in adult situations that determine the strength of moral or immoral reinforcers and thus, together with past moral learning, the rate of conformity and deviation. A hypothesis is next presented on the relation between the strength of conditioners and age-grades, in order to explain the apparent decrease in the rate of socialization as persons move toward adult life. This apparent decrease is important to our theory because it is often invoked in support of the claim that the maintenance of moral commitment does not depend on sanctions. We illustrate the hypothesis by a review of literature on intensive adult socialization and its associated moral changes. The chapter closes with a brief review of the implications for moral commitment of commonplace status changes in adult life and a short reference to related topics not discussed in this book.

The Effect of Isolation

It would be profitable for us to study men who work in isolated occupations, because they can provide data on the maintenance of moral commitment when social contact and thus most social reinforcement is absent. Such occupations are rare. Men often work in small groups isolated for large periods of time from any larger society, and these isolated groups are frequently reported in the social-psychological literature; but seldom does a man work for long all alone. An isolated occupation differs from social isolation in general—as in the infrequent examples of "feral men" and children raised in attics—because it first requires extensive socialization in an ordinary social world followed by isolation from it. The hypothetical noble savage learns little from human society in the first place; the isolated worker first learns much and then moves to a situation where social reinforcement is terminated. Isolated work by its nature is not convenient for research: it tends to be located in remote areas and the observation itself contaminates the object of study (isolation) unless elaborate noninteractive instruments are used, such as hidden or long-range cameras and microphones. Since I am acquainted with a number of persons who at one time or another had worked in isolation, I conducted informal and exploratory interviews with some of them. In no case did the period of isolation exceed four months, but their responses strongly suggest that even this brief absence from commonplace social reinforcement erodes commitment to common norms.

Two types of workers were involved: fish wardens and fire lookouts. The fish wardens were employed by the U.S. Department of the Interior to watch for illegal fishing on the inlets of the very thinly populated southeastern coast of Alaska. The wardens were deployed one to each inlet and provisioned for a summer's stay. Once every week or two a mail boat brought mail and supplies, and wardens sometimes visited each other by motorboat; but generally the level of human interaction was quite low. The fire lookouts, employed by the U.S. Forest Service, were not so isolated. Their job was to watch for and report forest fires from observation stations built on peaks and promontories with an extensive view. Most of the lookout sites could be reached with a two-wheel-drive light truck and work was normally scheduled for a five- or six-day stretch, with two days' relief by a visiting observer. Most important, the fire lookout stations were equipped with radio or telephone communication, which the fish wardens lacked; though intended for timely fire reporting, it was widely used for informal conversation as well. A few of the fire lookouts were married and brought their wives to the lookout, whereas the fish wardens were required to be single.

My interviewing concentrated on conformity to norms of excretion. Because in ordinary life in middle-class Anglo-American society these norms appear to be well learned, evidence of extinction or "disinternalization" in the absence of social reinforcement favors a reinforcement theory. The interviewing did elicit reports of such extinction, and of more rapid attenuation of commitment to the norms than I had expected. The respondents themselves mentioned the unanticipated extent to which their behavior fell into patterns of indirection and sloth, exemplifying in concrete detail the abstract notion of *anomie*. Most wardens and lookouts were college students working during the summer recess, and most of my respondents took many books with them to their job sites, to spend their many hours of free time in instructive reading. Most of the books returned unopened at summer's end. The respondents also noted that in the absence of "anything to do" they slept 12 to 18 hours a day: social contact evidently reinforces not only reading good books but also getting out of bed. The reported rate of descent into inactivity appeared to vary inversely as the degree of isolation: married fire lookouts changed least, unmarried ones somewhat more, and the fish wardens most of all.

Arriving at their job site, the fish wardens set about to pitch a summer's camp, and selected a site for a latrine physically segregated from the camp itself and "private," that is, out of sight of the camp. But as time passed and no other possible witnesses of the latrine appeared, the conventionally private location that was a long walk from the tent was replaced by one that was closer, with no attention paid to segregation and privacy.

The segregation of excretion from other activities among the fire lookouts was affected by the fact that many lookout stations were built on towers in order to provide vantage beyond surrounding trees, and some were eighty feet off the ground. Since the duties of the position required constant occupation of the tower, it was equipped for eating and sleeping. Only the privy was built at ground level. Privacy and segregation in excretion thus required the descent and ascent of the tower, thus contributing substantially to the cost of conformity to conventional norms.

Among both the fish wardens and the fire lookouts, the segregation of excretion declined, especially of urination. A stronger aversion to the odor of feces was reported to be a factor, yet one of the fish guards said that he endured the odor of a latrine that was close at hand rather than go to the trouble of moving either the camp or the latrine. The fish wardens, when interviewed, tended to be somewhat embarrassed about recounting their behavior, suggesting the importance of human interaction and reinforcement to morality even in a retrospective interview. The interview was the first occasion of social interaction in which the excretory deviation of camp life had been an object of public attention.

The lookouts, on the other hand, reported themselves as more faithful about segregating their latrines, even though the architecture of the lookout tower made conformity more inconvenient. The reason for the difference might lie in the important, if occasional, interaction that the lookouts had with other persons. Though most of this occurred when the lookouts left the tower on their days off, to visit friends or go shopping, some of it consisted of visits to the towers by others, including Forest Service supervisory personnel. Deviation was therefore a more public matter and more subject to sanctions. Not that the lookouts climbed down the ladder every time they wanted to relieve themselves; usually they simply urinated off the tower balconies. Defecation, less frequent than urination, tended to take place during times they were performing other activities which also required climbing down the tower.

These exploratory interviews suggest the importance of reinforcement in the maintenance of common norms. In any event, the effect of isolation on behavior deserves more systematic study. Perhaps one reason why morality is so little studied is that conventional wisdom often associates the distinctively moral—or immoral—character of an act with its rarity: martyrdom or murder are much more likely to be brought up for debate than anything more commonplace. Such rare events are hard to study; this makes it difficult to find evidence against the claim that moral actions are in some way independent of sanctions. They seem to be independent because we have less information on the conditions on which they do in fact depend. If commonplace activities were our moral examples, we would know their determinants too well to assert that they are independent.

Information, Vicarious Reinforcement, and Moral Commitment

The notion of information appears often in the analysis of norms, conformity, and deviation in the context of what is called "small-group" research. In such a context, norms are generally defined as statements, and thus as verbal behavior. Sanctions are usually construed as verbal behavior in the form of information about norms and about the attitudes toward them of other members of a group. (See, for example, Rommetveit [1955, pp. 18 ff.]; and Thibaut and Kelley [1959, Chaps. 8 and 13].) This point of view is not radically different from the one we are advancing, although the terminology is different and the small-group approach is less general insofar as it stays close to verbal behavior and short periods of time.

One point of agreement is that "information" is usually information about sanctions. The verbal representation of sanctions can serve as symbolic or vicarious reinforcement, as we observed earlier. Moreover, a distinctive place for information as a variable may be derived from our emphasis on the role of cognition as a constraint on commitment: internalization involves the expectation of sanctions; at anything less than the theoretical maximum degree of commitment, this expectation leads to a quest for information about sanctions. The relevance of information about sanctions is therefore a function of the degree of internalization, or moral learning. When moral learning is relatively complete, situations with morally relevant stimulus properties elicit emotional and gross muscular reactions rather than discriminatory behavior; the person leaps before he looks, or at least before he looks very closely. The language he is likely to use and to which he is likely to respond will be highly moral and emotive, and it will obscure the conditions and consequences of action more than it will clarify them. When moral learning is relatively weak, situations which offer opportunities to conform or to deviate elicit discrimination and an assessment of the relative rewards: the actor looks before he leaps. The language he is likely to use and to which he is likely to respond will be realistic and will facilitate analysis of relative reward and punishment: it is thus informative in a very literal sense.

The learning-theoretical argument that the absence of reinforcement extinguishes learning led (in Chapter III) to the thesis that most people live in a state of "partial internalization": their moral behavior depends partly on learned commitment and partly on calculation of sanctions, with the latter maintaining or weakening the former. Since the interests of social control—the maintenance of institutionalized or other structurally important norms—lie in maintaining commitment rather than in weakening it, these interests are best served by providing information about sanctions, which, true or false, will serve to convince people that their future interests will be served by conformity. We often mean by the term "psychopath" a person who calculates with extraordinary, and thus conspicuously amoral, precision the value of conformity as against the rewards for transgression, the windfall reward that deviation brings along with the possible punishment for it. But psychopaths often conform. When their calculations are based on false information, they conform because of ignorance and error. This is also true of those whose moral commitment is partial: they too respond to false information and conform partly because of their commitment and partly due to ignorance and error.

Here it is useful to distinguish two concepts: the "moral environment" and the "moral world view." Both of these are involved in symbolic anticipatory socialization of the young and tend to lose their force as the young gain adult status. An environment may be considered a "moral environment" to the extent that all deviation is punished and all conformity rewarded. This is a theoretically limiting case and is, for all practical purposes, impossible. But many highly solidaristic or *gemeinschäftliche* communities approximate the moral environment by effectively segregating, stigmatizing, or isolating chronically deviant activities and persons so that many members of the community lack information about the amount of unpunished deviation that does occur. Even in diverse and *gesellschäftliche* societies certain groups, such as adolescents and "respectable" women, generally live within a moral environment that is largely cut off from the more heterogeneous and immoral elements of the larger society.

The "moral world-view" is the symbolic representation of the moral environment. It depicts a world where all virtue is rewarded and all vice punished. Like all symbolic representations, it is far easier to produce than what it represents and thus is at least not an obvious practical impossibility. It is very difficult consistently to reward virtue and to punish vice, less difficult to isolate part of the population from situations where vice may be rewarded and virtue ignored, and still less difficult to produce elaborate and sophisticated arguments to prove that virtue is rewarded and vice punished: virtue triumphs in the long run in spite of apparent exceptions; the vicious endure anxiety and sink into mental imbalance; the suffering of the virtuous turns out in the end to benefit them; and so on. The promulgation of a moral world-view is an efficient form of social control, and such world-views are therefore widespread. Thus the isolation of particular groups of people in genuinely moral environments is accompanied by the vigorous presentation of a moral world-view. As we observed in Chapter IV, Anglo-American society does much to contain its adolescents in a moral environment, systematically shielding them from contaminating experience and conditioning them to conform in adult life by anticipatory socialization based on moral world-views.

The following excerpt illustrates the moral world-view. Too extreme and orderly to persuade secular adults, it is addressed to middle-class adolescent girls only partly committed to premarital chastity and thus curious (but also largely ignorant) about the details and consequences of sexual intercourse. The author is concerned to show that chastity is rewarded and its lack punished; her article (from a popular women's magazine) is entitled "Too Much Sex on Campus."

> ...One girl who came to me for help had brought from home moral standards that many of her pseudo-sophisticated dormmates found amusing. They told her she would have a dull time unless she quit being so old-fashioned.
>
> In her sophomore year...she was "pinned" by a sophisticated young man, a senior. He began to demand privileges, arguing about "the rightness" of intimacy between two people in love. The girl discussed his arguments with her dormmates, many of whom were already sleeping with their dates. Their advice was to forget scruples.
>
> Exposed to this atmosphere, suggesting that sex was exciting, desirable, even healthy, she submitted to her young man. As she became more deeply involved, she began to tell herself that what she was doing was right....
>
> Her affair was conducted in a nearby woods, in the boy's room and in motels. There was no hint of trouble until she received an unexpected letter from the boy, telling her he was returning home to marry a girl he had known since childhood. She was stunned with disbelief. A short time later she discovered she was pregnant.

It was at this point she arrived in my private chambers appealing for help. I tried to persuade her to confide in her parents, so that they could help her in this frightening experience. She refused. Then she had an abortion performed in another state over a weekend.

This girl was the victim of male indifference. Most coeds do not seem to realize that the average young college man, even today, adheres to the "double standard." And this is true even among those who advocate sex equality for women. As these young men have admitted to sociological researchers, and in confidence to me, the motto is "Love 'em and leave 'em." Usually they put an end to liaisons by marrying someone else—a chaste girl if they can find one. Deserted girls of sensitivity feel they have been merely objects of lust, and their distress is overwhelming.

There is abundant psychiatric and medical evidence that illicit sex usually inflicts deep psychic wounds. The sensitive, naive girl, developing into maturity, cannot foresee what the experience will do to her, nor can anyone tell her. This "depersonalized, meaningless and degrading pattern of courtship," as one educator called it, could develop over the years into ruinous promiscuity.

...It is a parent's duty to talk frankly to a college-bound daughter.... The parent's advice must be shrewd as well as frank. It is foolish, for example, to base the argument against premarital sex on the danger of pregnancy. The daughter may avail herself of contraceptive measures, widely used on campuses, and feel that she has met her mother's objections.

If the girl is unmoved by ethical or religious injunctions against premarital sex—and she should be made to face the issue—then the parent must help her to see the fraudulence of boys' pleadings. Can sex before marriage be an act of love? Almost never. The force driving a young man to break a girl down, girls must realize, is not love. Rather, it is the craving for ego-nurture. In his college years, often the most emotionally disruptive years of his life, a young man seeks sex to ease physical and psychological anguish. A parent should put the matter bluntly: Even the nicest young man may be selfish. No intelligent college girl who has been properly alerted would willingly submit to him.[1]

Few details that might contribute to moral persuasiveness among those ignorant of the realities of courtship are omitted from this formidable narrative. It rigorously excludes any information that might reinforce female sexuality. The counterarguments of the boy friend and dormitory companions are presented and then shown to be insincere or ill-advised, the better to elicit future conformity among readers of the article who might subsequently encounter such arguments. Although sexual intercourse is often a strong primary reward, it is described here, with the appropriate punishing connotations, as "submission." Although intercourse is often used in exchange (for example, for a prospect of marriage) and is thereby

---

[1] From Barron (1964). By permission of Judge Barron and the publisher.

extrinsically reinforced, in this narrative the expected reward is lost: the boy marries a competitor who offers less of herself. This point is repeated in the claim that college men adhere to a double standard and seldom marry girls they seduce. Pregnancy is of course not inevitable in such liaisons, depending on the variables of fecundity, coital frequency, and contraception, but it occurs in this narrative to suggest whatever conclusions about its inevitability a technically uninformed audience might draw. Causal efficacy is imputed to deviant acts: affairs produce "psychic wounds" and "ruinous promiscuity." Parents, for their part, are advised to present symbolically the sanctions that will be applied in the future, but not to stress those (such as pregnancy) whose actual occurrence can be avoided by relatively simple discriminative behavior (such as contraception). Instead the author suggests teaching the doctrine that boys' entreaties are motivated by personal defects: selfishness, insecurity, psychological anguish. Conformity is finally identified with intelligence: those who deviate are stupid.

Those conversant with the facts on sex, courtship and marriage in this or any other society will know that this moral view of the matter, though not false on every count, is certainly false on many of them. That is not the point. Though moral world-views appear to be accounts of facts, a true empirical account is the last thing they need to be in view of their function. Judge Barron's article would probably amuse most sociologists and many college girls as well, but it is not addressed to them. Its intended audience consists of adolescent girls, ignorant and curious about sex, and of their mothers, on whom falls a major responsibility for the moralization of the young and who might regard such a narrative as a wholesome influence on impressionable daughters. Indeed, the moral world-view is ubiquitous in material used in instructing the young. American high-school civics texts notoriously present as fact not what the nation's political and social processes really are, but what educators think they ought to be. Judge Barron's account seems less extreme when compared with the putatively scientific facts about premarital celibacy presented in most college textbooks on "Marriage and Family Living."

Moral world-views sustain conformity both by reinforcing past learning and by providing information which calculating individuals may assess. The extent to which they sustain conformity, however, also depends on the location of people in amoral environments and their exposure to amoral world-views. Other things being equal—in this case the strength of previously learned commitment and the strength of other sanctions—persons with exceptional access to amoral situations and ideas will have relatively high rates of deviation. Even if their moral commitment were originally as strong as the moral commitment of those exposed only to moral environments and world-views, the reinforcement of their commitment solely by actual sanctions (without additional symbolic representation) will lead to its more rapid attenuation. It might be profitable to study those whose positions in society enable them to move to an exceptional degree outside the moral environment and who thereby gather much evidence against which the claims of the moral world-view may be compared.

One such group will be those who in the course of their work gain exceptional access to reliable information about conformity, deviation, and its consequences. These will be specialists in some part of the sanctioning process, especially as it deals with institutionalized norms. Roman Catholic priests provide one example, for they listen to confessions (some of which may be relatively accurate verbal reports of behavior) and apply symbolic sanctions. The environment of the priest is carefully designed to be a highly moral one, and much of the symbolic world to which he is exposed consists of a sophisticated and systematic moral world-view. Yet ministry and the confessional provide him with strong "temptations"—that is, information about circumstances under which deviation will be rewarded and probably untouched by ordinary institutional sanctions. The Roman Church has therefore evolved a strong set of sanctions specifically to counter the reinforcing effect of these temptations, including the interdiction of "solicitation"—the seduction of female penitents, who, having revealed in their confessions how they were seduced in the past, give tempting information about how they might be seduced in the future.[2]

The sociologist Erving Goffman has discussed immoral environments and tempting information in a number of contexts. Much of his book, *The Presentation of Self in Everyday Life* (1959), deals with a distinction between the places and situations where institutionalized norms are conformed to and those where they are not. Goffman's distinction, made in terms of "regions" and "region behavior," "backstage" and "discrepant roles," can also be viewed as one between places and situations where certain classes of general or "public" sanctions are likely to be encountered and those where they are not. Private occasions, small groups, interaction limited to family members or to peers in age, sex, and stratified status, and so on, all lend themselves to certain types of deviation. Goffman also describes how access to the "backstage" presents information which tempts those who are supposed to be particularly moral to become particularly immoral: thus the hotel detective, armed with specialized knowledge of sanctions and entrusted to maintain property rights within his domain, becomes especially well informed about techniques by which such

---

2 I draw here from the discussion of clerical celibacy in Blake and Davis (1956, pp. 364–65, especially the references in their note 26). See also Ranulf (1938, pp. 135–37).

rights may be trespassed against with little risk. Insulated against the reinforcing effect of sanctions by the knowledge of how poorly they sometimes
work, he often succumbs to the alternate rewards of theft. Westley, in his
study of police (1951, pp. 256 ff.) finds the same process operating in their
case, including the special organizational sanctions that have been evolved
to counteract the extraordinary temptations of much police work. Lawyers
are considered poor risks by credit specialists because their familiarity with
the operation, and thus with the limitations, of legal sanctions enables them
to avoid the quasi-contractual and often unenforceable requirements on which
much credit is based. A similar situation among tax accountants is controlled by special rules and sanctions. Such accountants are expert in the
complexities of the United States tax laws; many of them are also former
employees of the Internal Revenue Service and well informed about how
much of the law the government actually has the resources to enforce. To
adapt Parsons' metaphor, they have audited the "power bank" and know
where it has overextended itself. This enables them to profit from false
and fraudulent tax returns filed for their clients and themselves. The government therefore requires every accountant who prepares a tax return to sign
it, and to stand jointly liable with the taxpayer for any misinformation
which the accountant knows the return to contain. The taxpayer's punishment is usually only a fine based on the amount of the attempted fraud;
but the accountant may suffer the indefinite loss of lucrative business privi-
leges extended to him by the government—the pleading of cases in the tax
court, advising clients, and preparing tax returns. Thus the long-run pecu-
niary interest of the accountant is made to accord with the submission of
strictly legal returns.

These examples should be enough to make the general point: information
about sanctions generally weakens their capacity to reinforce moral behavior,
and information about the reward that accrues to deviation tends to extinguish moral commitment. Of course, if norms were typically stronger than
they are represented to be, information would strengthen rather than weaken
their capacity to reinforce. But a pattern of strong sanctions, weakly ad-
vertised, would be a wasteful form of social control. Economy in social
control follows from representing sanctions symbolically as compared to applying the sanctions themselves; weak sanctions are therefore generally adver-
tised as strong ones. The implication for the role of moral learning in social
control is thus made clear: it cannot be relied on to vouchsafe conformity for
any long period of time in situations which provide a great deal of information about the *actual,* as distinguished from the *reputed,* operation of sanctions. Social control in such situations therefore requires special sanctions,
strong enough to offset the strong effect of information about opportunity
and impunity. This leads to the old question: *quis custodiet ipsos custodes?*

Those who control, if they are to be controlled themselves, must be subject to specialized sanctions. Often such sanctions cannot be applied, and the result is the ruthless immorality of the powerful. If the moral action of rulers depended solely on their early commitment to good intentions, Lord Acton's observation that power corrupts would not be a truism of politics.

Age-Grades and the Strength of Reinforcers

The claim that the rate of change of behavior in socialization (or in learning generally) decreases as a function of age is frequently made in theoretical derivations. It supports the doctrine that "the child is father of the man," and thus the idea that the important events of adult life are to be studied in the childhood of the adults. On an empirical basis, the decreasing-rate argument has been fully developed by Benjamin Bloom in his review of research, *Stability and Change in Human Characteristics* (1964). The principal claim of this work is summarized in a graph in the Preface (p. vii) showing "level of development" as a function of age, increasing at a decreasing rate; with the variation in the value of this function that may be produced by environmental factors also decreasing as a function of age. Bloom marshals 200 pages of review (mostly of research on small "samples of convenience" reported in American journals of psychology, education, and child development) to show that the correlation between two measurements of the same characteristic at different ages is generally quite high. Some of his measurements are not of behavior (for example, height). Most of the behavior he does measure consists of highly abstracted bits of verbalization selected for its manipulability in quantitative analysis (such as I.Q. scores) ; as such it reflects the research preoccupations of the scientists whose work Bloom reports. It remains an interesting and open question whether behavior in more natural environments is equally stable. Despite his thesis of environmental invariance Bloom reaches the same conclusion. "We are of the opinion," he states at the end of his book, "that much of the stability we have reported in this work is really a reflection of environmental stability. . . . What is needed are a number of studies in situations where the environment changes over the same span of time" (p. 223). Bloom mentions his own surprise when, in correlating height at two ages, the association rose from a Pearsonian r for two variables of .74 to a multiple correlation of .90 when a variable of social class position was added (p. 184). Given the precision with which height can be measured (especially compared with most measures of behavior) this is an impressive increase in an already high correlation and shows the influence that the environment can have even on what is generally regarded primarily as a genetically determined variable.[3]

The effect of choosing variables for longitudinal assessment with an eye to easy quantification has led to an emphasis on precise, repeatable, and accessible characteristics which can be measured readily at all ages. Necessarily, then, most variations linked to aged-graded statuses have been excluded, and it should not be surprising to sociologists that longitudinal studies find little instability in rates of change. Rates of such activity as the use of obscene words, grooming, interaction with the opposite sex, and so on have not been studied in the research that Bloom reports, and it would be most surprising if they were to fit his "decreasing rate of growth" curve.[4] The implication for the process of moral development is clear. It is, as we already noted, often spoken of as a process in which the early years are crucial, and data such as Bloom reports are cited as analogical evidence: early conditions—or at any rate early behavior—are pretty good predictors of most later characteristics: Will not this then be true also of moral commitment? The answer of this theory is that it need not be if the activity in question (or moral commitment generally) is reinforced differently at different ages. Chapter IV outlined one kind of age-graded shift in moral commitment. If such changes can be shown to be widespread, then it suggests that constancy of adult commitment results not from the adult's autonomous fundamental values, but rather from the relative constancy of the reinforcing environment, the persistent sanctions of which a stable and secure status is composed.

---

[3] It is, of course, logically possible that certain class variations might themselves depend to an important degree on a genetic component. Thus one can imagine rules of marital selection (hypergamy based on the bride's height) that would concentrate a genetic factor favoring taller offspring in higher strata. An environmental factor is more likely: the upper classes historically eat more meat. For an attempt to revive sociological interest in genetic factors see Eckland (1967). Eckland attempts to show the importance of genetic inheritance in intelligence. This is probably the worst of all possible dependent variables for his purpose, because of the protean nature of the concept of "intelligence" and the extremely wide range both of genetic and environmental factors to which it might be related. Most of Eckland's references are not to literature in genetics but to work in psychology, education, and child development (including that of Bloom, to whom he refers as a "leading proponent of the environmentalist view"). This body of work egregiously exemplifies "experimental positivism" as discussed above in Chapter III and thus is quite ill suited for the assessment of environmental variables. It supports Eckland's arguments mainly by default. "Intelligence" and many other aspects of behavior might eventually be shown to rest much more on genetic factors than many social scientists believe today. But they will not be shown to do so by research which fails adequately to assess and control for environmental effects—the distinctive failing of experimental positivism.

[4] A further stabilizing bias in longitudinal studies occurs because those who are most likely to change their environment are also those most likely to disappear from the original sample. Few longitudinal studies are free from a "dropout" sampling bias in this direction.

A social reinforcement theory of morality accounts for changes in moral behavior by explaining it in terms of changes in status. This is consistent with the decreasing rate of change that Bloom's review finds so widespread. The latter need not be explained as the operation of some developmental process apart from reinforcement, but as the result of interaction between the ongoing sanctions of which socialization is composed and what the person being socialized has already learned. In many cases the same stimuli will have less reinforcing effect on adults than on children. This occurs first, because stronger stimuli will be needed to reinforce a given response where a previously learned competing response has to be extinguished first; and second, because there is a decrease in both the relative and absolute strength of reinforcers that societies will allow to be applied to occupants of older statuses. We cannot do with impunity to adults what we can do with impunity to children.

A growing child is constantly reinforced for increasing generalization in discrimination and response in a way which entails the extinction of many specific responses learned earlier. At one time it will be reinforced for emitting the vocal operant "mommy" in the presence of any adult female, for eager and anticipating parents tend to reinforce vocalization in any form in its earliest stages. But soon the child comes to be reinforced also for increasingly specific and subtle discriminations in connection with emitting the word "mommy," so that he emits it when his mother and only when his mother is present, while he is also reinforced for emitting new and additional names for previously undiscriminated stimuli. If he is to learn these new names, the operant "mommy" must in this context be "unlearned" or extinguished. Later on, he forms sentences with the casual syntax of babytalk, while still later this too must be unlearned and replaced by more regular grammar. Much the same pattern of change and transition goes on in other areas as well. The more new behavior is learned, the more old behavior has to be extinguished; and the more old secondary reinforcers have to be replaced by newer "tertiary" ones. The marginal amount of novel behavior produced by each given unit of reinforcement therefore declines.

Some evidence for this is seen in the few studies of socially isolated children. Most such studies show that any substantial period of isolation of very young children—or even isolation from the mother, with physiological needs met by others—results in "retardation" or low rates of subsequent learning. But most such studies report children who were not only isolated during part of infancy, but who also received institutional care (as in an orphanage) rather than conventional familial attention after the isolation. One student of institutional care has concluded that it provides only 6 to 8 per cent as much attention as a "normal mother" (Spitz, as cited in Stone [1954, p. 12]). Although the specific proportion may be questioned, whatever difference does exist between institutional and familial care will almost certainly produce different reinforcing effects. The slow learning of isolates may be more a result of limited later reinforcement than of limited early maternal care. Indeed, there is evidence that children whose early isolation was followed by a return to conventional level of maternal reinforcement "soon...made up for their lost development" (Stone, 1959, p. 11). The celebrated case of Isabelle, reported by the parapatetic Kingsley Davis, shows what happened when a child, after years in an extremely limited environment, was subjected to a program of intensive long-term care. After a slow start, Isabelle began to learn at a rapidly accelerating rate, going "...through the usual stages of learning characteristic of the years one through six not only in proper succession but far more rapidly than normal.... She eventually entered school where she participated in all school activities as normally as other children."[5] Such cases as Isabelle's illustrate how rapidly human learning can occur when various acts learned according to a relatively slow age-graded schedule do not have to be extinguished first. As Robert Burgess has pointed out in conversation, many developmental changes that ordinarily occur only over a long period of time can possibly be produced much more quickly simply by accelerating the appropriate schedule of reinforcement beyond its more leisurely natural pace.

As we have observed in the natural social situation, however, new learning requires the extinction of much past learning. Further, as the individual moves closer to adult status, the reinforcements that may be applied get weaker. Textbook definitions of "status" and "role" usually speak of the "rights and obligations" that limit what their occupants can do. This continues the voluntaristic emphasis on the actor rather than the environment. Less remarked are the limits thereby placed on what other people (the social environment) can do to the occupant. The two limitations are not always equal: insofar as statuses are stratified, persons in high positions command strong reinforcers which can be applied to those below them, while those below them command only weak reinforcers that may be applied to those above. This bears on age-grading because it has some properties of social stratification itself, involving between different ages the same persistent and unequal access to scarce and widely valued properties that define stratification in general. The difference, of course, lies in the rate and conditions of mobility: in the conventional sense of "stratification" the unequal access is inheritable across generations from parents to children, whereas in a

---

5 Davis (1949, pp. 206–7). Similar evidence is reported in World Health Organization (1962). This volume is a sequel to Bowlby (1951), in which Bowlby concluded from evidence available to him that early deprivation definitely constrained later development. In the later volume some of the contributors are not so sure. See especially Ainsworth (a colleague of Bowlby's) (1962, pp. 97–169, especially 152 ff.).

purely age-graded system everybody automatically moves through all the ranks (if they live long enough) just by growing old. Rank does not increase monotonically by age in all societies; in many the old and infirm are worse off than the younger and more vigorous adults. But all societies rank adult statuses more highly than pre-adult ones, so that the older group, who already know the society's culture, can use efficient schedules of reinforcement in teaching the younger group who have yet to learn it. This is not to say that other factors have no effect in cultural continuity, or that the young never teach anything to the old, but that adults will generally be less subject to those reinforcers that produce rapid learning and will thus learn more slowly. And we must add to this our previous observation that adult learning requires especially strong reinforcement if previously learned competing responses are to be extinguished.

It is therefore to be observed that when rapid rates of learning are required of adults, they are placed in special situations, separated from everyday life in time and place, where the conventional limitation on the strength of reinforcers—especially, perhaps, negative reinforcers—is relaxed, and they are strongly reinforced and more or less treated as children. Such child-like treatment can now be seen to be required if rapid rates of learning are to occur.

The extensive literature on "total institutions" provides many examples where adults are not given the respect due their age-grade. I review this literature below, but I want first to discuss the implication for moral learning of age-grading and the decreasing strength of conditioners. Clearly, the implication is that, other things being equal, moral behavior does come to be increasingly stable with age. This is not to say that it also becomes more *moral,* in the sense that rates of conformity are higher, for the morally weakening effect of adult information, also a function of passage through age grades, tends to make adults less moral than adolescents. Rather the *rate of change* in morality declines, because of *a parallel decline in the rate of change of the social variables of which it is a function.* The apparent stability of adult morality, usually explained in terms predicable of the actor (functional autonomy, superego strength, and diverse other aspects of "personality") and thus as independent variables operating upon his environment, is explained instead in terms predicable of the environment, that is, the stable schedules of reinforcement which operate on the actor as a result of his position in an ongoing social structure. Where psyche was, there shall sanction be. This in turn suggests an examination of moral behavior where schedules of reinforcement change. Any of the various forms of status mobility exemplify such change, and it has already been discussed in connection with age-grading and symbolic anticipatory socialization of the young. We now turn to studies of changes of status and morality in adult life.

Recent Studies of Deviation
and the Notion of a "Deviant Career"

A new direction in the sociological study of normative deviation has been taken in the last two decades by a group (sometimes called the "interactionist school"), some of whose influential authors are Edwin Lemert, Erving Goffman, and Howard S. Becker.[6] While most sociological commentators on normative matters have been influenced by the idealistic legacy, the writers of this school generally have not. The former group generally considers norms in symbolic forms, as rules, laws, or other verbal utterances, and concentrate on broad institutionalized normative patterns; whereas the interactionist school attends instead to sanctions—of whose variety and subtlety they are generally careful observers—and to what has been called the "subinstitutional level" of normative organization. Especially do they avoid "the phenomenology of the moral man," most of whose component parts they have criticized in different terms. When they discuss the process of learning of or habituation to deviant roles, it is in terms surprisingly consistent with our own theory. Learning a deviant role might be regarded as "immoral" rather than "moral" learning, but this presents no difficulty here. The most direct contrast to "moral" in our theory is "amoral"; the "contranormative forces" that students of deviation study work against institutionalized norms but are otherwise no less normative than the more widespread prescriptions to which these forces are opposed. Ever since Sutherland pointed out that criminal behavior is learned, students of deviation have presented considerable evidence that much deviation is not notably "psychopathic" or calculating (as analyzed in Chapter III) but involves normative learning, presumably by the same mechanisms that account for the learning of institutionalized norms. The difference resides in what gets learned.

The involvement of moral learning in deviation is emphasized in a major theme of the interactionist school, the process which Lemert first distinguished as "secondary deviation."[7] In this theme, "primary deviation" occurs prior to sanctions, while "secondary deviation" occurs after inauguration of sanctions, an important part of which is the labeling not simply of a specific act or set of acts but of the whole individual and (by implication)

---

6 See Lemert (1951, 1967); Goffman (1961, 1963); and Becker (1963). Other authors of book-length works of this persuasion are Matza (1964); Erikson (1966); and Scheff (1967).

7 Lemert first published a statement of the distinction in "Some Aspects of a General Theory of Sociopathic Behavior" (1948, pp. 27 ff.), elaborated it throughout his treatise, *Social Pathology* (1951), and reviewed its use and relation to other concepts in the field of deviation in "The Concept of Secondary Deviation" (1967).

his entire behavioral repertory as "deviant," through such names as "delinquent," "radical," "ne'er-do-well," "eccentric," "cripple," and "slut." Such labels isolate the deviant and help maintain moral world-views; the resultant economy of social control probably accounts for their ubiquity and persistence. Some of these writers sometimes seem to deny either that primary deviation exists or that it is of any sociological interest, as in Becker's oft-quoted claim:

> Social groups create deviance by making the rules whose infraction constitutes deviance, and by applying those rules to particular people and labelling them as outsiders. . . . Deviance is not a quality of the act the person commits, but rather a consequence of the application by others of rules and sanctions to an "offender." The deviant is one to whom that label has been successfully applied; deviant behavior is behavior people so label [1963, p. 9].

From our point of view, this assertion is largely unobjectionable as it stands. But it also seems to imply that social groups have unlimited degrees of freedom with regard to what they label as deviant. Such an implication is inconsistent with the hypothesis presented in Chapter I that the major limits of institutionalized norms are set by the requirements of viable social organization.[8] But this hypothesis is not inconsistent with the general distinction between primary and secondary deviation. It merely implies that among all the varieties and instances of "primary deviation," some are much more likely than others to evoke the societal response that produces secondary deviation. It also suggests that the names by which secondary deviants get stigmatized will imply that they have violated institutionalized norms. This priority of institutionalized norms is noted in the many instances reported by writers of the interactionist school, in which secondary aspects of deviation appear to be far more important than its primary aspects in shaping a deviant career. It is also not inconsistent with the interactionists' implication that much deviation does not consist of operant behavior but is essentially ascribed, or with the related claim that many or most primary deviants go unpunished while many primary conformers get punished. Here the empirical support for the interactionist school is strong. But these contentions are not inconsistent with a claim of the relative primacy of conventionally institutionalized norms.

Punishment (by stigmatization or other means) of "innocents," that is, persons whose primary deviation has been trivial or nonexistent, can abet the efficiency of social control and the maintenance of institutionalized norms. Since notorious and unpunished deviation from important norms

---

8 In a conversation I had with him in 1962, Becker allowed that "there are probably some kinds of activity that society will always have to prohibit."

constitutes evidence that sanctions are not applied, according to the hypotheses of Chapter III such deviation tends to weaken moral commitment for that large part of society for whom moral learning is not complete. To counter this effect social control requires someone to be punished, and what is important for this purpose is not so much that the victim of punishment be in fact a primary deviant to the important norm as that his identification as a primary deviant be unambiguous and his punishment exemplary (see Dentler and Erikson [1959] for a related argument). For this reason the roster of persons labeled as deviant runs to those who are convenient for labeling because they are easy to locate, conspicuous, and defenseless—the young, the poor, the genetically distinguishable ("races"), the deformed—as much as (or more than) to persons who are in fact primary deviants. The roster also includes few primary deviants who are skillful in hiding their primary deviation or in avoiding a reputation for it—the educated, the powerful, the hypocritical. Lemert and Goffman provide numerous examples where a disreputable status of great generality is assigned in a presumed connection with a particular violation of institutionalized norms, when in fact the events that resulted in the assignment (as in most cases of blindness or genetic deformity) had no such connection—for example, the attribution of the blindness of a child to the wrongdoing of parents, or of a harelip to incestuous procreation.[9]

Any conclusion that such facts as these upset the notion of the priority of institutionalized norms is unwarranted. At most they tell us that particular putative institutionalized norms are not institutionalized at all. The ubiquitous reliance of social control on "victims of convenience" tells us, for example, that a norm of "justice," that is, "due process" of "responsible and thorough determination of facts" in the assessment of guilt, is not as strongly institutionalized as liberal intellectuals may believe it is. The vulnerability of the poor to sanctions, and the invulnerability of the rich, together with the persistence of the mechanisms that account for the difference, suggest that stratification may also be a major social institution in this normative sense.

The distinction between primary and secondary deviation is valuable to our theory in two additional respects. First, in emphasizing the manner in which deviation not only produces a societal response, but, in its secondary form, is also caused by it, the distinction expands the realm of behavior that the mechanism of social reinforcement can explain. In *Stigma,* Goffman illustrates in manifold ways how the daily routine of the stigmatized person consists of adaptations not so much to the primary event that elicits the stigma (which may be purely physical) as to the social response to the

---

9 Goffman (1963), illustrated in the fictional epigraph and *passim*; Lemert (1951, *passim*, and especially pp. 111–13).

stigma. Second, the distinction helps us to outline the sequence of events—the "schedule of reinforcement"—associated with a deviant career and with the eventual learning of a commitment to deviant norms and the roles they define. The deviant so labeled moves into a world where rewards for conventional conformity are no longer applied to him, and where the reinforcements that follow sustained deviation become the ones that control his behavior. Regardless of the extent to which putatively negative sanctions actually reinforce the deviation they are supposed to control (as probably occurs in drug addiction under current United States law), Lemert's point is sound that putative sanctions produce effects other than reduction of the deviation, often including further deviation. Thus stutterers withdraw and adopt the deviant habits of the isolate; and youthful radicals, after being so labeled, become unemployable and alienated, and move from socialist revisionism to revolutionary anarchism or communal quietism. In *Social Pathology* (1951, Chaps. 5–11), Lemert illustrates such sequences of deviation with skill and thoroughness, and the learning of the deviant roles in which the process terminates shows all the persistence and stability we conventionally associate with learned conformity to institutionalized norms.

Stratification, Mobility, and Conformity: The Case of the American "Skid Row"

Among all the properties that a status or position in a social structure may possess, the property of stratification is probably the most pervasive, at least in complex societies. Recalling the definition of stratification as the aggregate ranking of inheritable positions according to their access to whatever may be scarce yet widely valued, then it is clear that extensive status mobility apart from statuses based on age or marriage is likely to involve some degree of change in stratum. Indeed, the sociological term "social mobility" is usually an elliptical reference to "upward" or "downward stratum mobility." Since this essay has already argued that moral commitment is a function of social reinforcements largely organized by status, so that status mobility leads to moral change, it will be instructive to review the moral posture of men who have undergone substantial downward mobility. Indeed, the "deviant career" just reviewed is usually a movement down the ranks of stratified statuses, since successful stigmatization of deviant statuses requires that they be ranked lower on the average than statuses labeled as conventional and conforming. For more evidence on downward mobility we look now at a group of men who (though widely studied in other connections) most students of deviation have until recently overlooked: the inhabitants of "Skid Row."

Skid Row is a common area in American cities, characterized by a "central" location, old buildings, a low level of economic activity as shown by rent or sales revenue, and essentially defined by its largely male population of persons who, however they got there, occupy a low position in the overall system of American stratification.[10] A few of these men are Negroes and as members of this highly subordinated quasi-caste probably never enjoyed any status very much more respectable than the one they now occupy in Skid Row. Therefore their behavior bears only slightly on the relation of status mobility to morality. But most of the men are white: not only are they thereby members of this superordinate group, but their present disreputable status mainly follows an earlier more reputable one. The behavior of these men does bear on the relation of status mobility to morality.

The mechanisms of this movement vary. Some Skid Row inhabitants are simply retired old men, devoid of relatives with whom they can or will reside, who find Skid Row a place where food and lodging are cheap and companionship of age-mates readily at hand. This form of mobility is age-graded, representing a shift from "working" to "retired," usually at a fixed and predictable age. Strictly speaking this is not stratum mobility, but it shares many of its characteristics such as change in income and prestige. These men constitute the "aristocracy" of Skid Row. Their income, for example, though not great, is assured, and it is more than the others have. Correspondingly, their moral behavior is more conventional. These men, who conform to rules even where few sanctions defend them and where rewards are obtainable through deviation, may be judged to act in response to commitments learned in the past. They express conventional disgust with the deviations of others (see the quotations in Bogue [1963, pp. 153 ff.]) which, *ceteris paribus,* is probably a good verbal indicator of learned moral commitment. Many other Skid Row residents, however, have moved down the ladder not in retirement and old age but during their active adult years, generally because of some kind of failure or occupational disadvantage. Their income derives from panhandling, scavenging, and petty theft. They have a very low status—so low, in fact, that they have none left to lose.

Here it will be useful to outline the general relation between stratified position and social control. Most of the sanctions a society is able to use are combined into broad institutionalized levels of status, so that it becomes impossible to present a person with a large number of positive sanctions without thereby raising his status, nor expose him to many negative ones without lowering it. This is demonstrated in the technique used in total institutions for forcefully removing the symbols of the inmates' prior

---

10 This account of Skid Row draws mainly from two sources: Bogue (1963), and Wallace (1965). The latter volume shares much of the perspective of the "interactionist" school.

status so that a new and usually inferior one can be established in the interest of efficient control. But the relation between status and sanction is more general than this. That conventional middle-class conformity is the price to be paid for the rewards of middle-class status is seen in the loss of that status—often quite separate from legal punishment—that follows upon the discovery of deviation on any large scale. The removal of most pretentions to conventional repute is a prerequisite for thorough stigmatization as deviant (cf. Garfinkel, 1956). This is clearly when we consider strong norms, such as those that prohibit fraud, grand larceny, homosexuality, child molestation, and so forth: their violation not only entails legal sanctions but also the loss of the deviant's employment and his public reputation. Indeed, the informal sanctions are much stronger than the formal legal ones. Even weaker norms may be enforced the same way. Professional debt collectors have learned that debts can usually be collected easier through letters to employers, voluntary arrangements with employers for garnishment of wages, the parking of vehicles marked "Collection Agency" in front of the debtor's home and so forth, than they can by recourse to merely legal sanctions that will be enforced by the courts. If the object is to gain a relatively great amount of conformity at a given cost in sanctions then it is better, in short, to threaten the status and embarrass its occupant in general terms than to apply particular sanctions to particular acts.

This advantage of sanctioning a person's status rather than his particular acts is additionally sustained in many industrial societies by the constraint placed on legal sanctions which American jurists call "due process of law." This is the attempt to guarantee, among other things, that an individual will be visited with legal sanctions only after an accurate and limited inquiry into whether a person accused of a crime has in fact committed it. Notions of due process severely limit the mechanisms of social control, which adapt not so much to protect persons and their status from arbitrary sanctions as to control overall rates of deviation. Where legal processes are so constrained, social control tends in the interests of efficiency to run more to extra-legal sanctions. Just as convenient and exemplary persons tend to get labeled as deviants rather than inconvenient and ordinary primary deviants, so the application of sanctions to individuals tends not so much toward isolated reinforcement of particular acts with no contingency on other activities as to reinforcement of a broad range of activities by making the person's tenure in a particular stratum level dependent upon the more or less regular performance of these activities.

To the extent that society maintains control over its members by threatening to take away valuable statuses (the member must conform to hold the status) then control of those who have no status to lose is attenuated. Although methods of control exist which are not closely related to stratified status, so many methods are so related that we may expect, and do in fact observe, a general negative association between stratum level and conformity to broad institutionalized norms. Almost all empirical studies show higher rates of deviation in the lower classes.

We observe this association among the younger inhabitants of Skid Row. Although deviant behavior tends to be under-reported in demographic statistics, Bogue's study cited above offers many data which suggest that deviation is widespread on Skid Row. Doorways, alcoves, areas only nominally removed from public scrutiny are used for urination, personal assault —"jack-rolling"—and theft of personal property are reported to be frequent; conventional standards of cleanliness and privacy are widely ignored; police, hotel employees, and so forth are perfunctory and rude in their treatment of the inhabitants; and so on. Deviation of this sort draws complaints from most Skid Row inhabitants (Bogue, 1963, pp. 154 ff. and photographs throughout). On the other hand, because Skid Row is also an environment in which conventional sanctions are attenuated, it is therefore an attractive place to live for those who are ineligible to gain the rewards of higher statuses. Dress and grooming are casual, no pretence of industriousness need be maintained, and large and small economies of daily life can be practiced which in more respectable environments would be prohibited. Wallace's book, in fact, is largely organized around the thesis that Skid Row is attractive to many of its inhabitants precisely because middle-class morality is not enforced there. Whatever the reason, it appears to be a social environment with high rates of deviation.

Deviant behavior on Skid Row probably occurs not because its inhabitants never learned the norms in question, but through the extinction or "disinternalization" of past learning through termination of reinforcement. While some of the men on Skid Row are of such low social origins that they probably received little in the way of genteel socialization, Bogue's data (1963, Chap. 14) show that most of the men are downwardly mobile. At one time they probably learned well the norms they now violate. They learned not to urinate in doorways, to shave regularly, to respect the person and property of their fellows, and to exhibit at least a superficial and public respect for the conventions of everyday life. If so, then their current behavior on Skid Row is evidence for the hypothesis that learned moral commitment is not maintained in the absence of ongoing reinforcement.

Total Institutions

The phrase "total institution" was coined by Erving Goffman to name that sort of social agency in which "a large number of like-situated individuals, cut off from the wider society for an appreciable length of time, together lead an enclosed, formally administered round of life."[11] These are features that hospitals, monasteries, prisons, and boarding schools have in common, as against the more regularly observed diversity of functions served and groups processed. Structurally, total institutions divide into two groups, *staff* and *inmates*; for Goffman, the important feature of such institutions lies in the techniques by which the staff applies exceptionally strong sanctions to the inmates and in the changes thereby produced in what he calls "the structure of the self."

In some respects, Goffman appears to be advancing a mentalistic conception of social psychology. He states that his object in mental hospital field work is to "learn about the social world of the hospital inmate, as this world is subjectively experienced by him" (1961, p. ix). Then too, Goffman writes with an eye to literary effect. His style is artfully plain and the clumsy neologisms of psychiatry, psychology, and sociology almost never appear in his work. Nevertheless, in *Asylums,* as in his other writings, he is a good and true friend of a reinforcement theory of morality because he reports so much on inmate behavior.

Total institutionalization informs us also on the relationship among age-grading, the strength of reinforcers, and the rate of learning. If the limitations on the strength of reinforcers associated with a particular status are ignored, so that the rich are treated like the poor, or the old like the young; if the reinforcers are strong enough to extinguish prior learning, then changes occur in adult behavior at a rate usually associated with the behavior of children. The moral autonomy of the adult reduces to the social stability of his status: change the status and in time you change the behavior.

In "The Moral Career of the Mental Patient" and other papers in *Asylums,* Goffman outlines the mechanisms whereby childlike rates of moral change are produced in adults. These follow in a generally regular order as inmates move from an "outside" civil status to their new environment. The rate of movement varies. For most mental patients it is gradual and often anticipated; for most concentration-camp prisoners and Marine Corps recruits, abrupt and often surprising. In all cases the individual tends to emit responses learned in his pre-institutional status, which must be extinguished if the institution is to do its work.

To facilitate this extinction, total institutions use a process often called "depersonalization," or the undoing of those habits and properties of a person that are conventionally called his "personality" (Goffman, 1961, p. 20). But if social processes are the principal source of personality character-

---

11 Goffman (1961, p. xii). For a related discussion, see also Wheeler (1966, especially the typologies on pp. 57 and 61).

istics, then depersonalization is also a form of status degradation. In its extreme form this often involves strong aversive stimuli such as kicks, blows, exposure to extreme cold, and so forth, but the main effect of the stimuli is symbolic or secondary rather than primary. Stimuli equally strong and aversive are often applied outside the total institution without any degrading meaning. Thus within the total institution they are used not indiscriminately but only in ways that conventional respect of the inmate's prior status would prohibit. They thus inform the inmate that his old status has been vacated. Sometimes this starts with a straightforward explanation of the new situation, as when Marine Corps drill instructors, for example, first plead with their new recruits to give them mindless and instant obedience. But words alone are usually not enough to change old and well-learned habits; the verbal admonitions are therefore supported by non-verbal symbolic degradations. The process is distilled in the Ozark anecdote wherein the muleskinner, discovered beating a mule with a wooden beam, explains that he is not punishing the animal but simply trying to get its attention.

Goffman's discussion of "self" or "personality" in terms of what he calls an "identity kit" brings comfort to the behaviorist's heart. Whatever may be the components of the self on a purely subjective level, Goffman reminds us of its dependence on various routine habits and even on physical accoutrements, such as cosmetics, clothing, and grooming aids, and the periodic renewal of these accoutrements. Total institutions change the self not by focusing on its subjective aspects but by removing the physical pieces of old identity kits and by making the continuation of old habits impossible. Thus personal variations in clothing and grooming get replaced with "regulation" haircuts and uniform dress, "typically. . . 'coarse' . . . ill-fitting, often cold, and the same for a wide variety of inmates." Because the total institution has such control over its inmates, they may be required to assume demeaning postures and say silly things in order to get objects to which access in the civilian world can be taken for granted. Similarly the staff may call the inmate "obscene names, curse him, point out his negative attributes, tease him, or talk about him or his fellow inmates as if he were not present." While in the civilian world most persons have a secure access to what Goffman calls "ecological niches"—a private place to defecate, to store personal possessions, to avoid interaction, and so forth—these are generally inaccessible in the total institution. The privacy usually accorded the body is often not respected in medical and other examinations. Inmates often must mix with other inmates whom they would avoid in civilian life for risk of contamination of their status; for example, political prisoners must mix with sex offenders, twice-born with despised castes, women with men, and so on. Contact with the outside environment, which is likely to reinforce the inmate's former status, is cut off completely or monitored so as to attenuate its effects: mail is opened or censored, visits are ritualized by heavy surveillance, and so on.

In a study of socialization of nuns in religious orders, Douglas (in press) reports some distinctive aspects of this isolated and regimented environment: the notiviate hears that "she puts away her past when she takes the veil," that "singularities" (idiosyncrasies) are to be exorcised, that all conversation is prohibited unless three or more novitiates are present, and that use in speech of the first person singular should cease, so that "I like the gift you gave me" becomes "We like the gift you gave us." The total institution, in sum, depersonalizes its inmates by systematically countering the support given to their prior status and by punishing the responses to and learned during their enjoyment of that status, replacing it with a single new status, more or less the same for all.

Goffman outlines a technique common in total institutions whereby the rate of extinction of responses learned in a previous status is increased. It is important here because of its analogy to the mechanisms (outlined in Chapter III) involved in the learning of guilt, resting on the same distinction between an act and the actor's verbal report of it. The technique is evidence for the hypothesis that the verbal report of an act reinforces to some extent the act itself, although in the present case the distinction is better put as one between an act and the actor's expression of sentiments about the act.

In formal or "impersonal" settings for social control there is generally little proximate interaction between sanctions following a deviant act and the response of the deviant to these sanctions (although there may be important ultimate interaction, as in secondary deviation.) The sanction for a given deviation is more or less the same regardless of how the deviant reacts to it. But in informal or "personal" settings, such as families or other primary groups, there is generally a great deal of proximate interaction between sanctions and the deviant's response to them, and the length of the sanctioning process as a whole is a function of the response of the deviant to the first part of that process (cf. with Wheeler's distinction between "differentiated" and "undifferentiated" processing systems [1966, p. 57]). This occurs especially in the familial training of children and, in terms of our theory (adapting that of Winfred Hill), is essential to the acquisition of guilt. It can be found too in some formal processes, as in the notion of "contempt of court," wherein the legal punishment for an act can be in part contingent upon the response to the legal sanctioning process and the determination of punishment.

When sanctions do not interact with the response to them they cannot reinforce that response; following the sanction the actor therefore makes whatever response he is otherwise reinforced for making. Often this is a verbal expression of hostility, or, as Goffman puts it, a "face-saving reactive expression . . . sullenness . . . *sotto voce* profaning asides, or fugitive expressions of contempt, irony, or derision" (1961, p. 36). In total institutions, however, the totalitarianism of the family and the primary group is reasserted and the interaction between sanctions and the response to them is reestablished; he who protests the sanctions finds them applied to him that much more strongly. Their termination or attenuation is contingent on his own response, and whatever response terminates them most quickly and consistently is thereby reinforced. Hostility thus comes to be replaced with contrition. The "fugitive expressions of contempt, irony, or derision," since they derive comparison between the inmate's present and past statuses, reinforce the behavior learned in the past status. Punishing such expressions thus helps extinguish the previously learned behavior. Goffman tells us that hostile reactions tend to occur in private places or occasions, where staff cannot observe inmates, and that they are often made in the presence of the staff, but in a style which, though plain to other inmates, is too subtle for staff to understand. These mechanisms, a part of what Goffman calls "underlife" or " secondary adjustments," enable inmates to resist the institution's program and maintain some of the previously learned behavior that the institution is trying to extinguish. But these secondary adaptations occur only because total institutions are seldom absolutely total. Such complete totality could be achieved only at a very high cost, and even the most ruthless of total institutions operates under budgetary constraints. The primary fact in the total institution is still not the continuity of inmates' behavior but the change of that behavior.

Now that we have seen how total institutions work, we can appreciate what they produce. Their relevance for our theory derives from the fact that the new forms of behavior they produce are often saliently moral. The inmates unlearn old norms which they had learned well and learn new ones in their place. They not only conform to the new norms themselves but in time come to sanction other inmates. Relevant here are two discussions of moral learning in total institutions: "identification with the aggressor" and other responses, as observed by Bruno Bettelheim during his own imprisonment in a Nazi concentration camp; and the development of the "Sambo" personality among American blacks as discussed by Elkins (1963). Because both these cases provide an example of commitment to norms which are repugnant to middle-class conventions and which are hardly the kinds of commitments implied by developmental, self-actualizing, or other nonenvironmental theories of moral commitment, they raise serious questions about such theories and contain a strong argument for a reinforcement theory.

Bettelheim's discussion (1960, pp. 107 ff.), like Goffman's, concentrates on what strong schedules of reinforcement can do to the ego, self, or person-ality.[12] In concentration camps, he found degradation of an extreme degree. Starting with transportation to the camp, the staff used various symbolic means to inform new inmates that their old status was well and truly lost. The degree of "trauma" this produced was largely a function of how much downward mobility it represented: upper-middle-class prisoners became the most disoriented. Aspects of the "self" often presented as evidence of its autonomy from reinforcement crumbled when their reinforcement was re-moved:

> Those familiar with the mores of this group (the German middle class) well appreciate what a blow it was when raw privates in the SS addressed them not as *Herr Rat* (or some other title of office) but with the degrad-ing "thou"; even worse, they were forbidden to address one another with the titles of office that were their greatest pride, and were forced to use the much too familiar "thou" form when they spoke to each other. Up to then they had never realized just how much extraneous and superficial props had served them in place of self-respect and inner strength. Then all of a sudden everything that had made them feel good about themselves for so long was knocked out from under them...[and eventually] they disintegrated as autonomous persons....
> Nearly all of them lost their desirable middle-class characteristics, such as their sense of propriety and self-respect. They became shiftless, and devel-oped to an exaggerated extent the undesirable characteristics of their group: pettiness, quarrelsomeness, self-pity....[Some] became chiselers and stole from other prisoners....Some followed the behavior pattern set by the criminals. Only a very few adopted the ways of the political prisoners, usually the most desirable of all patterns....Many more tried to submit slavishly to the SS [Bettelheim, 1960, pp. 121–22].

Bettelheim observed that "childish" behavior emerged among the in-mates, and his explanation for it is the same one we are offering: the inmates were reinforced on a schedule similar to that defining the status of children in civilian society. The complete domination of the inmates by

---

12 Bettelheim himself experienced and wrote about the earlier concentration camps where various types of felons, political prisoners, and ethnic groups were brought together for isolation and oppression, but before large-scale extermination was practiced. In the later camps, a majority of the inmates were murdered by gasing only a few days after their "selection" from various Jewish ghettos, and the remainder were decimated by slave labor. Treatment of prisoners in the later camps, though extremely adverse, was more or less unstructured or anomic. In the earlier camps, the treatment of prisoners was designed to produce docile behavior, and it is to these, with their strong schedules of reinforcement, rather than the later ones with their strong reinforcers, that the literature on personality changes in such situations refers. Besides the discussions of moral change by Goffman and Bettelheim, see Kogon (n.d., pp. 63 ff.) and E. Cohen (1963, Chaps. 3 and 4).

the Gestapo and the SS is characteristic of the domination of children by parents. Bettelheim decribes, for example, how prisoners were required to beg permission from the attendant guard to defecate at other than regular times, just as a child might ask his parents to locate a toilet for him: "...it was as if the education to cleanliness were being repeated all over again." Moreover, the familiar form of second-person address (*du*) "in Germany is never used indiscriminately except among small children" (1960, pp. 121–22). This return to the child's status was most strikingly shown in older prisoners.

Though mortality in the camps was high (Bettelheim estimates 30 per cent per year during his stay), some prisoners lived on for several years. This group drew away from the standards of civilian life and became committed instead to the norms of the SS. Most "developed types of behavior... usually characteristic of infancy or early youth." They came to be oriented solely to the present, and they apparently spent much of their time in "primitive and contradictory daydreams" (1961, pp. 168–69). In what Bettelheim calls "the final adjustment," the result was a "personality structure willing and able to accept SS values and behavior as its own." The special pejorative vocabulary of the SS came to be used, and in time "it was not unusual, when prisoners were in charge of other prisoners, to find old prisoners...behaving worse than the SS." They did what they could to modify their prison costume so that it resembled the SS uniform. They prided themselves in standing stiffly at attention. One episode illustrates the essential element of moral learning—conformity to a norm in the absence of sanctions to maintain it:

> Often an SS man would for a while enforce some nonsensical rule, originating in a whim of the moment. Usually it was quickly forgotten, but there were always some old prisoners who continued to observe it and tried to enforce it on others long after the SS had lost interest. Once, for example, an SS man was inspecting the prisoners' apparel and found that some of their shoes were dirty on the inside. He ordered all prisoners to wash their shoes inside and out with soap and water. Treated this way, the heavy shoes became hard as stone. The order was never repeated, and many prisoners did not even try to carry it out the first time, since the SS, as was often the case, gave the order, stood around for a few minutes and then left. Until he was gone, every prisoner busied himself with carrying out the order, after which they promptly quit. Nevertheless there were some old prisoners who not only continued to wash the insides of their shoes every day but cursed all who failed to do so as being negligent and dirty. These prisoners believed firmly that all rules set down by the SS were desirable standards of behavior, at least in the camp [p. 172].

Theories of moral commitment which argue that sanctions alone cannot account for it and which hold that personality variables which are not dependent on reinforcement must figure in the explanation are difficult to square with what happened in the dismal reaches of the concentration camps. Even that resolute advocate of social invariance, Gordon Allport, was moved by this evidence: "No one," he acknowledged, "however intense his efforts, [can] permanently withstand complete collapse of his social supports" (1961, p. 188). To be sure, Bettelheim mentions individual variations in the pattern of adjustment, but it is not at all inconsistent with a reinforcement theory to claim that the past history of the individual—which is mainly a history of his past reinforcements—will affect the rate at which he will be conditioned even by the strong schedules of total institutions. The overall conclusion, from the literature on total institutionalization and especially on concentration camps, is that human behavior and morality are much more dependent on social environment than conventional wisdom and the naive phenomenology of moral men indicate. Most who lived through camp life and were still in shape to write about it afterward were medical men, and many were psychoanalysts with a strong prior commitment to the doctrine of the immutable superego. Their new despect for environmentally induced change is well expressed for these professionals by Alexander:

> The psychiatrist stands in amazement before the thoroughness and completeness with which this perversion of essential superego values was accomplished in adults.... It may be that the decisive importance of childhood and youth in the formation of [these] values may have been overrated by psychiatrists in a society in which allegiance to these values in normal adult life was taken too much for granted because of the stability, religiousness, legality, and security of the 19th Century and early 20th Century society [1948, p. 173].

In view of the moral shifts that movement from civilian to inmate life can produce, it is interesting to consider whether the inmate can be "re-moralized" by a return to civilian status. Some qualified evidence on this is presented by Eitinger (1964), who compared the subsequent adaptation of two groups of concentration camp survivors. One group consisted of Norwegians who returned to Norway; the other, of European Jews from many countries, who later settled in Israel. Generally, the Norwegians made a "more successful" return to civilian life. Eitinger reports that physical conditions within the camps were approximately the same for the two groups, but that the context of incarceration varied, involving more symbolic degradation and a longer prior period of anxiety for the Jews. But also important was that "the Norwegian groups returned home to almost normal conditions of life, while the Israeli groups had lost their homes and their contacts and were isolated in the truest sense of the word" (p. 181). Perhaps the high levels of neurosis and disorientation that Eitinger observed among the Jews in Israel can be explained in part by their marginal status in a new nation with few stable positions for much of its refugee population. His data are not conclusive, but they add some support to the hypothesis that the stability of moral commitment is principally a function of the stability of its social reinforcement.

Total institutionalization shows the moral changes in persons who have passed through the age-graded steps in the moral careers of ordinary society and who are then abruptly subjected to novel and strong schedules of reinforcement. This may be compared to the behavior of persons who have been subjected to such schedules since birth—or even for several generations, wherein relatively extreme control throughout life by others becomes something of a social institution in itself. Such an institution is discussed by Elkins (1963). The controversy attends the ideologically delicate question of a "slave personality" and the pejorative stereotype of "Sambo." Elkins's book is also the first comparative study of North and South American slavery of Africans. It compares the effects not only of different slave regimes but also of concentration camps.

In his introduction (1963) to Elkins's book the sociologist Nathan Glazer notes the salient characteristics of American slavery and its impact on contemporary Negro behavior. As a slave regime it was "the most awful the world has ever known." The slave was

> ...totally removed from the protection of organized society..., his existence as a human being was given no recognition by any religious or secular agency, he was totally ignorant of and completely cut off from his past, and he was offered absolutely no hope for the future. His children could be sold, his [conjugal unions] not recognized, his wife could be violated or sold..., and he could also be subject, without redress, to frightful barbarities....The slave could not, by law, be taught to read or write; he could not practice any religion without the permission of his master,... could never meet with his fellows, for religious or any other purposes, except in the presence of a white; and finally, if a master wished to free him, every legal obstacle was used to thwart such action [Glazer, 1963, p. ix].

Here Glazer has cataloged what might be called the "rudiments of citizenship" in the sense that they are extended to adult humans of almost every status—even, in most cases, to the lowest groups in a stratified system—but which were systematically denied to the black slave. The American slave's status was in fact most succinctly defined by its lack of what is accorded to others. It therefore occasions no surprise that the behavior of persons who have for generations been reduced to such a position should also lack what we conventionally find in the behavior of others who experience different reinforcements. This lack is what is embodied in the stereotype of "Sambo."

Glazer has remarked, in another context, that most stereotypes contain a large measure of truth (Glazer and Moynihan, 1963, p. 33, paraphrased). This was said to counter the belief of liberal-left intellectuals that most stereotypes are mostly false. In order to offset the effect of this belief among his readers, Elkins marshals an extravagance of support for the thesis that the Negro under slavery did develop a distinctive personality.

> Sambo, the typical plantation slave, was docile but irresponsible, loyal but lazy, humble but chronically given to lying and stealing; his behavior was full of infantile silliness and his talk inflated with childish exaggeration. His relationship with his master was one of utter dependence and childlike attachment [Elkins, 1963, p. 82].

Sambo was not the universal Negro under slavery, but he was the distinctive plantation type; and the plantation was the most total of all concrete institutions that shaped the life of the slave. Elkins draws a series of persuasive analogies between the concentration camp and the slave's situation. The decline of the African typically began with his capture in tribal wars, from which he was sold to the Europeans waiting at the coast. Then followed the terrible "middle passage"—the shipment of slaves in unbelievably crowded ships from Africa to the West Indies. Elkins estimates mortality among the slaves at 60 per cent by the time the West Indies were reached; those who survived had been conditioned by the death of their fellows. The slave's new environment was totally new; his novel status a totally dependent one. Just as infants are completely in the hands of their parents, so the slave was completely in the hands of his master. The "familial care" provided the slave was of course very rudimentary in character, somewhat like that given bastard children who are raised in attics.

Elkins points out that the frequent literary reference to the Sambo personality among American slaves and its persistence as a stereotype is not found elsewhere in the New World, particularly not in Brazil and Jamaica. Our explanation would be in line with his, that is, while the slaves outside the United States also went through the deprivations of the middle passage, their status after that was not one in which a pattern of servility and infantile dependence was so consistently reinforced. The Latin-American slave, though in the lowest stratum, still shared some rights held by others. It further served the interest of powerful institutions to protect his status— notably the Roman Catholic Church, which viewed the consistent suppression of the slave's family relations as a threat to its then emerging attempt to control the institution of marriage. Moreover, the European colonists in

Latin America were mostly men, and lacking European women they tended to take slave women first as concubines and later as wives (Glazer, 1963, p. xii; cf. Davis, 1941, p. 391). This produced some social mobility, first for women and later for their half-caste offspring, weakening the caste system and thereby the slave system with which it was implicated. Under such circumstances the patterns of operant behavior denoted by such terms as "planning," "initiative," "foresight," "ambition"—aspects of stratum mobility aspirations—received some reinforcement in Latin America, whereas in the North American system they were ignored or punished.

The contemporary impact of the different antecedent status of North American as compared to Latin American and West Indian blacks is discussed elsewhere by Glazer in accounting for the relative stratum immobility of American Negroes in contemporary urban settings. The American Negro is simply too recently released from the extreme state of slavery to be reached by the institutions from which he might learn enough of the behavior that produces mobility. West Indian Negroes, on the other hand, whose ancestors were not slaves in this country (and who once accounted for about 17 per cent of the black population of New York City), accounted for most of the political leadership, business enterprise, and mobility among Negroes during the period that they were a differentiated group (Glazer and Moynihan, 1963, pp. 34–37).

The argument presented by Elkins deals with the impact of institutions on personality rather than directly with the effect of sanctions on morality. But this is a difference only in vocabulary and scope. "Institutions" are complexes of sanctions; "personality" is a pattern of behavior more conveniently predicable of a particular person than of the variables (both environmental and genetic) of which the pattern is a function; and "morality," as we have defined it, is learning to delimit the range of operant behavior to what is consistent with some type of social organization— in the case at hand, that of a neofeudal plantation economy. The black man was subject to a slave morality, and it was not less normative because his masters taught it to him for their own economic advantage. The slave remained helpless and childlike after emancipation because he had learned so well an earlier complex of norms defining his status as helpless and childlike, and because emancipation did not provide either strong or long-lasting reinforcements for self-reliant and adult behavior (especially after the return of white political domination in the American South after 1876). Elkins's argument thus accords with the examples of adult moral change that we have already discussed, and it calls attention to the same important points. First, adult moral commitment depends on reinforcement from the social environment, and it changes as that environment changes. Second, the mechanisms of reinforcement are able to produce behavior which, though inexplicable in terms satisfactory to the moral world-view usually implicated in nonreinforcement theories of morality, represents "moral commitment" in the sense discussed here: conformity to a norm at a remove from sanctions to maintain it.

Adult Incontinence

The norms defining the circumstances of excretion are well defined, and for the most part quite thoroughly learned. Violations of them are therefore theoretically relevant. Evidence of their extinction, however, would provide strong support for the theory being advanced in this book.

The basic norms governing excretion—those delimiting it to particular times and places, defining appropriate attitudes toward and uses of excrement, and so forth—are, within any one society, highly invariant. However, many ancillary norms vary greatly, both as to what is prescribed and in rates of conformity, according to status, institutional settings, and more transitory social institutions. These ancillary norms relate to privacy, location, prophylaxis, symbolic reference, and differences in types of excretion. All of these vary with the main axes of status—age, sex, and social class. The young are often denied the privacy extended to most adults, and they are taught special circumlocutions to describe excretion that are not the same ones that adults use. Because of the anatomical association of excretory and sexual functions, women are accorded greater privacy and learn more stringent standards for environmental and personal prophylaxis, since their sexual functions are more thoroughly regulated by norms. Members of the higher strata conform more, in general; among other scarce and valued properties they can claim, they have more access to specialized locations for excretion—more plumbing in their homes and readier access to it elsewhere. One reason respectable men do not urinate in hallways, as do the urban poor, is that their respectability opens more restroom doors. Variations in these ancillary norms thus may not bear on theories of moral commitment. Men who do not wash their hands after urinating may never have learned such a rule in the first place. Adult incontinence becomes theoretically relevant when it involves the central norms—bladder and sphincter control.

The literature on incontinence suggests that it varies with age, and probably depends more on physiology than conditioning. What is needed are cases where operant and nonoperant incontinence can be concretely rather than only analytically separated. Such cases, though rare, are available. First is urinary incontinence in youth or young adults, symptomatically named "enuresis." That this is an operant activity is clearly established by the frequent use of operant conditioning techniques for its cure (see, for example, Lovibond, 1963). The second is incontinence in total institutions.

Incontinence in coercive total institutions, such as prison camps, is less relevant to our argument than incontinence in therapeutic ones such as mental hospitals. Since people of almost any status are allowed considerable flexibility in the timing of excretion, a rigid and infrequent schedule constitutes an unmistakable sign of disrespect. It is a mark of the more coercive total institutions (Bettelheim, 1960, p. 132; Goffman, 1961, pp. 25, 41). Under such circumstances, the inmate may become an "involuntary deviant" from the core excretory norms: physiological reflexes overpower operant control and the inmate "soils himself." The attendant responses of guilt, contrition, and "abuse to self-respect" facilitate the degradation and extinction of old statuses and promote the rapid learning of new ones.

Incontinence in a therapeutic setting is discussed by Schwartz and Stanton (1950). The mental hospital these authors studied was exceptional. It was small and private, with high fees and intensive psychotherapeutic treatment, and had a staff that was disinclined to use the more homely and economical forms of punishment which Goffman and others report to be common in public mental hospitals. Yet if we recall that punishments are defined by their effects, it will be seen that any mental hospital that will not let its inmates quit "voluntarily," where no operant activity can lead to any substantial improvement of status (that is, a status outside the hospital), that treats them as only children are treated in ordinary life, and which requires demeaning supplication to gain from others the small amenities and useful objects that in ordinary life one can gain for oneself, will constitute a punishing environment—at least until inmates' commitment to prior statuses has been extinguished.[13] The exceptional hospital that Schwartz and Stanton studied evidently was of this pattern. In such a setting, the only rewards that would have effectively reinforced "abiding by the ordinary social conventions" would be the prospect of increased independence and possible release. But the mission of this hospital—the application of intensive psychotherapy—required (unless the patients already deeply believed in psychotherapy) just the sort of strong reinforcement that incarceration facilitates. It is also unlikely that psychiatrists with a strong belief in psychotherapy would believe that the attendant constraints, rather than the psychotherapeutic dialog itself, was the main reinforcement affect-

---

13 This point tends to get overlooked in conventional psychotherapeutic ideology, which often seems to maintain that the rewarding or punishing effect of a stimulus is mostly a function of the name by which it is called. It is indeed such a function, but it is a function of other factors too, usually more immutable than the name. The preoccupation with symbolic value results in an elaborate set of transformations from plain words to circumlocutions, especially the attachment of the suffix "therapy." This extraordinarily adaptable word is sometimes attached to stimuli which, in the absence of psychiatric legitimation, are usually regarded as a form of torture. For descriptions of electro-shock therapy and its effect as an exemplary punishment in mental hospitals, see Belknap (1956, p. 194).

ing the behavior that they were trying to cure. What the psychotherapists saw as a reward (the therapy) may have been punishing in terms of its effects. If the incontinent patients were placed in the back ward because they were resistant to psychotherapy under more humane conditions, then it may have been that they were in the back ward not so much because they were incontinent as that they were incontinent because they were in the back ward.

The cases discussed by Schwartz and Stanton show very clearly that continence and incontinence can depend on social reinforcement. Those who learn continence have their commitment complemented by equally strong sanctions for incontinence. Indeed, gross incontinence would probably result in the loss of whatever status they occupied in society, for others, committed to the proprieties, would not continue the interaction with them which maintained that status. The patients in question, however, had already lost any such status. If status reinforces continence, we would not be surprised to find it extinguished among mental patients.[14]

Even among patients in the back ward, however, one can still imagine rewards and punishments that could produce and maintain continence. The special circumstances of this hospital apparently prevented this, since deliberate punishment was prohibited. The staff was instructed to pay no attention to incontinence. To the extent that they complied, therefore, continence would be reinforced only intrinsically and by its effect in such interaction with other patients as the patient still engaged in—and only so long as the back ward was not "solitary confinement." The behavior of very young children suggests that the products of excretion are not intrinsically aversive. Further, incontinent behavior may become a stimulus in interaction, a means of drawing attention to oneself or of fending off others. Schwartz and Stanton provide much evidence of the use of incontinence as such a social stimulus. After an incontinent act, the patient would usually call for the hospital staff to come and clean things up (1950, pp. 404, 406 ff.). These patients tended to exhibit "clinical symptoms" and various bizarre habits apart from their incontinence, and both the staff and the other inmates tended to avoid them. This cut them off from the ordinary social interaction that all social animals value, and thus increased the frequency of any activity that would reestablish interaction. Just as a child whines and cries not because he has any complicated "good reason" to but simply because this activity is subsequently reinforced by the attention of his mother, so the isolated back ward case is incontinent not because he is afflicted with some arcane psychopathological condition but because in

---

14 Apparently incontinence is common among back ward cases. See the advertisements for special clothing for incontinent patients mentioned in Goffman (1961, p. 79).

his rather threadbare setting incontinence is the most efficient way he has to get attention. Staff reaction to incontinence resembles the commentaries of parents:

Female Aid: "She does it to be defiant."
Female Nurse: "She does it because she is being hostile."
Another Female Nurse: "She wants to be waited upon or served."
Another Female Nurse: "She wants to put the personnel in an uncomfortable position."
Another Female Nurse: "Miss Adams enjoys watching a man clean it up; that's why she does it."
Another Female Aide: "She does it to get attention"[15] [Schwartz and Stanton, 1950, p. 409].

Better, perhaps, to have interaction based on cleaning up feces than no interaction at all.

Incontinence can be rewarding also because it can provide potent sanctions for others. Apparently this occurred at least once, even though the consequences were eventually punishing:

Miss Bell was being teased by two patients who were much more adequate socially than she. They chased her off living room chairs when her pants were wet, called her "filthy" and in general directed much invective against her for her soiling activities. After that she selected the beds of these two patients and voided on them. This in turn produced renewed attacks [Schwartz and Stanton, 1950, pp. 407–9, 415].

In another case, the other patient repeatedly tried to "engage the investigator in discussion" during a group therapy session. "She was met by a rebuff. Immediately after this the patient voided." But the excretory insult was not invented in the back ward. It also occurs in civil society, especially in such of its less civil moments as riots, insurrections, and adolescent rites of passage (for example, initiation into the "Hell's Angels" motorcycle group and college fraternities).

Schwartz and Stanton are concerned to show that incontinence is a function of interaction, and noted that "none of the patients were ever observed to be incontinent immediately after having received something they requested." They view incontinence as sustained by exposure of the patient to punishing social situations, and suggest that it may be checked by "positive situations" in which the person is rewarded. They also generalize from incontinence to mental illness in general, and thus partly

---

15 No psychoanalytic fallacy is committed by these commonplace (and, given the pattern of recruitment for nurses and aides, probably working-class) explanations. The world-view from the boiler room usually has the virtue of parsimony.

anticipate the more systematic sociological theories of that process by Lemert, Goffman, Szasz, and Scheff: that is, that regardless of what else may be involved in the *omnium gatherum* called "mental illness," its symptoms are first and foremost violations of social norms. Thus the conclusion of Schwartz and Stanton is applicable, *mutatis mutandis,* to moral learning:

> Our conception that mental illness is not a phenomenon occurring within the individual independent of his environment but rather a phenomenon of the total situation of which the patient is an active part has the following implications for social psychological theory: autistic behavior is not solely a product of past history but—like realistic behavior—is part of and takes into account the social situation. Thus, a consideration of pathological behavior, and in particular deeply regressive behavior, should not exclude consideration of the current reality situation. And finally, it is possible that a "symptom" is stable *only* because it is part of a stable social equilibrium and not because it is by its nature irreversible [p. 416].

A Note on Moral Change and Status in Ordinary Social Life

In this chapter we have tried to show that moral commitment, acquired through social reinforcement in youth, is maintained by ongoing reinforcement in adult life. The stability of adult commitment has been explained by the stability of adult statuses and of the schedules of reinforcement of which these statuses are composed. To that end, we have discussed cases in which reinforcement has changed through isolation or a pronounced change in status and where previously learned norms have been extinguished and new ones learned in their place.

The extremity of many of these situations—especially those of total institutions—tends to obscure the point that the processes by which these institutions wreak their effects and so drastically shape the moral career of their inmates differ only in degree and not in kind from less rapid changes in status, especially with age, in everyday life. Most of the techniques found in the total institution were not invented by it, but operate—less systematically and in weaker form—in ordinary changes in status. The extreme mechanism of extinction and relearning in "brainwashing" and concentration camps, in which the deviant must not only report the deviant act but must also, as it were, embrace the sanction against it, profess his guilt, his admiration of his punishers, and his own worthlessness, corresponds to the totalitarian control by parents of their children, whose "sense of personal autonomy," however sensitive and liberal their parents, gets short shrift if it involves incest or homicide among siblings or other important violations of institutionalized norms. The difference between parental and institutional domination is not in means but in the legitimacy, or degree of social support, of the ends to which they are applied. Older children often depreciate the conduct of younger ones, and sometimes this assumes very degrading forms. The process of degradation and depersonalization that reaches its extreme form in prison camps is practiced less severely in many rites of passage elsewhere. Officer candidates who come up through the ranks, who once greatly valued the comaraderie of their former fellows, gradually, through the constant reinforcement of their new status by the deference paid it, come to expect enlisted men to salute them and grow indignant if they do not. All these situations erode old moral commitments and replace them with new ones, just as do the more spectacular environments reviewed in this chapter.

Conclusion

This volume now comes to an end, and I have to repeat my earlier statement that what has been said here to explicate and defend a simple thesis is only a small part of what might have profitably been said. There remains one major unremarked topic which deserves mention, at least for the record: this is the *propensity to sanction*. Visible deviation is manifestly variable in its capacity to elicit sanctioning responses from those who witness it. What accounts for the variation? What, for example, is the relation between degrees of moral commitment and the propensity to sanction? Does the cognitive expectation of sanctions by a person increase the rate at which he is likely to apply them to others? A variety of "soft" evidence does suggest that commitment and a propensity toward sanctioning are positively associated, operating over and above the institutionalized division of labor that assigns specific responsibilities for sanctioning to parents, priests, teachers, supervisors, and police. The notion of such an association is of course not new: it was probably first advanced by Svend Ranulf in his interesting volume *Moral Indignation and Middle-Class Psychology* (1938). Ranulf's views about the determinant of "the disinterested tendency to inflict punishment" are probably not entirely satisfactory to present-day social scientists, but his question remains an interesting and pre-eminently sociological one.

Moral commitment has traditionally been accounted for in terms of psychical and, often, voluntary processes. Our object has been to try to explain it in terms of social reinforcement; in short, to replace psyche with sanction wherever there has appeared an opportunity to do so. How well the attempt has succeeded is for the reader to judge.

Bibliography

Ainsworth, Mary D., 1962. "The Effects of Maternal Deprivation: A Review of Findings and Controversy in the Context of Research Strategy," in *Deprivation of Maternal Care: A Reassessment of Its Effects.* Geneva: World Health Organization.

Alexander, Leo, 1948. "War Crimes: Their Social Psychological Aspects," *American Journal of Psychiatry,* **40:** 173.

Allport, Gordon, 1937a. *Personality: A Psychological Interpretation.* New York: Henry Holt.

——, 1937b. "The Functional Autonomy of Motives," *American Journal of Psychology,* **50:** 141–56.

——, 1955. *Becoming: Basic Considerations for a Psychology of Personality.* New Haven: Yale University Press.

——, 1961. *Pattern and Growth in Personality.* New York: Holt, Rinehart & Winston, Inc.

Alpert, Harry, 1939. *Emile Durkheim and His Sociology.* New York: Columbia University Press.

Anderson, Alan Ross, and Omar Khayyam Moore, 1957. "The Formal Analysis of Normative Concepts," *American Sociological Review,* **22:** 9–17.

Aronfreed, Justin, 1963. "The Effects of Two Experimental Socialization Paradigms upon Moral Responses to Transgression," *Journal of Abnormal and Social Psychology,* **66:** 437–48.

——, 1964. "The Origins of Self-Criticism," *Psychological Review,* **71:** 193–216.

——, 1968. *Conduct and Conscience: The Socialization of Internalized Control over Behavior.* New York: Academic Press, Inc.

———, and A. Reber, 1963. "The Internalization of Social Control through Punishment." Unpublished manuscript.

Ausubel, David, 1955. "Relationships between Shame and Guilt in the Socializing Process," *Psychological Review,* **62**: 378–90.

Bandura, Albert, and Aletha C. Huston, 1961. "Identification as a Process of Incidental Learning," *Journal of Abnormal and Social Psychology,* **63**: 311–18.

Bandura, Albert, and Richard H. Walters, 1963. *Social Learning and Personality Development.* New York: Holt, Rinehart & Winston, Inc.

Banfield, Edward C., 1958. *The Moral Basis of a Backward Society.* New York: The Free Press.

Barker, Roger, and Herbert Wright, 1954. *Midwest and Its Children.* New York: Harper & Row, Publishers.

Barron, Jenny Loitman, 1964. "Too Much Sex on Campus," *Ladies Home Journal* (February): 47 ff.

Becker, Howard S., 1963. *Outsiders.* New York: The Free Press.

Belknap, Ivan, 1956. *Human Problems of a Mental Hospital.* New York: McGraw-Hill Book Company.

Benedict, Ruth, 1934. *Patterns of Culture.* Boston: Houghton Mifflin.

———, 1943. *The Chrysanthemum and the Sword.* Boston: Houghton Mifflin.

Berlyne, D. E., 1966. "Reply [to Fodor]," *Journal of Verbal Learning and Verbal Behavior,* **5**: 408.

Bertocci, Peter A., 1945. "A Reinterpretation of Moral Obligation," *Philosophy and Phenomenological Research,* **6**: 270–83.

Bettelheim, Bruno, 1960. "Behavior in Extreme Situations," in *The Informed Heart.* New York: The Free Press, 107ff.

Black, Max, ed., 1961. *The Social Theories of Talcott Parsons.* Englewood Cliffs, N.J.: Prentice-Hall, Inc.

Blau, Peter, 1964. *Exchange and Power in Social Life.* New York: John Wiley & Sons, Inc.

Bloom, Benjamin S., 1964. *Stability and Change in Human Characteristics.* New York: John Wiley & Sons, Inc.

Blumer, Herbert, 1962. "Society as Symbolic Interaction," in Arnold Rose, ed., *Human Behavior and Symbolic Processes: An Interactionist Approach.* Boston: Houghton Mifflin, 179–92.

———, and Robert F. Bales, 1966. Exchange of letters on G. H. Mead, *American Journal of Sociology,* **71**: 535–48.

Bogue, Donald J., 1963. *Skid Row in American Cities.* Chicago: Community and Family Study Center, The University of Chicago.

Boring, Edwin G., 1950. *A History of Experimental Psychology,* 2nd ed. New York: Appleton-Century-Crofts.

———, 1961a. "A History of Introspection," in *Psychologist at Large.* New York: Basic Books, Inc., 210–45. Originally published 1953.

——, 1961b. "Humanizing Psychology," in *Psychologist at Large*. New York: Basic Books, Inc., 342–46. Originally published 1958.

——, ed., 1961c. *Psychologist at Large*. New York: Basic Books, Inc.

——, 1961d. "Was This Analysis a Success?" in *Psychologist at Large*. New York: Basic Books, Inc., 127–40. Originally published 1940.

——, 1963. *The Physical Dimensions of Consciousness*. New York: Dover Publications, Inc. Originally published 1933.

Bowlby, John, 1951. *Maternal Care and Mental Health*. Geneva: World Health Organization.

Bronfenbrenner, Urie, 1961. "Parsons' Theory of Identification," in Max Black, ed., *The Social Theories of Talcott Parsons*. Englewood Cliffs, N.J.: Prentice-Hall, Inc., 191–213.

——, 1964. "The Role of Age, Sex, Class and Culture in Studies of Moral Development." Unpublished manuscript.

Brown, Roger, 1965. *Social Psychology*. New York: The Free Press.

Chomsky, Noam, 1959. Review of B. F. Skinner's *Verbal Behavior, Language,* **35:** 26–58.

——, 1965. *Aspects of the Theory of Syntax*. Cambridge, Mass.: The M.I.T. Press.

——, 1967. "The Responsibility of Intellectuals," *New York Review of Books,* **23:** 21ff.

Cohen, Albert K., 1965. "The Sociology of the Deviant Act," *American Sociological Review,* **30:** 5–14.

Cohen, Elie A., 1953. *Human Behavior in the Concentration Camp*. New York: W. W. Norton & Co., Inc.

Costner, Herbert, and Robert K. Leik, 1964. "Deductions from Axiomatic Theory," *American Sociological Review,* **29:** 819–35.

Dahrendorf, Ralf, 1958. "Out of Utopia: Towards a Reorientation of Sociological Analysis," *American Journal of Sociology,* **64:** 115–27.

Davis, Allison, and John Dollard, 1940. *Children of Bondage*. Washington, D.C.: American Council on Education.

Davis, Kingsley, 1937. "The Sociology of Prostitution," *American Sociological Review,* **2:** 744–55.

——, 1939. "Illegitimacy and the Social Structure," *American Journal of Sociology,* **45:** 215–33.

——, 1940a. "The Child and the Social Structure," *Journal of Educational Sociology,* **14:** 217–29.

——, 1940b. "The Sociology of Parent-Youth Conflict," *American Sociological Review,* **5:** 523–35.

——, 1941. "Intermarriage in Caste Societies," *American Anthropologist* (N.S.), **43:** 391.

——, 1949. *Human Society*. New York: The Macmillan Company.

————, 1961. "Prostitution," in Robert K. Merton and Robert A. Nisbet, eds., *Contemporary Social Problems.* New York: Harcourt, Brace & World, Inc., 262–88.

————, 1966. "Sexual Behavior," in Robert K. Merton and Robert A. Nisbet, eds., *Contemporary Social Problems,* 2nd ed. New York: Harcourt Brace Jovanovich, Inc., 322–72.

————, and Judith Blake, 1962. "Social Structure and Fertility," in S. M. Lipset and N. J. Smelser, eds., *Sociology: The Progress of a Decade.* Englewood Cliffs, N.J.: Prentice-Hall, Inc., 364–65. Originally published 1956.

————, 1964. "Norms, Values, and Sanctions," in R. E. L. Faris, ed., *Handbook of Modern Sociology.* Skokie, Ill.: Rand McNally & Co., 456–84.

Dentler, Robert A., and Kai T. Erikson, 1959. "Some Functions of Deviance in Groups," *Social Problems,* **7:** 98–107.

Deutscher, Irwin, "Words and Deeds: Social Science and Social Policy," *Social Problems,* **13:** 235–52.

Dollard, John, 1949. *Caste and Class in a Southern Town,* 2nd ed. New York: Harper.

Douglas, Dorothy J., in press. "The Novitiate: Socialization to a Deviant Sexual Role," in Jack Douglas, ed., *Deviance and Respectability.* New York: Basic Books, Inc.

Durkheim, Emile, 1953. "The Determination of Moral Facts," in D. F. Pocock, trans., *Sociology and Philosophy.* London: Cohen & West. Originally published 1903.

————, 1961. *Moral Education,* trans. Everett Wilson and Herman Schnurer. New York: The Free Press. Written 1903–1906. Originally published 1925.

Eckland, Bruce K., 1967. "Genetics and Sociology: A Reconsideration," *American Sociological Review,* **32:** 173–94.

Eitinger, Leo, 1964. *Concentration Camp Survivors in Norway and Israel.* Oslo: Universitetsforlaget.

Elkins, Stanley M., 1963. *Slavery: A Problem in American Institutional and Intellectual Life.* New York: Grosset & Dunlap, Inc. Originally published 1959.

Erikson, Kai, 1966. *Wayward Puritans: A Study in the Sociology of Deviance.* New York: John Wiley & Sons, Inc.

Faris, Ellsworth, 1937. "Of Psychological Elements," in *The Nature of Human Nature.* New York: McGraw-Hill Book Company, 173–89. Originally published 1928.

Faris, Robert E. L., ed., 1964. *Handbook of Modern Sociology.* Skokie, Ill.: Rand McNally & Co., Inc.

Fodor, Jerry, 1965. "Could Meaning Be [a mediating response]?" *Journal of Verbal Learning and Verbal Behavior,* **4:** 73–81.

————, 1966. "Rejoinder [to replies by Berlyne and Osgood]," *Journal of Verbal Learning and Verbal Behavior,* **5:** 413–15.

Gardner, Martin, 1957. *Fads and Fallacies in the Name of Science.* New York: Dover Publications, Inc., 1957.

Garfinkel, Harold, 1956. "Conditions of Successful Degradation Ceremonies," *American Journal of Sociology,* **61:** 420–24.

Gibbs, Jack P., 1965. "Norms: The Problem of Definition and Classification," *American Journal of Sociology,* **70:** 586–94.

———, 1966. "Sanctions," *Social Problems,* **14:** 147–59.

Glazer, Nathan, 1963. "Introduction," to Stanley M. Elkins, *Slavery: A Problem in American Institutional and Intellectual Life.* New York: Grosset & Dunlap, Inc.

———, and Daniel Patrick Moynihan, 1963. *Beyond the Melting Pot.* Cambridge, Mass.: Joint Center for Urban Studies, The M.I.T. and Harvard University Presses.

Goffman, Erving, 1959. *The Presentation of Self in Everyday Life.* Garden City, N.Y.: Doubleday Anchor Books.

———, 1961. *Asylums.* Garden City, N.Y.: Doubleday Anchor Books.

———, 1963. *Stigma.* Englewood Cliffs, N.J.: Prentice-Hall, Inc.

Goode, William J., 1951. *Religion among the Primitives.* New York: The Free Press.

Hansel, C. E. M., 1966. *ESP: A Scientific Evaluation.* New York: Charles Scribner's Sons.

Harlow, Harry F., 1949. "The Formation of Learning Sets," *Psychological Review,* **56:** 51–65.

———, 1962. "Social Deprivation in Monkeys," *Scientific American,* **207:** 136–46.

———, 1963. "Basic Social Capacity of Primates," in Charles H. Southwick, ed., *Primate Social Behavior.* New York: Van Nostrand Reinhold, 153–60. Originally published 1959.

———, and Margaret K. Harlow, 1963. "A Study of Animal Affection," in Charles H. Southwick, ed., *Primate Social Behavior.* New York: Van Nostrand Reinhold, 174–84. Originally published 1961.

Hempel, Carl G., 1959. "The Empiricist Criterion of Meaning," in A. J. Ayer, ed., *Logical Positivism.* New York: The Free Press, 108–20. Originally published 1955.

Hill, Winfred, 1960. "Learning Theory and the Acquisition of Values," *Psychological Review,* **67:** 317–31.

Hirschi, Travis, and Hanan C. Selvin, 1967. *Delinquency Research: An Appraisal of Analytic Methods.* New York: The Free Press.

Hobbes, Thomas, 1958. *Leviathan: Or, the Matter, Form and Power of a Commonwealth Ecclesiastical and Civil.* Indianapolis: The Bobbs-Merrill Co., Inc. Originally published 1651.

Hockett, Charles F., 1967. *Language, Mathematics, and Linguistics* (Janua Linguarum, Series Minor, No. 60). The Hague: Mouton.

———, 1968. *The State of the Art* (Janua Linguarum, Series Minor, No. 73). The Hague: Mouton.

Holmes, Oliver Wendell, Jr., 1896. "The Path of the Law," *Harvard Law Review,* **10:** 447–58.

Homans, George C., 1961. *Social Behavior: Its Elementary Forms.* New York: Harcourt Brace Jovanovich, Inc.

————, 1964a. Autobiographical Introduction, in *Sentiments and Activities.* New York: The Free Press, 1–49.

————, 1964b. "Bringing Men Back In," *American Sociological Review,* **29:** 809–14.

Hymes, Dell, 1967. "Why Linguistics Needs the Sociologist," *Social Research,* **34:** 632–47.

Inkeles, Alex, 1963. "Sociology and Psychology," in Sigmund Koch, ed., *Psychology: A Study of a Science,* Vol. 6. New York: McGraw-Hill Book Company, 320–60.

James, William, 1931. *Principles of Psychology.* New York: Henry Holt. Originally published 1890.

Johnson, Harry M., 1960. *Sociology: A Systematic Introduction.* New York: Harcourt Brace Jovanovich, Inc.

Kagan, Jerome, and H. A. Moss, 1962. *From Birth to Maturity.* New York: John Wiley & Sons, Inc.

Keniston, Kenneth, 1968. *Young Radicals: Notes on Committed Youth.* New York: Harcourt Brace Jovanovich, Inc.

Kluckhohn, Clyde, et al., 1952. "Values and Value-Orientations in the Theory of Action," in Talcott Parsons and Edward A. Shils, eds., *Toward a General Theory of Action.* Cambridge, Mass.: Harvard University Press, 413–463.

Kluckhohn, Florence, and Fred L. Strodtbeck, 1961. *Variations in Value Orientations.* New York: Harper & Row, Publishers.

Koch, Sigmund, 1964. "Psychology and Emerging Conceptions of Knowledge as Unitary," in T. Y. Wann, ed., *Behaviorism and Phenomenology: Contrasting Bases for Modern Psychology.* Chicago: The University of Chicago Press.

Kogon, Eugon, n.d. *The Theory and Practice of Hell.* New York: Berkeley Books.

Kohlberg, Lawrence, 1963. "Moral Development and Identification," in Harold W. Stevenson, ed., *Child Psychology* (The 62nd Yearbook of the National Society for the Study of Education). Chicago: National Society for the Study of Education, 277–332.

————, 1964. "Development of Moral Character and Moral Ideology," in Martin L. Hoffman and Lois Waldis Hoffman, eds., *Review of Child Development Research,* Vol. 1. New York: Russell Sage Foundation, 383–431.

————, 1966. "A Cognitive-Developmental Analysis of Children's Sex-Role Concepts and Attitudes," in Eleanor E. Maccoby, ed., *The Development of Sex Differences.* Stanford: Stanford University Press, 82–172.

LaPiere, Richard T., 1934. "Attitudes v. Actions," *Social Forces,* **13:** 230–37.

La Rochefoucauld, Francois de, 1959. *"Les Maximes,"* in Louis Kronenberger, ed., *The Maxims of la Rochefoucauld.* New York: Random House Vintage Books. Originally published 1665–1678.

Leighton, Dorothea, and Clyde Kluckhohn, 1947. *Children of the People: The Navaho Individual and His Development.* Cambridge, Mass.: Harvard University Press.

Lemert, Edwin, 1948. "Some Aspects of a General Theory of Sociopathic Behavior," in *Proceedings of the Pacific Sociological Society: 1948*. Research Studies 16, No. 1, State College of Washington.

———, 1951. *Social Pathology*. New York: McGraw-Hill Book Company.

———, 1967a. "The Behavior of the Systematic Check Forger," in *Human Deviance, Social Problems, and Social Control*. Englewood Cliffs, N.J.: Prentice-Hall, Inc., 109–18. Originally published 1958.

———, 1967b. "The Concept of Secondary Deviation," in *Human Deviance, Social Problems, and Social Control*. Englewood Cliffs., N.J.: Prentice-Hall, Inc., 40–64.

———, 1967c. *Human Deviance, Social Problems, and Social Control*. Englewood Cliffs, N.J.: Prentice-Hall, Inc.

Levinson, Daniel J., 1959. "Role, Personality, and Social Structure in the Organizational Setting," *Journal of Social and Abnormal Psychology*, **58:** 170–80.

Levy, Marion J., Jr., 1952. *The Structure of Society*. Princeton: Princeton University Press.

———, 1963. "Some Problems for a Unified Theory of Human Nature," in Edward Y. Tiryakian, ed., *Sociological Theory, Values, and Sociocultural Change: Essays in Honor of Pitirim A. Sorokin*. New York: The Free Press.

Lewis, Oscar, 1951. *Life in a Mexican Village: Tepoztlan Restudied*. Urbana: University of Illinois Press.

———, 1961. *The Children of Sanchez*. New York: Random House, Inc.

Linton, Ralph, 1936. *The Study of Man*. New York: Appleton-Century-Crofts.

Lipset, Seymour Martin, 1959. "Democracy and Working-Class Authoritarianism," *American Sociological Review*, **24:** 482–501.

———, 1965. "Students and Politics," in S. M. Lipset and Sheldon S. Wolin, eds., *The Berkeley Student Revolt*. Garden City, N.Y.: Doubleday Anchor Books.

Loomis, Zona K., and Charles P. Loomis, 1961. *Modern Social Theories*. New York: Van Nostrand Reinhold.

Lovibond, S. H., 1963. "The Mechanism of Conditioning Treatment of Enuresis," *Behavior Research and Therapy*, **1:** 17–21.

Lynn, David, and William Sawrey, 1959. "The Effects of Father-Absence on Norwegian Boys and Girls," *Journal of Abnormal and Social Psychology*, **59:** 258–62.

Malcolm, Norman, 1964. "Behaviorism as a Philosophy of Psychology," in T. Y. Wann, ed., *Behaviorism and Phenomenology: Contrasting Bases for Modern Psychology*. Chicago: The University of Chicago Press, 141–55.

Malinowski, Bronislaw, 1926. *Crime and Custom in Savage Society*. London: Routledge & Kegan Paul Ltd.

Mason, William A., 1963. "The Effects of Environmental Restriction on the Social Development of Rhesus Monkeys," in Charles H. Southwick, ed., *Primate Social Behavior*. New York: Van Nostrand Reinhold, 161–73.

Matthews, Fred H., 1966. "The Americanization of Sigmund Freud: Adaptations of Psychoanalysis before 1917," *American Studies*, **1:** 1–24.

Matza, David, 1964. "Position and Behavior Patterns of Youth," in Robert E. L. Fairs, ed., *Handbook of Modern Sociology*. Skokie, Ill.: Rand McNally & Co., Inc.

————, 1964. *Delinquency and Drift*. New York: John Wiley & Sons, Inc.

————, 1966. "The Disreputable Poor," in N. J. Smelser and S. M. Lipset, eds., *Social Structure and Mobility in Economic Development*. Chicago: Aldine, 310–39.

May, Mark A., 1941. Preface to Neal A. Miller and John Dollard, *Social Learning and Imitation*. New Haven: Yale University Press.

Mead, George Herbert, 1903. "The Definition of the Psychical," *University of Chicago Decennial Publications in Psychology*, III.

————, 1936a. *Mind, Self, and Society*. Chicago: The University of Chicago Press.

————, 1936b. "Psychology of Punitive Justice," in *Mind, Self, and Society*. Chicago: The University of Chicago Press. Originally published 1917.

Mead, Margaret, 1949. "Social Change and Cultural Surrogates," in Clyde Kluckhohn and Henry A. Murray, eds., *Personality in Nature, Society, and Culture*. New York: Alfred A. Knopf, Inc.

————, 1959. "Some Anthropological Considerations concerning Guilt," in M. L. Remert, ed., *Feelings and Emotions*. New York: McGraw-Hill Book Company, 313–63.

Merton, Robert K., 1949. *Social Theory and Social Structure*. New York: The Free Press.

Milgram, Stanley, 1971. "Behavioral Study of Obedience," in Robert M. Stutz, William N. Dember, and James J. Jenkins, eds., *Exploring Behavior and Experience: Readings in General Psychology*. Englewood Cliffs, N.J.: Prentice-Hall, Inc., 355–65. Originally published 1963.

Miller, Daniel R., 1966. Review of Albert Bandura and Richard H. Walters, *Social Learning and Personality Development, American Sociological Review*, **31:** 128–30.

Miller, Neal A., and John Dollard, 1941. *Social Learning and Imitation.* New Haven: Yale University Press.

Minturn, Leigh, and William W. Lambert, 1964. *Mothers of Six Cultures*. New York: John Wiley & Sons, Inc.

Moore, George Edward, 1903. *Principia Ethica*. Cambridge: Cambridge University Press.

Morris, Charles W., 1946. *Signs, Language, and Behavior*. Englewood Cliffs, N.J.: Prentice-Hall, Inc.

Mowrer, O. Hobart, 1960a. *Learning Theory and Behavior*. New York: John Wiley & Sons, Inc.

————, 1960b. *Learning Theory and the Symbolic Processes*. New York: John Wiley & Sons, Inc.

Murdock, George Peter, 1948. *Social Structure*. New York: The Macmillan Company.

Mussen, Paul Henry, John Janeway Conger, and Jerome Kagan, 1963. *Child Development and Personality,* 2nd ed. New York: Harper & Row, Publishers.

Omvedt, Gail, 1967. "The Social Sciences and Linguistic Revolution," *Berkeley Journal of Sociology,* **7**: 220–28.

Osgood, Charles E., 1963. "Psycholinguistics," in Sigmund Koch, ed., *Psychology: A Study of a Science,* Vol. 6. New York: McGraw-Hill Book Company, 244–316. Originally published 1956.

———, 1966. "Reply [to Fodor]," *Journal of Verbal Learning and Verbal Behavior,* **5**: 402.

Parsons, Talcott, 1934–1935. "The Place of Ultimate Values in Sociological Theory," *International Journal of Ethics,* **45**: 288–90.

———, 1937. *The Structure of Social Action.* New York: McGraw-Hill Book Company.

———, 1952. *The Social System.* New York: The Free Press.

———, 1959. "An Approach to Psychological Theory in Terms of the Theory of Action," in Sigmund Koch, ed., *Psychology: A Study of a Science,* Vol. 3. New York: McGraw-Hill Book Company.

———, 1964a. *Social Structure and Personality.* New York: The Free Press.

———, 1964b. "Social Structure and the Development of Personality," in *Social Structure and Personality.* New York: The Free Press, 78–111. Originally published 1958.

———, 1964c. "The Superego and the Theory of Social Systems," in *Social Structure and Personality.* New York: The Free Press, 17–33. Originally published 1952.

———, and Edward A. Shils, eds., 1952a. *Toward a General Theory of Action.* Cambridge, Mass.: Harvard University Press.

———, 1952b. "Values, Motives, and Systems of Action," in *Toward a General Theory of Action.* Cambridge, Mass.: Harvard University Press, 313–63.

Piaget, Jean, 1962. *The Moral Judgment of the Child.* New York: Crowell-Collier and Macmillan, Inc. Originally published 1928.

Potter, Stephen, 1948. *The Theory and Practice of Gamesmanship; or, The Art of Winning Games without Actually Cheating.* New York: Henry Holt.

Price, George K., 1956. "Science and the Supernatural," *Science,* **122** (August 26).

Ranulf, Svend, 1964. *Moral Indignation and Middle-Class Psychology.* New York: Schocken Books. Originally published 1938.

Redfield, Robert, 1930. *Tepoztlan: A Mexican Village.* Chicago: The University of Chicago Press.

Rommetveit, Ragnar, 1955. *Social Norms and Roles.* Oslo: Akademiskforlag.

Rose, Arnold M., ed., 1962a. *Human Behavior and Symbolic Processes: An Interactionist Approach.* Boston: Houghton Mifflin.

———, 1962b. "A Systematic Summary of Symbolic Interaction Theory," in *Human Behavior and Symbolic Processes: An Interactionist Approach.* Boston: Houghton Mifflin, 3–19.

Ross, Edward A., 1901. *Social Control.* New York: The Macmillan Company.

Ross, Sir David, 1930. *The Right and the Good.* Oxford: Clarendon Press.

Russell, Bertrand, 1952. "The Elements of Ethics," in Wilfred Sellars and John Hospers, eds., *Readings in Ethical Theory.* New York: Appleton-Century-Crofts, 1–34. Originally published 1910.

Sachs, Hanns, 1961. "Comment [on Boring, 'Was This Analysis a Success?'],'" in Edwin G. Boring, ed., *Psychologist at Large.* New York: Basic Books, Inc., 140–42. Originally published 1940.

Sanford, Nevitt, 1955. "The Dynamics of Identification," *Psychological Review,* **62:** 106–18.

Santayana, George, 1952. "Hypostatic Ethics," in Wilfred Sellars and John Hospers, eds., *Readings in Ethical Theory.* New York: Appleton-Century-Crofts, 263–72. Originally published 1913.

Schachter, Stanley, 1963. "Birth Order, Eminence and Higher Education," *American Sociological Review,* **28:** 757–68.

Scheff, Thomas J., 1966. *Being Mentally Ill: A Sociological Theory.* Chicago: Aldine.

Schein, Edgar H., 1964. "Brainwashing," in Warren G. Bennis et al., eds., *Interpersonal Dynamics.* Homewood, Ill.: Dorsey Press of Richard D. Irwin, 454–74.

———, Inge Schneier, and Curtis Barker, 1961. *Coercive Persuasion.* New York: W. W. Norton & Co., Inc.

Schilpp, Paul Arthur, ed., 1942. *The Philosophy of G. E. Moore.* Evanston, Ill.: Northwestern University Press.

Schwartz, Morris, and Alfred H. Stanton, 1950. "A Social Psychological Study of Incontinence," *Psychiatry,* **13:** 399–416.

Scott, John Finley, 1962. "The Impossible Theory of Action: Some Questions on Parsons' Prewar Classification of Action Theories," *Berkeley Journal of Sociology,* **7:** 51–62.

———, 1963. "The Changing Foundations of the Parsonian Action Scheme," *American Sociological Review,* **28:** 716–35.

———, 1965. Review of William A. Scott, *Values and Organizations: A Study of Fraternities and Sororities, American Sociological Review,* **30:** 971.

———, 1968. Review of Talcott Parsons, *Sociological Theory and Modern Society, American Sociological Review,* **33:** 453–56.

Sears, Robert R., Eleanor E. Maccoby, and Harry Levin, 1957. *Patterns of Child Rearing.* New York: Harper & Row, Publishers.

Sellars, Wilfred, and John Hospers, eds., 1952. *Readings in Ethical Theory.* New York: Appleton-Century-Crofts.

Sidman, Murray, 1960. *The Tactics of Scientific Research: Evaluating Experimental Data in Psychology.* New York: Basic Books, Inc.

Skinner, B. F., 1953. *Science and Human Behavior.* New York: The Macmillan Company.

———, 1957. *Verbal Behavior.* New York: Appleton-Century-Crofts.

———, 1961a. *Cumulative Record.* New York: Appleton-Century-Crofts.

———, 1961b. "The Operational Analysis of Psychological Terms," in *Cumulative Record*. New York: Appleton-Century-Crofts, 272–86. Originally published 1945.

———, 1961c. "Superstition in a Pigeon," in *Cumulative Record*. New York: Appleton-Century-Crofts, 404–9. Originally published 1948.

———, 1964. "Behaviorism at Fifty," in T. Y. Wann, ed., *Behaviorism and Phenomenology: Contrasting Bases for Modern Psychology*. Chicago: The University of Chicago Press, 76–96.

———, and C. B. Ferster, 1957. *Schedules of Reinforcement*. New York: Appleton-Century-Crofts.

Slater, Philip E., 1961. "Toward a Dualistic Theory of Identification," *Merrill-Palmer Quarterly*, **7**: 113–26.

Smelser, Neil J., 1963. *Theory of Collective Behavior*. New York: The Free Press.

Soal, S. G., J. B. Rhine, P. E. Meehl, and Michael Scriven, 1956. Rejoinders and commentaries to George K. Price, "Science and the Supernatural," *Science*, **123** (January 6).

Southwick, Charles H., ed., 1963. *Primate Social Behavior*. New York: Van Nostrand Reinhold.

Spiro, Melford, 1951. "Culture and Personality: The Natural History of a False Dichotomy," *Psychiatry*, **14**: 19–46.

———, 1965. *Children of the Kibbutz*. New York: Schocken Books.

Spitz, René, 1954. Cited in Joseph L. Stone, "A Critique of Studies of Infant Isolation," *Child Development*, **25**: 12.

Staats, Arthur W., and Carolyn K. Staats, 1963. *Complex Human Behavior*. New York: Holt, Rinehart & Winston.

Stevenson, Charles, 1944. *Ethics and Language*. New Haven: Yale University Press.

Strauss, Leo, 1952. *The Political Philosophy of Hobbes*. Chicago: The University of Chicago Press.

Sumner, William Graham, 1906. *Folkways*. Boston: Ginn and Company.

Swanson, Guy E., 1960. "Internalization," in Julius Gould and William Kolb, eds., *A Dictionary of the Social Sciences* (compiled under the auspices of UNESCO). New York: The Free Press.

Thibaut, John W., and Harold H. Kelley, 1959. *The Social Psychology of Groups*. New York: John Wiley & Sons, Inc.

Tinbergen, Niko, 1953. *Social Behavior in Animals*. London: Methuen & Co. Ltd.

Tiryakian, Edward Y., 1965. "Existential Phenomenology and the Sociological Tradition," *American Sociological Review*, **30**: 258–71.

Tolman, Edward C., 1932. *Purposive Behavior in Animals and Men*. New York: Century.

———, 1943. "Identification and the Post-war World," *Journal of Abnormal and Social Psychology*, **38**: 141–48.

———, 1951a. "A Behaviorist's Definition of Consciousness," in *Collected Papers in Psychology*. Berkeley: University of California Press, 63–83. Originally published 1927.

————, 1951b. *Collected Papers in Psychology*. Berkeley: University of California Press.

Verplanck, William S., 1955. "Since Learned Behavior Is Innate, and *Vice Versa, What Now?" Psychological Review,* **62**: 139–44.

Wallace, Samuel E., 1965. *Skid Row as a Way of Life*. Ottowa: Bedminster.

Waller, Willard, 1928. *The Sociology of Teaching*. New York: John Wiley & Sons, Inc.

Walters, Richard H., and Lillian Demkow, 1963. "The Timing of Punishment as a Determinant of Resistance to Temptation," *Child Development,* **34**: 207–14.

Wann, T. Y., ed., 1964. *Behaviorism and Phenomenology: Contrasting Bases for Modern Psychology*. Chicago: The University of Chicago Press.

Washburn, Sherwood, and Irven DeVore, 1963. "The Social Life of Baboons," in Charles H. Southwick, ed., *Primate Social Behavior*. New York: Van Nostrand Reinhold. Originally published 1961.

Westley, William, 1951. "The Police: A Sociological Study of Law, Custom and Morality." Ph.D. dissertation, The University of Chicago.

Wheeler, Stanton, 1966. "The Structure of Formally Organized Socialization Settings," in Stanton Wheeler and Orville G. Brim, Jr., eds. *Socialization after Childhood*. New York: John Wiley & Sons, Inc., 53–116.

Whiting, Beatrice B., ed., 1963. *Six Cultures*. New York: John Wiley & Sons, Inc.

Whiting, John W. M., 1959. "Sorcery, Sin, and the Superego," in Marshall R. Jones, ed., *Nebraska Symposium on Motivation: 1959,* Vol. 7. Lincoln: University of Nebraska Press, 174–95.

————, and Irwin R. Child, 1953. *Child Training and Personality*. New Haven: Yale University Press.

Winch, Robert F., 1962. *Identification and Its Familial Determinants*. Indianapolis: Bobbs-Merrill Co., Inc.

World Health Organization, 1962. *Deprivation of Maternal Care: A Reassessment of Its Effects*. Geneva: World Health Organization.

Wrong, Dennis, 1961. "The Over-Socialized Conception of Man in Modern Sociology," *American Sociological Review,* **26**: 183–93.

Index